MURDER
AT THE
INN

MURDER
AT THE
INN

A HISTORY
OF CRIME IN
BRITAIN'S PUBS
AND HOTELS

JAMES MOORE

The
History
Press

First published 2015

The History Press
The Mill, Brimscombe Port
Stroud, Gloucestershire, GL5 2QG
www.thehistorypress.co.uk

British Library Cataloguing in Publication Data.
A catalogue record for this book is available from the British Library.

ISBN 978 0 7509 5683 3

Typesetting and origination by The History Press
Printed in Great Britain

CONTENTS

INTRODUCTION

In the early 1930s, archaeologists working at Housesteads Roman fort on Hadrian's Wall in Northumberland made a shocking discovery. Underneath the floor of a building in the civilian settlement, just outside the main fort, which was believed to be the remains of a Roman tavern, they found two skeletons. One was a man and the other was a woman. The male skeleton had the blade of a knife still stuck in its ribs. The bodies had been buried in the back room under a clean layer of clay. Not only did they appear to have been hurriedly hidden, but it was usual Roman practice to bury the dead outside the walls of a town or military post. The archaeologists came to a gruesome conclusion – that they had uncovered a double murder thought to have been committed before the year AD 367.

The origins of modern-day pubs and inns in Britain can be traced back to Roman 'tabernae' that sold wine and food to travellers and advertised their wares by displaying vine leaves outside. These were often rowdy places where arguments could suddenly erupt, leading to brawls and, sometimes, death. And, for the next 2,000 years, the development of drinking institutions across the nation would go hand in hand with the history of both crime and punishment. Our pubs and hotels have long been places of solace offering good company, welcome liquid refreshment, a hearty meal and perhaps a bed for the night. Yet they have always had the potential to be crucibles of crime too.

With a need for drinks that were safer than water and places where the community could meet and relax, the alehouse thrived in Saxon times and into the medieval era. Inns, which grew out of the tradition of monastic hospices, were, from around the twelfth century, places where you could not only get a drink but a bed for the night. And by this time there were a few taverns too, selling wine to a well-to-do crowd. By the nineteenth century all these hostelries had become part of the fabric of the nation and begun to morph into the pubs and hotels we recognise today. The word 'pub', or 'public house', was first coined in the late seventeenth century, but did not become common until 1800, while inns only began being called hotels from the eighteenth century. The modern-day equivalent of the tavern is the wine bar. The distinctions between all these establishments have, however, become blurred over the years.

Sir William Harcourt, a nineteenth-century Home Secretary, once said that 'As much of the history of England has been brought about in public houses as in the House of Commons.' It is also true that many of the most dramatic episodes in both English and British criminal history feature pubs and hotels. Over the centuries they have acted as dens of thieves, pirates, smugglers, highwaymen and those plotting terror. They have also been the scenes of mass brawls, riots and grisly murders. Serial killers, too, have often made them their haunts as they search for more victims. Yet pubs and hotels have also served the community when it comes to solving and punishing crime. For they have been used as venues for post-mortems, inquests, court sessions and even as places of execution.

In *Murder At The Inn* the fascinating connection between crime and the hostelry is brought to life in detail for the first time. Part one, a drinker's guide to crime, explores the different kinds of felony that have been linked to pubs and hotels and the different functions they have performed in the legal process throughout history. Part two looks at fifty criminal cases from the last 400 years where pubs and hotels were at the heart of the story. These include half-forgotten but gripping tales of wrongdoing as well as celebrated cases involving the likes of Dick Turpin, Jack the Ripper and Lord Lucan. In all of the examples at least one pub or hotel was involved. Some, like The Blind Beggar in London's East End, where one of the Kray brothers shot a gang rival in 1966, have achieved international notoriety. Most of the pubs and hotels mentioned in this book can still be visited to this day and, where they are still open, directions on how to find them are included. All provide a vital link with an important aspect of our shared history and are still places in which to enjoy a drink, along with a good yarn, serving just the same purpose as their forerunners did in ancient times.

James Moore, 2015

DISCLAIMER ...

Writing about the history of pubs and hotels is a slippery business. The names of venues change, sometimes frequently, while others suddenly close. Some reopen, only to move to new locations. And, like many of the good bar room tales told within their walls, the exact truth about a pub's past is often tricky to pin down. I have endeavoured to stick to the facts, where they are known, and to correctly link old hostelries and inns to the crimes in question, but apologies for any inaccuracies that may have crept in. These will, of course, be corrected in future editions.

ACKNOWLEDGEMENTS

Without the help and support of a whole host of people, this book would not have been possible. So I'd like to raise a toast to the following: Jim Addison, Gurdish Bansal, Peter Biddle, Fran Bowden, Adele Clay, Philip Cutter, Deborah Dickeson, Sophie Enever, Alex Evans, Michael Evered, Leila Gibson, Susannah Harvey, Felicity Hebditch, Jan Hebditch, Kate Hebditch, Max Hebditch, Rick Hebditch, George Hoare, Gary Hodgson, Catrina Hudson, Judi James, Kevin Kemp, Rod Leitch, Lana Matile Moore, Alex Moore, Charlie Moore, Geoff Moore, Laurie Moore, Philippa Moore, Sam Moore, Saskia Moore, Tamsin Moore, Dr Tom Moore, Tommy Moore, Paul Nero, Dr Claire Nesbitt, Fiona Poole, Will Poole, Sarah Sarkhel, Daniel Simister, Robert Smith, Peter Spurgeon, Jason Stredder, Samm Taylor and Julia Wherrell.

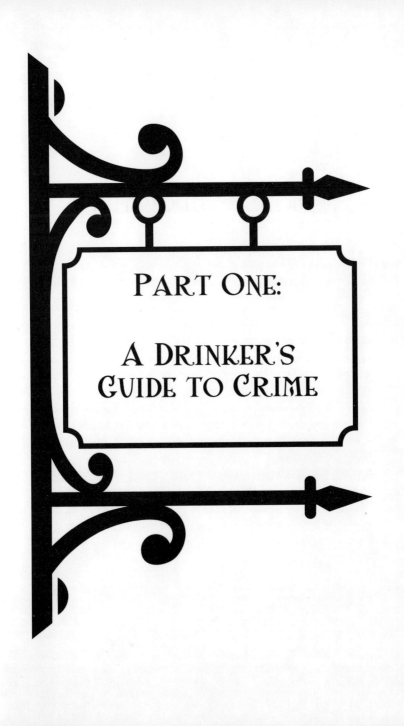

PART ONE:

A DRINKER'S
GUIDE TO CRIME

1

HOMICIDE AND THE HOSTELRY

For many years The Crown and Dolphin pub in Shadwell, East London, displayed a macabre item of memorabilia behind the bar – a genuine human skull. It was purported to be that of John Williams, the man supposedly responsible for the Ratcliff Highway murders which had rocked the capital in 1811. The story goes that in the 1880s his skeleton had been dug up near the now closed Crown and Dolphin during building works. They knew it was Williams' body not only from the location in which he was known to have been buried, but also because the skeleton had a wooden stake through it – just like Williams when he'd been buried.

The Ratcliff Murders saw seven people killed in two separate incidents over twelve days within a square mile of each other, and were later described as 'the sublimest and most entire in their excellence that ever were committed'. The first murder occurred on the night of 7 December 1811 when a 24-year-old draper, Timothy Marr, along with his wife, Celia, 22, their 3-month-old son and a shop assistant were all found dead at their shop in Wapping. The adults' skulls had been crushed in and the baby's throat cut. Then, on 19 December, 56-year-old John Williamson, landlord of the nearby King's Arms, along with his wife and a servant, were murdered in their own pub. A serial killer appeared to be on the loose and initially the Bow Street Runners, a precursor of the Metropolitan police force, had little to go on. However, John Williams, who lodged at another defunct Wapping pub, The Pear Tree, became a suspect when he was linked to a ship carpenter's hammer thought to be the murder weapon in the first killings. The evidence was shaky, but Williams was arrested. He was never brought to trial, committing suicide in jail. The public were outraged that Williams had cheated the hangman, and to assuage them the Home Secretary ordered that his body be paraded through the streets. An estimated 180,000 people attended the procession before Williams' dead body had a stake hammered through the heart according to ancient custom, and was unceremoniously buried in a hole at a crossroads.

The case became a media sensation and was instrumental in the growing fascination with murders among the nineteenth-century public which saw many high profile killings such as the Red Barn Murder of 1827 (see page 98) dramatised in plays. Our obsession with murder has continued to this day, fuelling countless TV dramas, films and books. But one aspect that has been largely ignored is how pubs and inns have often provided backdrops or even the stage for murder, just as they did in the Ratcliff Highway killings. Indeed it is startling just how many of the famous murder cases in history involve a pub or hotel in some capacity. Sometimes they feature as murder scenes, sometimes as places where despicable crimes are planned or simply as locations where the villains have been arrested. In other cases they provide vital evidence to police and prosecutors as places where victims or suspects were last seen.

Sharing a drink can bring people together and induce a convivial, friendly atmosphere. Yet too much drink can get the better of any of us, and the records of the earliest alehouses show that beer and blood have always been bedfellows. Just as now, fights and brawls could break out over anything from religion and politics to sex or money. In 1641, for example, the constable of East Grinstead found people fighting in an alehouse. He reported 'a great deal of bloodshed' and the ale-wife 'covered with gore'. At worst, of course, this behaviour could lead to murder. For many

The Bull Hotel in Long Melford, Suffolk, which was the scene of a shocking murder in 1648. (*Courtesy of the Bull Hotel*)

years it was said that the famous playwright Christopher Marlowe had been killed in a simple tavern brawl, though this is now in dispute among historians. Whether or not the esteemed author of works like *Doctor Faustus* was indeed stabbed in a row over a bar bill as it is alleged, there are plenty of other examples from history where violence flared up in drinking venues and led to death. On 10 February 1355, two university students drinking in the Swyndlestock Tavern in Oxford complained about the quality of the wine. In the argument that ensued they ended up throwing the jug at the head of the taverner, John Croidon. What had begun as a low-level row soon erupted into a full-scale riot in the streets of the city, with hundreds of scholars taking on groups of locals. The trouble lasted several days and only ended after the deaths of ninety of those involved. During the English Civil War, inns and alehouses were often melting pots for heated debate, and in 1648 at The Bull in Long Melford it may well have been a disagreement over politics which led Roger Greene to stab Richard

Evered. The murder took place in the entrance hall of the half-timbered inn, which dates back to 1580. Greene was swiftly tried and executed.

Disputes over more trivial matters can always get out of hand too – but never more spectacularly than when Lord Byron, an uncle to the famous poet, killed his cousin William Chaworth in a disagreement over who had more game on their respective estates. On 26 January 1765 the pair fell out over the issue whilst drinking at the Star and Garter tavern in London's Pall Mall, and a duel in one of the rooms of the building resulted in Chaworth being run through with a sword. Although Byron was brought to trial he got special treatment, being a peer of the realm. He got off with a conviction for manslaughter and a small fine.

Although often outlawed, or the subject of regulation, gambling in alehouses and pubs has been popular for more than 1,000 years. It has also led to murderous disputes. The Maid's Head in Norwich, Norfolk, has a proud history going back 800 years, but in 1519 it was the setting for a shameful episode when John Ganton was slain with a dagger in a disagreement over who was winning in a game of dice. In the following century a game of shove ha'penny, still a bar room favourite today, resulted in a man being stabbed to death in a Hertfordshire alehouse, while the ghost that is reputed to haunt The Grenadier, in London's Belgravia, is said to be of a former soldier murdered there after cheating in a game of cards.

Money is often a motive for murder and plain old robbery has accounted for plenty of killings linked to hostelries. In 1734, for instance, a pedlar called Jacob Harris slashed the neck of the landlord at the now demolished Royal Oak in Ditchling Common, West Sussex, killed his wife and maid too and then made off with the night's takings. Before he died, however, the taverner named his victim and Harris was tracked down to the Cat Inn, West Hoathly, where he was found hiding in a chimney. Another murder and robbery, that of William Stevenson, in 1859, by two men with whom he had been drinking in The Ship at Sibsey, Lincolnshire, even gave rise to a ditty:

At the public-house he called for ale,
His lowly spirits for to cheer,

He little thought that night to die,
And being to his home so near;
But he was followed from that house,
By some ruffians you shall hear,
Who robbed and murdered the poor old man,
In Sibsey village in Lincolnshire.

An equally invidious crime took place in June 1922 when an 18-year-old pantry boy at the Spencer Hotel in London, today known as the DoubleTree, went to the gallows after killing a guest there, Lady Alice White. Henry Jacoby had battered the 65-year-old to death with a hammer in Room 14 of the hotel. She had made the mistake of waking up during his attempt to rob her. Seven years later, Sidney Harry Fox was also hanged after he strangled his mother in the Metropole Hotel in Margate, Kent, to cash in on an insurance policy. His attempt to disguise the murder by lighting a fire in her room had failed.

Plans to bump people off have often been hatched over a drink in a pub. In 1551 Thomas Arden, the mayor of Faversham in Kent, was strangled, beaten and stabbed to death in his own home. His wife Alice and her lover, Richard Mosbye, planned the murder at an inn called the Fleur-de-Lis, now a museum. Alice was burned at the stake and others who took part were also executed. In another case, from 1741, a captain in the Royal Navy, Samuel Goodere, ordered some of his men to assemble in the White Hart in Bristol before kidnapping his own brother, Sir John Goodere, who was then murdered aboard the HMS *Ruby*.

Pubs can be the venue for criminal 'hits' too, most famously in the case of the Krays (see page 240). That case took several years to solve. But the police have had even more difficulty in bringing anyone to justice for the murder of Russian spy Alexander Litvinenko. After taking tea at the Millennium Hotel in London on 1 November 2006, in the company of two other Russians, the 44-year-old former secret service agent fell ill. He died a few days later. His death was attributed to poisoning with the radioactive substance polonium-210, traces of which were found at the hotel. While British police identified a Russian man as the main suspect, no one has, to date, faced charges.

It's always worth being wary about whom you're talking to in a pub or hotel bar. In the last 200 years they have been the haunts of a number of serial killers, many of whom appeared to be charming characters on the surface, as they lured victims to their doom. Among these were Neville Heath, John George Haigh and Dennis Nilsen.

Numerous pubs crop up in the evidence surrounding the most famous serial killer of all, Jack the Ripper, whose murders shocked London in 1888. Many Whitechapel watering holes were later declared as places where possible suspects and victims were seen drinking in the run up to the crimes. And, while the Ripper murders have remained frustratingly unsolved, sightings of murder victims in pubs just before their disappearance have been crucial in many a murder trial. In April 1937, Ruby Keen, 23, was killed in a lane near Leighton Buzzard, Bedfordshire, by a former boyfriend, Leslie George Stone. The pair had been seen drinking in several pubs in the town including the Golden Bell, the Cross Keys and the Stag in the hours before the murder, and witnesses were able to testify that Stone, well-oiled with beer, had been trying to persuade the port-drinking Ruby to break off her engagement with a local policeman on the night she died. Stone, 24, was eventually hanged at Pentonville Prison on 13 August 1937.

In an earlier case, heard at the Old Bailey, George Foster denied killing his wife and child by drowning them in the Paddington Canal. He swore that, though he had been in the Mitre tavern with them on the day in question, he had left alone. A waiter at the pub testified that he had seen them leaving together. Foster was hanged on the 18 January 1803.

Sometimes, however, such evidence would lead to the wrong verdict. In March 1949 the Cameo Cinema Murders rocked the city of Liverpool when the manager and assistant at the picture house were robbed and shot dead. Chillingly, the plot of the film that had been showing that night involved a double murder. The police made little headway with their investigations until 23-year-old local prostitute Jackie Dickson and her boyfriend, pimp James Northam, came forward. The couple said that they had seen labourers George Kelly, 27, and Charles Connolly, 26, both of whom had minor convictions to their name, planning the crime in a pub called The Beehive in Mount Pleasant that night. According to them, Kelly had been showing off his gun in the bar. Kelly and Connolly claimed not even to know each other and to have alibis. They both maintained that they had not been in The Beehive on the evening in question. Despite more shaky evidence from a convict who had claimed to have overheard the two accused men plotting whilst behind bars, Kelly and Connolly were put on trial. While Kelly was convicted and hanged in March 1950, Connolly got ten years behind bars. Both convictions were eventually quashed in 2003.

Sex and troubled relationships account for a vast number of murders, and again pubs and inns play their part in these tragic episodes, perhaps most famously in the case of Ruth Ellis (see page 236) but also in the case of another female killer, poisoner Mary Blandy (see page 85). A man who could not bear to see his relationship fail was behind a less famous murder in Catton near Norwich in 1908. Horace Larter killed his 19-year-old sweetheart Nellie Howard and later that night stumbled into The Maid's Head in Old Catton, dripping blood and spilling beer. He pleaded guilty to the crime, telling police, 'In a fit of passion I stabbed her in the neck.'

Some murders do, of course, seem completely senseless, such as the 1922 murder by 15-year-old Jack Hewitt of Sarah Blake, the landlady at the Crown and Anchor pub, which was located by the aptly named Gallows Tree Common near Pangbourne in Berkshire. Before Hewitt was convicted he put his actions down to watching too many movies, telling police to 'blame it on the pictures'.

For some reason, after committing their crimes, murderers often seek refuge in the comforting surroundings of pubs and hotels. When Harry Roberts and two accomplices killed three police officers in 1966 in what would become known as the Massacre of Braybrook Street, the felons went on the run. Roberts checked into London's grand Russell Hotel. While staying here he bought camping equipment, subsequently managing to avoid capture for three months before being apprehended and locked up for life. Thankfully the long arm of the law usually does catch up with murderers, and they have often been arrested in pubs, such as William Wilton who killed his wife, Sarah, in Brighton in 1887. He was picked up just hours later in the Windmill, now The Dyke Pub & Kitchen, confessing there and then.

Murder victims have even turned up in pubs many years after the event! In October 2010, workmen were redeveloping a derelict pub in Richmond-upon-Thames called the Hole in the Wall for the naturalist and filmmaker David Attenborough who lived next door. They discovered a skull which had been buried where the pub's stables had once stood. Scientific tests concluded that it was the missing head of Julia Martha Thomas, a widow who was known to have been murdered by her maid, Kate Webster, on 2 March 1879 in a house nearby. Webster first pushed her victim down the stairs, then boiled her body before disposing of the body parts around south-west London. She even tried to sell the fatty remains of the dead woman as dripping to the landlady at the Hole in the Wall. Webster was hanged in July 1879 at Wandsworth Prison.

LOCATIONS: **The Bull**, Hall Street, Long Melford, Sudbury, Suffolk, CO10 9JG, 01787 378494, www.oldenglishinns.co.uk; **Maid's Head Hotel**, No. 20 Tombland, Norwich, NR3 1LB, 01603 209955, maidsheadhotel. co.uk; **The Grenadier**, No. 18 Wilton Row, London, SW1X 7NR, 020 7235 3074, www.taylor-walker.co.uk; **The Cat Inn**, Queen's Square, West Hoathly, West Sussex, RH19 4PP, 01342 810369, www.catinn.co.uk; **Double Tree**, No. 4 Bryanston Street, Marble Arch, London, W1H 7BY, 020 7935 2361, doubletree3.hilton.com; **Millennium Hotel**, No. 44 Grosvenor Square, London, W1K 2HP, 020 7629 9400, www.millenniumhotels.co.uk; **The Golden Bell**, Leighton Buzzard, No. 5 Church Square, Leighton Buzzard, Central Bedfordshire, LU7 1AE, 01525 373330, www.thegoldenbell.co.uk; **The Stag**, No. 1 Heath Road, Leighton Buzzard, Bedfordshire, LU7 3AB, 01525 372710; **The Beehive**, No. 14 Mount Pleasant, Liverpool, L3 5RY, 0151 525 8967; **The Maid's Head**, No. 85 Spixworth Road, Old Catton, Norwich, Norfolk, NR6 7NH; **Hotel Russell**, Nos 1–8 Russell Square, London, WC1B 5BE, 020 7837 6470; **Dyke Pub & Kitchen**, No. 218 Dyke Road, Brighton, East Sussex, BN1 5AA, 01273 555672, www.connaughtpub.co.uk

2

MURDEROUS LANDLORDS

Most pub landlords and landladies are genial folk. They are people with whom you can share a joke and enjoy a chat. Sometimes they even provide a shoulder to cry on. But there are exceptions to this rule, and a few have been truly villainous. Tales of murderous landlords date back centuries and the concept of the psychopathic innkeeper has a rich heritage in literature and film. This tradition first arose because travel, until relatively recent times, was an extremely hazardous business. There was not only the threat of being robbed by bandits or highwaymen on your journey, but it was difficult to know whom you could trust as you bedded down for the night in an unfamiliar place. At even some of the best inns you could awake to find your possessions gone in the morning, only taking comfort from the fact that you hadn't been murdered in your bed too.

The Ostrich Inn at Colnbrook, Berkshire, can trace its history to around 1100 when it was a hospice for travellers, though the present building dates to around 1500. It was probably the Crane Inn, mentioned in Thomas Deloney's 1600 work, *The Pleasant Historie of Thomas of Reading*. This tome included the anything but pleasant account of a landlord by the name of Jarman who robbed rich travellers by boiling them. He constructed a special bed in

The Ostrich Inn, Colnbrook, West Berkshire, was the setting for the story of a killer innkeeper. (© *James Moore*)

one of the chambers of the inn above the kitchen. When he was sure his unwitting guest was asleep, the poor soul would then be tipped through a trapdoor into a bubbling cauldron beneath. Jarman, aided by his wife, did away with some sixty people before his ruse was finally rumbled when enquiries were made about one of his missing guests, Thomas Cole. His body was found in the local brook, supposedly giving the village its name. Deloney's work was, in fact, designed as a fictional tale, but the tale about Jarman, which is supposed to have happened in the reign of Henry I, may well have been based on a true story. After all, serial killers are not a new phenomenon and some of Deloney's details are quite specific.

Just a few years after Deloney's work was published, there was a true story of a murder by an innkeeper. In 1654 Thomas Kidderminster, a farmer from Ely in Cambridgeshire, was travelling to London and happened to stay at the now lost White Horse in Chelmsford, Essex. Here he was robbed of the £600 he was carrying and killed by a Mr Sewell, who subsequently gave up running the inn. The murder did not come to light until 1663 when some remains were dug up in the inn's yard by its new owner, a Mr Turner. They appeared to be of a man who had a hole in the side of his skull. Kidderminster's widow read a report in a newspaper asking if anyone might have information regarding the case and realised that the rough date of the supposed killing matched the time that Thomas had gone missing. She conducted her own enquiries and in the end witnesses who had been working at the inn spilled the beans about the crime. Sewell and his wife, who was also implicated, died before they could be tried, but Moses Drayne, the inn's ostler (stableman) at the time of the killing, who had helped bury the body, was hanged for his part in the bloody business.

Other very real tales of killer landlords are not difficult to come by. William Wyatt, landlord of the former Rose and Crown in Fowey, Cornwall, went to the gallows in 1812 after robbing and murdering Isaiah Folk Valentine, drowning his victim near the quay. In January 1878 James Donoghue, the 31-year-old landlord of the Spinner's Arms in Bradford, was convicted of killing Michael Dunn after an argument. Dunn's body was discovered at the back of the pub. In December 1899 Samuel Crozier, landlord of the Admiral Rous Inn at Galleywood Common, Essex, was hanged for murdering his wife, Ann, in a room above the bar. The pub is now a private home.

Perhaps the most infamous publican to have been convicted of murder was George Chapman, a man later linked to the Jack the Ripper murders. His real name was Severin Koslowski and he was thought to have left his native Poland for England in 1888, the year that the Ripper killings began. What is more, he was living in Whitechapel, the area in which the murders took place. By 1890 he was working as a barber underneath the White Hart pub on Whitechapel High Street. He married a Polish woman called Lucy Baderski but another woman from Poland turned up accusing him of already being her husband. Chapman soon left for America. Strangely, around the same time the Ripper murders dried up too.

By 1895 he was back, without his wife, and hooked up with a woman called Mary Spink. They lived in Hastings, Sussex, where he worked as a hairdresser while she played the piano. Soon they were back in London where Chapman became landlord of a former pub, The Prince of Wales in Bartholomew Square. Mary soon became ill with vomiting attacks and died in December 1897. Her death was put down to consumption. Chapman employed a new barmaid, Bessie Taylor, who soon became his 'wife'. The couple moved to the now demolished Grapes in Bishop's Stortford, Herts, where they lived for eighteen months before moving back to London. In 1900 they took on the Monument Tavern in Union Street, Borough. In February 1901, Bessie died too, with similar symptoms to Mary's. Again Chapman moved on, this time to The Crown in Borough High Street, taking on another new barmaid, Maud Marsh. The pair were soon living as husband and wife, but within a year she would be dead. Maud's symptoms were largely the same as the others, but this time the victim's mother, who nursed her, became suspicious and alerted the authorities. A post-mortem found that Maud had been poisoned with antimony. An investigation followed and the bodies of Mary Spink and Bessie Taylor were exhumed. They, too, were found to have been poisoned, and in March 1903 Chapman was found guilty of murder. He was hanged at Wandsworth Prison on 7 April. While Chapman may have been in the right place at the right time and was clearly a man who was habitually cruel towards women, his method of murder, using poison, does not seem to fit with the violent attacks attributed to the Ripper.

A much more modern serial killer also had a history as a landlord. Steve Wright is currently serving life for the murder of five prostitutes in a horrendous killing spree in Ipswich, Suffolk, in 2006. Discovering that their former publican had been a serial killer sent shivers down the spines of drinkers at The White Horse in Chislehurst, south-east London, a pub which has more recently been called The Lounge. Wright also ran two other pubs, the now defunct Ferry Boat Inn at Norwich and the Rose and Crown in Plumstead, south-east London.

Of course being a landlord or landlady can be a dangerous business in itself and they have, themselves, often been the victims of murder. For example, on 10 December 1827, James Winter was executed at Chelmsford for the murder of Thomas Patrick, who ran the Yorkshire Grey pub in Colchester. Patrick had called a constable to the pub after a fight had broken out involving Winter, who then struck the unfortunate landlord with a board. In 1832 William Bradbury, the landlord of the Moorcock Inn, also known as Bill O'Jacks, on lonely Saddleworth Moor, was murdered along with his son Thomas. As he lay dying, the 84-year-old William managed to mutter the words 'pats' before expiring. It was not enough information to help solve the killings and the case remains unsolved. The pub was demolished in 1937. A policeman, Herbert Burrows, was the culprit in 1925 when he shot Ernest and Doris Laight, the landlord and landlady of the Garibaldi Inn, Worcester, along with their son. The 23-year-old, who lived across from the pub – which has since become a takeaway – had done it for the meagre sum in the till and managed to give himself away when he foolishly asked fellow officers if they had heard anything about the killings. They hadn't, as the crime had yet to be reported by anyone else. Burrows was hanged at Gloucester in February 1926.

LOCATIONS: **The Ostrich**, High Street, Colnbrook, West Berkshire, SL3 0JZ, 01753 682628, www.theostrichcolnbrook.co.uk; **White Hart**, No. 89 Whitechapel High Street, Aldgate, London, E1 7RA, 020 7247 1546

3

HOLD-UPS, HIDEOUTS AND HEISTS

Whilst most alehouses, pubs and hotels have been primarily venues for a bit of honest drinking and relaxation, some have seethed with thieves and rogues. For centuries they have been convenient places in which criminals of all types have congregated to plan crimes, get some Dutch courage before their exploits and even share out their ill-gotten gains. As early as 1370 it was recorded that Juliana Fox of Thornbury, Gloucestershire, was charged not only with running a brothel in her alehouse (once a very common practice) but knowingly using it as a rendezvous for robbers. Alehouses, which were often little more than rooms with a few benches before the eighteenth century, were places where impoverished tipplers could make a bit on the side by hiding goods or fencing them. By the early 1600s alehouses were being denounced as 'dens of sheep stealers and robbers'. The concerns were not without basis. During the reign of James I, for instance, a villain called Hampshire Will and fellow thieves met up at a hostelry called The Old Chopping Knife at Wokingham to plan their crime sprees. Yet the role of pubs as places where criminals gathered did not diminish – by the early nineteenth century writers were referring to certain pubs as 'flash houses' where thieves would congregate. Indeed this function has continued right up to the present day, and in the last 400 years the types of crime linked to pubs have only multiplied, while the concern about the link between drink and illegality remains as strong as ever.

Shakespeare's *Henry IV Part One* includes a robbery carried out by Falstaff and his lowlife associates at Gad's Hill in Kent, near Rochester. Indeed there is now a pub, the Sir John Falstaff, named after the character at the spot. After the hold-up they retreat to the Boar's Head Tavern in Eastcheap, London, a watering hole which really existed and burned down in the Great Fire of 1666. At the time the play was written, in the 1590s, Gads Hill was already an infamous haunt of robbers who regularly preyed on travellers, and Shakespeare's comic device reflected a serious real-life problem. The proliferation of alehouses and inns during Tudor times went hand in hand with the increase in highwaymen. In 1537, for example, an innkeeper at The Bear in Hungerford testified that three highwayman had lodged with him after robbing a clothier between Bagshot and Windsor Park.

Of course brigands had always held up travellers but during the seventeenth and eighteenth centuries bold new 'knights of the road' found rich pickings among the new stagecoaches and mail coaches which criss-crossed the country. The highwaymen used a multitude of drinking venues as their hideouts. They were both places to gather information and divide up the proceeds of their endeavours. One might think that after committing a robbery they would immediately head to the baser alehouses where a friendly tapster would be in on the act. While this was often the case, they also headed to upmarket inns on the basis that they were less likely to be searched. And whilst inns were grander than common alehouses, the reformed seventeenth-century highwayman John Clavell warned that even here the staff could be in league with the criminals. Clavell particularly highlighted the role of the ostler who, he said, was often a little too eager to help with a guest's bags in order to weigh them up and work out if they would make a good target on the road for the highwayman who would then give him a commission on a good haul. The Bull Inn at Shooter's Hill towards the south-east of London, which was first built in 1749 and still exists today, was legendary as a place where highwaymen would size up their victims – it would also be a spot where they were gibbeted once caught and executed. The sheer audacity of some highwaymen in the eighteenth century is exhibited at the Black Horse in Cherhill where there hangs a painting of the Cherhill Gang, a group of robbers who terrorised the roads west from London, apparently holding up travellers whilst totally naked.

The most famous of all highwaymen is Dick Turpin, the son of an innkeeper who was active in the early eighteenth century. During his years as a criminal, Turpin used many pubs and even lodged in them (see page 76). But there were plenty of other rascals of the road who made inns and alehouses their headquarters. George Lyon was one of the so-called 'gentlemen highwaymen', though by all accounts a rather cack-handed one. He was hanged at Lancaster in 1815 for holding up the Liverpool mail coach, his only successful robbery, which was planned at the Legs of Man in Wigan, a pub which closed in the 1970s. Lyon used horses loaned from the innkeeper at the Bull's Head Inn in Upholland, also now gone, where he returned to share out the loot with his accomplices. The Royal Anchor Hotel in Liphook, Hampshire, which survives as part of the Hungry Horse chain, was used by the highwayman Captain Jacques. He died there when shot whilst trying to make his escape using a secret passageway behind a fireplace. Meanwhile the highwayman Edward Higgins mixed with polite society at the George and Dragon in Knutsford, Cheshire, an inn which became the Royal George and is now a restaurant. Few of his fellow carousers realised that he was leading a double life as a criminal until he was arrested and hanged in November 1767.

However, as both inns and more humble drinking establishments became more refined towards the end of the eighteenth century, they themselves could be the victims of highwaymen and other robbers. By this era there was often plenty of cash and expensive chattels on the premises. In 1772 at The Sun Inn, Hitchin, three robbers held up the customers and landlord at gunpoint. On the way out with their loot they scratched their initials in the brickwork which can still be seen today. Towards the end of the eighteenth century, many innkeepers began to inform on the highwaymen as they had much to lose in terms of licences and reputation. By the 1830s the era of the highwayman had died out thanks to the development of better roads, tolls and more patrols. Thefts from 'victualing houses' continued, however, with figures showing that they made up the third largest type of robbery in Preston that same year.

During the heyday of smuggling in the late eighteenth and early nineteenth centuries bootleggers also used networks of pubs as bases for their activities, often with the cooperation of the publicans. Indeed in 1739 a government agent put the success of smugglers down to the fact that innkeepers often harboured them. Of course, the most famous of all smugglers' pubs is the Jamaica Inn on Cornwall's lonely Bodmin Moor, where there is even a museum dedicated to its treacherous history. The writer Daphne Du Maurier put Jamaica Inn on the map with her tales of ships being lured onto the rocks and wrecked so that their cargoes could be plundered. The inn, built in 1750, really was used by smugglers who used 100 different routes across the moors when transporting their contraband, and often made for the isolated Jamaica as a place to store the goods. Among the illicit items were tea, tobacco and brandy. In fact there were hundreds of pubs along England's south and east coasts which provided the cover for smuggling. The Lobster Smack on Canvey Island, which dates back to 1600, is one of the best known, while the history of the inns in the village of Alfriston in Sussex is interwoven with that of smuggling. Both the fourteenth-century Star and The Market Cross Inn were used by smugglers operating in the English Channel. The latter, which has now cashed in by renaming itself Ye Olde Smugglers Inn, was the headquarters of smuggling leader Stanton Collins. Like many such pubs it has a network of secret tunnels used to escape the beady eyes of the excise officers. It was one of these that met an untimely end when Collins' gang pushed him off a cliff nearby. Collins was finally arrested and transported to Australia for sheep stealing.

In more recent times, pubs have played roles in cases of organised crime. Members of the gang that took part in the Great Train Robbery of 1963 hatched their plans in the pubs and clubs of London. Chief among these was the Star Tavern in upmarket

The Star Tavern, Belgravia, West London, where the Great Train Robbery was planned. (© *James Moore*)

Belgravia, the favourite drinking spot of the heist's suave mastermind Bruce Reynolds. Other pubs, including The Spencer Arms in Putney and The Angelsea Arms in South Kensington, claim to have done their bit as the caper was organised. The robbers, who held up a Royal Mail train in Buckinghamshire, got away with £2.6 million. Then there was the Brinks–Mat robbery in 1983, which saw £25 million in gold stolen at Heathrow Airport, most of which was never recovered. George Francis, one of those thought to have laundered the loot, was gunned down dead in 2003. He had only narrowly avoided being killed in 1985 when he was shot by a hooded gunman at his pub, the Henry VIII, in Hever Castle, Kent.

LOCATIONS: *Sir John Falstaff*, Gravesend Road, Rochester, Kent, ME3 7NZ, 01634 717104, www.sirjohnfalstaff.co.uk; *The Bear Hotel*, No. 41 Charnham Street, Hungerford, West Berkshire, RG17 0EL, 01488 682512, www.thebearhotelhungerford.co.uk; *The Bull*, No. 151 Shooters Hill, London, SE18 3HP, 020 8856 0691; *The Black Horse*, Main Road, Cherhill, Calne, Wiltshire, 01249 813365, www.theblackhorsecherhill.co.uk; *Royal Anchor*, Nos 9-11 The Square, Liphook, Hampshire, GU30 7AD, 01428 722244, www.hungryhorse.co.uk; *The Sun Hotel*, Sun Street, Hitchin, Hertfordshire, SG5 1AF, 01462 432092, www.oldenglishinns.co.uk; *Jamaica Inn*, Bolventor, Launceston, Cornwall, PL15 7TS, 01566 86250, www.jamaicainn.co.uk; *The Lobster Smack*, Haven Road, Canvey Island, Essex, SS8 0NR, 01268 514297, www.thelobstersmackcanveyisland.co.uk; *The Star*, High Street, Alfriston, East Sussex BN26 5TA, 01323 870495, www.thestaralfriston.co.uk; *Ye Olde Smugglers Inne*, Waterloo Square, Alfriston, Polegate, East Sussex, BN26 5UE, 01323 870241, www.yeoldesmugglersinne.co.uk; *The Star Tavern*, No. 6 Belgrave Mews West, London, SW1X 8HT, 020 7235 3019, www.star-tavern-belgravia.co.uk; *The Spencer Arms*, No. 237 Lower Richmond Road, Putney, London, SW15 1HJ, www.thespencerpub.co.uk; *The Angelsea Arms*, No. 15 Selwood Terrace, South Kensington, London SW7 3QG, 020 7373 7960, www.angleseaarms.com; *The Henry VIII*, Hever Road, Edenbridge, Kent, TN8 7NH, 01732 862 457, www.shepherdneame.co.uk

PLOTS, RIOTS AND REBELLIONS

4

On 20 May 1604, a group of five men met for a secret meeting at an inn called the Duck and Drake near The Strand in St Clement's parish of London. The inn was the place where a Catholic called Thomas Winter usually stayed when he was in the capital. Joining Winter were a small band of co-conspirators: Robert Catesby, the leader, along with John Wright, Thomas Percy and Guy Fawkes. It was here, no doubt fuelled by a little wine, that they formulated their plan to kill King James I. As Thomas Winter later confessed:

> So we met behind St. Clement's, Mr. Catesby, Mr. Percy, Mr. Wright, Mr. Guy Fawkes, and myself, and having, upon a primer, given each other the oath of secrecy, in a chamber where no other body was, we went after into the next room and heard Mass, and received the blessed Sacrament upon the same.

As every history student knows, the plot involved hiding barrels of gunpowder in a cellar underneath the House of Lords. The intention was to blow up everyone inside, including the monarch, on 5 November, during the opening of parliament. The scheme was uncovered at the last moment thanks to a tip-off.

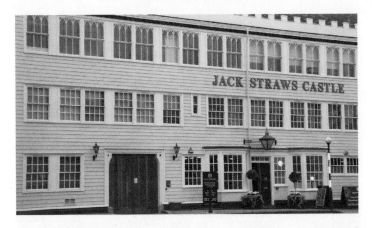

Jack Straw's Castle, a former pub which got its name from a fourteenth-century rebel. (© *James Moore*)

It was not the first occasion when one of the nation's inns had been at the centre of an attempt to overthrow the ruling elite, nor would it be the last. An earlier rebellion, which originated in Kent, had seen Jack Cade head a popular uprising against King Henry VI and lead an army to London. He made the White Hart in Southwark his headquarters before storming across London Bridge into the city. The revolt was soon put down after a battle on the bridge itself. The White Hart, which was next door to the existing George, a similar inn on Borough High Street, was pulled down in the nineteenth century. Another failed rebellion, that of Thomas Wyatt against Queen Mary in 1554, ended outside another of London's most historic lost inns, the Belle Sauvage. It was here that Wyatt rested in despair on a bench, realising that the game was up. Beheaded for treason, Wyatt didn't get the accolade of having a London pub named after him like former rebel Jack Straw. One of the leaders of the Peasant's Revolt, in 1381, Straw was also executed. But he was remembered at the Jack's Straw's Castle in Hampstead, North London. The pub, which closed in the 1990s, commemorated an earlier speech to followers made on the heath from a hay wagon.

In 1780, London was rocked by the Gordon Riots, which erupted after the government proposed legislation to reduce the

The Spaniards Inn, Hampstead, North London, where eighteenth-century riots were thwarted by the landlord. (*Courtesy of Mitchells & Butlers*)

The Boot in Cromer Street, London. Leaders of the Gordon Riots assembled in a previous incarnation here. (© *James Moore*)

restrictions imposed on Catholics. During the unrest 700 people were killed and 12,000 troops had to be deployed to put down the uprising. The leaders of the riots would meet at The Boot tavern in Cromer Street near King's Cross. At one point during the disturbances a mob marched on Kenwood House in Hampstead, the home of the pro-Catholic Lord Chief Justice, the Earl of Mansfield. They intended to burn the villa to the ground, but on the way they stopped at The Spaniards Inn, already nearly 200 years old, for refreshments. The Spaniards has since been mentioned in both Charles Dickens' *Pickwick Papers* and Bram Stoker's *Dracula*. On this occasion, a shrewd landlord plied his rowdy customers with free drink until cavalry arrived to protect the house. There were more religious disturbances in the Midlands in 1791 when the Birmingham Hotel in the city's Temple Row was attacked because it was the venue of a dinner held by dissenters to celebrate the French Revolution.

In the early nineteenth century another pub, the Horse and Groom in Cato Street, London, played a role in foiling the so-called Cato Street Conspiracy, an attempt to kill the Prime Minister Lord Liverpool and the cabinet. The conspirators were Spencean Philanthropists who believed in the common ownership of land and met in pubs like the Cock in Grafton Street and Nag's Head in Carnaby Market as well as the Horse and Groom in Marylebone. The latter overlooked a stable where, on 23 February, in a hayloft, the plotters assembled to finalise their plans. However, a police spy was watching them arrive from the Horse and Groom. A magistrate and some soldiers were alerted and arrived to arrest the gang. A scuffle ensued in which one man was killed. Five of those involved in the plot, including Thistlewood, were hanged for high treason at Newgate Prison on 1 May 1820. The Horse and Groom is long gone, but there is a plaque in Cato Street to show the location of the original hayloft.

Despite the failure of this conspiracy, threats to the establishment would increase in the 1830s as elements of society began to press for reform. At this time the Swing Riots swept Southern England as agricultural workers protested against their poor conditions. On 20 November a mob of 300 labourers in Andover, Hampshire, set out from the Angel Inn to smash up

Rioters set out from The Angel, Andover,
to destroy a local ironworks in 1830.
(© *James Moore*)

a local ironworks. Several of those who took part were transported for life.

In 1848, Europe was swept by a string of popular revolutions, and in England the Chartists, campaigning for electoral reform, were at the height of their influence. Members often met in pubs, like the One Bell in Crayford. The biggest Chartist meeting of some 150,000 people in April of that year on London's Kennington Common had failed to prompt the government to meet any of their demands. And now a group of frustrated, prominent Chartists planned an armed insurrection in the capital. They first met in June at the Albion beershop on Bethnal Green Road, East London. However, police spies had been at work again and on 16 August the ringleaders were caught at the Orange Tree pub on Orange Street in central London while others were rounded up at the Angel on Webber Street in Southwark. While Chartist leaders were locked up or transported, many of their demands, such as a secret ballot in elections and payment of MPs, did eventually become law. Today, in Huddersfield, there is even a pub named the Chartist.

In the twentieth century came a very different threat to the state in the form of terrorism. And during the Troubles in Northern Ireland para-military organisations would make pubs and hotels the focus of bombing campaigns both on and off the mainland. On 5 October 1974 the IRA targeted two pubs in Guildford, Surrey, because they were regularly used by British army personnel. The bomb that went off in the Horse and Groom at 8.30 p.m. killed five people and injured sixty-five. The Seven Stars was evacuated before the bomb there exploded at 9 p.m.

The following month, two more pubs in Birmingham were blown up. On 21 November bombs went off at the Mulberry Bush and the Tavern in the Town, killing a total of twenty-one people. The site of the Mulberry Bush is now a tourist centre and the Tavern in the Town was rebuilt as the Yard of Ale before becoming a Chinese restaurant.

In 1975 a device planted by the IRA went off in the lobby of the London Hilton on Park Lane, killing two people. Seven years later eleven soldiers and six civilians were killed by an INLA bomb at The Droppin' Well pub in Ballykelly, County Londonderry, which later became the Riverside Bar.

Perhaps the best known attack of the Troubles was the Brighton Hotel Bombing on 12 October 1984. The Victorian Grand Hotel, built in 1684, was ripped apart by a bomb during the Conservative Party conference. It was aimed at killing senior members of the British government. The Prime Minister narrowly escaped death but five people perished.

LOCATIONS: *The Boot*, No. 116 Cromer Street, King's Cross, 020 7837 3842; *The Spaniards Inn*, Spaniards Road, Hampstead, London, NW3 7JJ, 020 8731 8406, www.thespaniardshampstead.co.uk; *The Angel*, Andover, No. 95 High Street, Andover, SP10 1ND, 01264 365464; *One Bell*, No. 170 Old Road, Dartford, DA1 4DY, 01322 315444; *The Chartist*, No. 74 Commercial Road, Skelmanthorpe, Huddersfield, West Yorkshire, HD8 9DS, 01484 864322; *London Hilton*, No. 22 Park Lane, London, W1K 1BE, 020 7493 8000, www.parklanehilton.com; *The Grand Hotel*, Brighton, Nos 97–99 King's Road, Brighton, East Sussex, BN1 2FW, 01273 224300, www.grandbrighton.co.uk

BODIES IN THE BAR, POST-MORTEMS AND INQUESTS

5

Until well into the twentieth century, dead bodies that were discovered in mysterious circumstances were often taken to the local pub or hotel in the first instance. With few official mortuaries they were often simply the nearest 'public' place and usually had outbuildings where a corpse could be kept while investigations into how the person had come to die were carried out. In this way, many victims of murder have wound up in pubs, acting as temporary morgues, shortly after their deaths. Given the lack of refrigeration techniques, post-mortems needed to be done quickly and were often done in the pubs too by the nearest surgeon to hand.

On 7 May 1819 the corpse of Stephen Rodway, a coal merchant from Cricklade, was brought to the Bell at Purton Stoke in Wiltshire. The man had been travelling home with a good deal of money after conducting business in Wootton Bassett and had been found lying dead in the road. At 11 p.m. a local surgeon, William Wells, arrived at the Bell to examine the body and subsequently conducted an autopsy there. He found that Rodway had been shot three times. A man had been spotted riding away from the scene of the murder and a bare-knuckle fighter called Robert Watkins was arrested and tried for the murder. He was hanged in the village that July.

Conducting post-mortems in pubs was not always condu-
cive to proper scientific enquiry, as in the case of the serial killer
William Palmer. Palmer murdered a string of people in the mid-
nineteenth century (see page 116) but was only brought to book
after he poisoned his friend John Cook with strychnine at a hotel
in Rugeley, Staffordshire. His medical credentials meant that
Palmer was actually present at the post-mortem on Cook when
it was carried out at the hotel, during which he tried to disrupt
its conduct.

Unsurprisingly, when bodies turned up in a pub, gossip
soon spread locally and often there was a clamour to view the
body. Sometimes this was indulged, as in the strange case of the
Sir William Courtenay who took part in what was dubbed the
last battle in England in 1838. Courtenay was a self-styled knight
whose real name was John Nichols Thom. He was an innkeeper's
son and wine merchant from Cornwall who later spent time in an
asylum in Kent before becoming convinced he was the Messiah.
Somehow he managed to recruit a band of disaffected unemployed farm labourers and launch a minor uprising in the county.
The army had to be called out and, in a battle at Bossenden Wood
near Faversham, Courtenay and seven of his followers were killed
along with two soldiers. Having claimed he was immortal, the
authorities were keen to show that Courtenay was very much
dead in order to quash any more trouble. They exhibited his
body, along with those of his dead comrades, in the stables of the
Red Lion at Dunkirk. Such was the frenzy to see the bodies and
take away souvenirs that the landlord eventually had to nail shut
the windows and doors of the pub to protect his property from
being ransacked.

Even into the twentieth century, before the advent of
meticulous forensic examination of murder scenes and easy com-
munications, the first thought in an apparent murder was not to
leave the body where it lay but to remove it to a safe location.
The Royal Oak in Stapleford Abbots, Essex, was PC George
Gutteridge's local, just 100yds from where he lived. He often
popped in for a pint. And it was to the pub's coach house that his
body was brought after he was gunned down in 1927. George
had stopped two men driving a stolen car in a nearby lane who

The Red Lion in Dunkirk, Kent, where the body of Sir William Courtenay was put on view to the public. (*Courtesy of The Red Lion*)

had then shot him. The culprits were eventually tracked down and hanged.

Three years later, on 5 November, the charred remains of a body were found in a burning car in a lane near the village of Hardingstone in Northamptonshire. The remains were taken to the Crown Inn where they were the subject of a post-mortem conducted in the pub's garage. Alfred Arthur Rouse, a 36-year-old salesman aiming to dodge his debts and start a new life, had hoped police would think that the body was his. It had been found in the Morris Minor that he owned. However, police discovered that Rouse had actually picked up a hitchhiker, clubbed him to death and intentionally set light to the car before going on the run. Rouse, who later confessed to the crime, went to the gallows in Bedford on 10 March 1931, even though his murder victim was never identified.

Until the end of the nineteenth century, inquests into suspicious deaths were routinely carried out at pubs. It may seem strange today but, until the advent of dedicated coroner's courts, pubs and hotels were often the obvious choice, especially in rural districts, as they were large enough to accommodate all the necessary officials, witnesses and a jury. Plus, of course, refreshments were on tap. This fact led Charles Dickens to observe in his satirical novel *Bleak House*, published in the early 1850s, that the coroner 'frequents more public houses than any man alive'. As we have seen, the body of the deceased was often already at the pub, making it easy for a twelve-strong inquest jury – hastily chosen from the ranks of local men – to inspect the remains. Then in the same location, evidence would be heard in front of the coroner. Often the public would be allowed in too. After the jury's deliberations, sometimes aided by a little ale, the verdict on the cause of death was given; any murder or manslaughter suspect who had been identified was given up to the authorities for a full trial at the local assizes.

This state of affairs was often a recipe for chaos. Dickens was a noted campaigner for social reform and he, for one, did not approve of the habit of holding these serious affairs in an environment that was hardly sober or fitting for a modernising democracy. *Bleak House* features an inquest which is held at the fictional Sol's Arms. The coroner finds it almost impossible to be heard above the noise of the pub's customers busily playing skittles in the background. This was not a wild parody. In 1889 a medical journalist by the name of Sprigge wrote a scathing appraisal of the pub inquest, saying that 'The tint of the tavern-parlour vitiated the evidence, ruined the discretion of the jurors, and detracted from the dignity of the juror.' He went on to complain that 'the majesty of death evaporated with the fumes from the gin of the jury'. In 1847 an inquest at a pub into the deaths of three children in Ely, Cambridgeshire, descended into farce with the fathers of the deceased drunk in the bar and the mothers shouting obscene language. Despite the criticism, the practice of holding inquests in pubs was commonplace right up until the 1890s, with one piece of research showing that almost every inquest in Lancashire at the time was held in a pub.

The details of many of the most famous murder cases in British history first emerged at inquests in public houses. The case of Mary Ann Cotton, who has been described as Britain's first female serial killer, initially came to the public's attention following an inquest at the Rose and Crown, West Auckland, a pub which was then next door to the house in which she lived. By the time of the proceedings, Mary Ann had poisoned as many as twenty people, including three husbands, collecting lucrative insurance payouts along the way. In 1870 Mary Ann had hooked up with Frederick Cotton, but like many of her other victims, he died from stomach problems, followed by his son Frederick Junior and the couple's baby, Robert. In July 1872 the last remaining Cotton child, Charles, died too, apparently from gastric fever. Yet a parish official had become suspicious after Mary Ann told him, 'I won't be troubled long. He'll go like all the rest of the Cottons.' A hurried post-mortem was inconclusive and the jury at the inquest returned a verdict of death by natural causes. But newspaper reporters began to look into Mary Ann's past and found that a string of untimely deaths were linked to her. Meanwhile Charles' doctor had kept samples of the child's organs and they tested positive for arsenic. Mary Ann was found guilty of murder and executed at Durham Jail on 24 March 1873.

Another famous murder case where the initial inquest was heard in a pub was the killing of 3-year-old Francis Saville Kent in 1860 in the village of Rode, then in Wiltshire. His body had been found under a privy at the family home. Proceedings were initially held at the Red Lion in the village, where the verdict was 'wilful murder' by a person or persons unknown. Francis' half-sister Constance, who had been 16 at the time, was tried for the murder some five years later and imprisoned for life. The case would become the subject of a best-selling book, *The Suspicions of Mr Whicher, Or the murder at Road Hill House*, by Kate Summerscale.

Pub inquests only began to die away after the 1875 Public Health Act ordered the setting up of public mortuaries and coroners' courts across the country. The 1902 Licensing Act went further by forbidding the holding of inquests in public houses if any decent alternative existed, though some were still being carried out right up until the 1920s.

LOCATIONS: **The Bell Inn**, Purton Stoke, Swindon, Wiltshire, SN5 9JG, 01793 770434, www.arkells.com; **Red Lion**, Dunkirk, Faversham, Kent, ME13 9LL, 01227 750224, www.theredlionpubdunkirk.co.uk; **Crown Inn**, No. 57 High Street, Hardingstone, NN4 6BZ, 01604 708726.

6

COURTROOMS AND PRISONS

As well as venues for inquests, inns were used as courtrooms right up until the turn of the twentieth century. The practice of magistrates holding sessions in licensed premises was not outlawed until 1902. Before the widespread provision of police courts, large inns were sometimes the most convenient places for more minor cases to be heard, especially in rural areas. From the start of the eighteenth century, pubs were most often the setting for monthly petty sessions, the lowest tier of the court system where misdemeanours like theft and assault were handled along with, ironically, cases of drunkenness and the provision of licences for public houses. Matters were judged without a jury by local justices of the peace, who would decide whether the case needed to be passed on to the next level, the quarter sessions. The Cock Hotel in Stony Stratford, Buckinghamshire, was one inn that held petty sessions, as was The White Hart in Welwyn, Hertfordshire. Some, like the Sun Hotel in Lancaster, heard more serious cases in quarter sessions four times a year. Proceedings were often held in back or upstairs rooms. There were other types of court held at inns. The George and Dragon at Baldock, Herts, which dates back to 1465, had an archdeacons' court, while The Speech House in Coleford, Gloucestershire, is still the venue for meetings of the ancient verderers' court, charged with administering the Forest of Dean.

Down the centuries, inns have also been used as makeshift prisons. This was often linked to executions. Before modern methods of communication it might take several days to take a prisoner to the place at which they were to be tried or hanged. Constables and their charges would often lodge overnight at an inn, sometimes tied together while they slept (See the Red Barn Murder, page 98). In 1555, for example, George Tankerfield was kept overnight at the now demolished Cross Keys Inn at St Albans, Hertfordshire, before he could be burned at the stake for his heretical religious views. Prisoners were also kept overnight at the Boar's Head in Standish on their way to meet their executioners in Lancaster after being found guilty at the Chester Assizes. Even the most esteemed guests could be shut up at inns. In 1569 Mary Queen of Scots, confined by Queen Elizabeth I of England, was briefly moved from her 'prison' at Tutbury Castle in Staffordshire to the walled city of Coventry after an uprising in the north for safekeeping. She was lodged at the long gone Bull Inn. During the following years Mary was given a large degree of freedom and, although strictly a prisoner, was allowed to spend summers at the spa town of Buxton, staying at the New Hall or the Inne of the Sign of the Talbot. Her movements were strictly regulated but she enjoyed her stay.

The same building is now a hotel called the Old Hall and it was here that Mary scratched a message with a diamond ring into one of the bedroom window panes, which read 'Buxton, whose warm waters have made thy name famous, perchance I shall visit thee no more, farewell.' In the summer of 1586, after being implicated in a plot to assassinate Elizabeth, Mary was moved to Fotheringay from her imprisonment in another Staffordshire castle, staying at The Swan, now known as The Haycock Hotel, on her way. She was executed at Fotheringay on 8 February 1587. Mary wasn't the last supposed enemy of the state to be shut up at an inn. As recently as the Napoleonic Wars, high profile French prisoners could find themselves under a kind of 'public house' arrest. After the Battle of Trafalgar, the captured commander of the British and French forces, Admiral Villeneuve, did not find himself thrown in a rancid cell as you might expect, but lodged at the Crown Inn at Bishop's Waltham in Hampshire.

LOCATIONS: *The Cock Hotel*, No. 72 High Street, Stony Stratford, Milton Keynes, Buckinghamshire, MK11 1AH, 01908 567773; www.oldenglishinns. co.uk; *The White Hart Hotel*, No. 2 Prospect Place, Welwyn, Hertfordshire, AL6 9EN, 01438 715353, www.thewhiteharthotel.net; *The Sun Hotel and Bar*, Nos 63–65 Church Street, Lancaster, Lancs, LA1 1ET, 01524 66006, www.thesunhotelandbar.co.uk; *The George and Dragon*, No. 2 Hitchin Street, Baldock, Herts, SG7 6AL, www.thegeorgeatbaldock.co.uk; *The Speech House Hotel*, Coleford, Gloucestershire, GL16 7EL, 01594 822 607, www.thespeechhouse.co.uk; *Boar's Head*, Wigan Road, Standish, Lancashire, 01942 749747, www.boarsheadstandish.co.uk; *Old Hall Hotel*, The Square, Buxton, SK17 6BD, 01298 22841, www.oldhallhotelbuxton.co.uk; *The Haycock Hotel*, Wansford, Peterborough, PE8 6JA, 01780 782223; *Crown Inn*, St George's Square, Bishops Waltham, Hampshire, SO32 1AF, 01489 893350, www.crowninnbishopswaltham.co.uk.

INNS AND EXECUTIONS

From the twelfth century until 1783, Tyburn, near today's Marble Arch, was the principal place where criminals in the city of London would be executed. Over the centuries, hundreds of people were hanged here and each execution was a public spectacle, witnessed by hundreds of jeering onlookers. They were often provided with special stands constructed for the event. Even the traditional 2.5-mile journey from Newgate Prison in the city to Tyburn was a piece of theatre. Until the late eighteenth century, the route went via Holborn, St Giles and what is now Oxford Street, and the condemned person would be paraded in an open cart. On the way the prisoners also got to stop for a last alcoholic beverage, perhaps to steel their nerves and cause the hangman less trouble. The Bowl on St Giles High Street was one of the customary places to pause. In 1727 the author Jonathan Swift caught the atmosphere of these occasions when he wrote about the execution of Tom Clinch, based on the highwayman Tom Cox who had been hanged at Tyburn in 1691:

As Clever Tom Clinch, while the Rabble was bawling,
Rode stately through Holbourn, to die in his Calling;
He stopt at the George for a Bottle of Sack,
And promis'd to pay for it when he'd come back.

Jack Sheppard. *in the Room Called the* Caftle. *in* Newgate.

The notorious eighteenth-century thief Jack Sheppard, one of those condemned to die at Tyburn, who stopped at a tavern for a traditional last drink on the way to the gallows. (*Courtesy of Wellcome Images*)

The Mason's Arms in Berkeley Street was probably the last port of call on the way to Tyburn. It is said that the prisoners were manacled to the walls of the basement, in case their last draught on earth might inspire them to try and escape. Jack Sheppard, a notorious eighteenth-century English thief who became known for a string of ingenious escapes from London prisons, was finally hanged at Tyburn in November 1724. Sheppard, who was only 22, took his final drink at the City of Oxford pub where he downed a pint of 'sack' (fortified wine). Other reports say he also stopped off at The White Hart in Drury Lane. His hanging was witnessed by a staggering 200,000 people. Similar last drinks were offered to those facing the gallows in other cities around the country.

There was plenty of dark humour involved in these spectacles. Legend has it that in 1635 a condemned man by the name of Thomas Witherington asked for his procession from gaol to

The Angel and Royal Hotel in Grantham, Lincolnshire, where Richard III signed the Duke of Buckingham's death warrant in 1483 (*Courtesy of the Angel and Royal Hotel*)

Tyburn not to go via the usual route past the Three Cups Inn because he still owed money there and didn't want to be arrested for debt. Also, the phrase 'on the waggon', for being abstemious, is thought to allude to the convict's last drink in this world before getting back on the cart to make the final leg of their journey to the hangman.

Inns have also been the location for both the ordering and carrying out of executions. On 19 October 1483, Richard III was staying at one of the nation's grandest and oldest inns, The Angel in Grantham, now known as The Angel & Royal Hotel, when he signed the death warrant against his cousin, the Duke of Buckingham, for treason. Despite Buckingham's attempts to escape he was caught and brought to Salisbury. On 2 November he was executed in the courtyard of the Blue Boar.

In a remote part of Wales, executions may once have actually been carried out inside an inn. The Skirrid claims to date back to 1100, which would make it one of the oldest surviving pubs in Britain. Though there is little in the way of documentary evidence, local legend, passed down from generation to generation, has it that men sentenced to die by the local courts which sat in the inn were dispatched from a beam at the bottom of a set of stairs where rope marks can still be seen. According to the story, some 180 people were hanged this way, the last being for stealing sheep in the seventeenth century.

A number of old inns have 'gallows' signs – ones that extend out over the road from the premises. Most of these were purely for the purposes of advertising. But at the seventeenth-century George at Crawley in Sussex, later a haunt of serial killer John George Haigh (see page 233), there was an actual gallows outside the inn and condemned men were kept in cells beneath the Brewery Shades pub nearby, with subterranean passageways linking the two hostelries. In 1784 at Mudeford Quay there was a battle between smugglers barricaded inside the Haven House Inn and excise men. George Coombes, one of the bootleggers, was later hanged for his involvement and gibbeted outside the pub.

LOCATIONS: *The Mason's Arms*, No. 51 Upper Berkeley Street, London, W1H 7QW, 020 7723 2131; *The White Hart*, No. 191 Drury Lane, London, WC2B 5QD, 020 7242 2317, www.whitehartdrurylane.co.uk; *The Angel & Royal Hotel*, High Street, Grantham, Lincolnshire, NG31 6PN, 01476 565816, www.angelandroyal.co.uk, *The Skirrid Mountain Inn*, Llanvihangel Crucorney, Monmouthshire, NP7 8DH, 01873 890258, www.skirridmountaininn.co.uk; The George Hotel is now the *Ramada Crawley Gatwick*, High Street, Crawley, RH10 1BS, 01293 524 215, www.ramadagatwickhotel.com; *The Brewery Shades*, No. 85 High Street, Crawley, West Sussex, RH10 1BA, 01293 514105; *The Haven House Inn*, Mudeford Quay, Christchurch, Dorset, 01425 272609

8

LANDLORDS AND HANGMEN

Britain's best known hangman, Albert Pierrepoint, also ran a pub. Along with his job as an executioner during the middle of the twentieth century, he was landlord of the curiously named Help the Poor Struggler in Oldham, Lancashire. Pierrepoint took on the pub after the Second World War, when his reputation for expertly despatching the condemned was already well established. His persona at the pub could not have been more different from his grim job behind the walls of the nation's prisons.

At the Struggler he entertained customers with sing-a-longs and bar tricks. His identity as an executioner soon came to light after he was flown to Germany to hang Nazi war criminals, and many called at the pub, along with another hostelry he ran called the Rose and Crown at Hoole near Preston, to glimpse the dapper Pierrepoint pulling pints. The Rose and Crown is now an Indian restaurant, while the Struggler was demolished in 1972 for a new road.

During his twenty-five years at the gallows, Pierrepoint hanged more than 400 people, including the wartime traitor Lord Haw Haw, the acid bath murderer John George Haigh and Ruth Ellis, the last woman to be hanged in Britain. But the execution that probably made the biggest impression on Pierrepoint was of someone whose crime did not become a national sensation. In 1950 Pierrepoint was charged with hanging James Corbitt, one of the regulars at his own pub. The pair had even sung duets together there. In fact they had sung 'Danny Boy' together on the night that Corbitt had gone on to murder his girlfriend, Eliza Wood, at the now defunct Prince of Wales Hotel in Ashton-under-Lyne. Before escorting him to the noose in November 1950, Pierrepoint was said to have put Corbitt more at ease by using his nickname, Tish. The unpleasant task of hanging a friend from his 'other life' contributed to Pierrepoint's growing belief that the death penalty didn't work. In his 1974 autobiography, *Executioner: Pierrepoint*, he recalled returning to the pub after carrying out Corbitt's execution at Strangeways Prison in Manchester. He wrote:

> As I polished the glasses, I thought if any man had a deterrent to murder poised before him, it was this troubadour whom I called Tish. He was not only aware of the rope, he had the man who handled it beside him singing a duet. The deterrent did not work.

Pierrepoint is often referred to as England's last hangman, but that isn't quite correct. He retired in 1956 and one of the two final hangings were carried out on 13 August 1964 by Harry Allen. Like Pierrepoint, Allen was also a publican, running both the Rope and Anchor in Farnworth near Bolton and the Junction Inn at Whitefield, Manchester.

Interestingly drink had long been an issue with the job of hangman. Pierrepoint's own father, Henry, had been sacked from the role in 1910 after being found drunk before he was due to carry out an execution in Chelmsford, Essex. It wasn't the first incident of its type. In the 1880s the hangman Bartholomew Binns frequently turned up at the gallows worse for wear, botching executions. He was finally dismissed after his drunkenness was believed to have contributed to the horrible end of a man who was sentenced to death in Liverpool. The prisoner had choked to death over a quarter of an hour.

Another Victorian hangman, James Berry, would hold court in local pubs before a hanging, telling tales and singing songs.

Indeed, in October 1885, the Home Office became so concerned about the behaviour of hangmen that they wrote to the Prison Commission advising that executioners should reside in the prison on the night before undertaking their duties, presumably so that they would avoid the temptations of drink.

9
SIGNS OF THE CRIMES

We are used to encountering pubs with names that recall national heroes like Lord Nelson and the Duke of Wellington. But there are also plenty of watering holes named after some of the less upstanding citizens from our past, even where there is no direct link between the bar and the individual. When it comes to pubs named after criminals, Dick Turpin wins hands down. Scores more claim to have harboured the eighteenth-century rogue, who has become a much romanticised figure, though he was no stranger to committing violent theft and bloody murder (see page 76).

Turpin is not the only highwayman to find himself immortalised on a pub sign. John Nevison, nicknamed Swift Nick, was another of the supposed 'gentleman highwayman' operating in the century before, and details of his life, most notably his alleged flight to York from the south, have since been wrongly credited to the now much better known Turpin. But Nevison has not been forgotten by the brewing industry. His exploits are remembered at The Nevison's Leap in Pontefract and The Nevison Inn at Leigh in Lancashire. Sixteen String Jack, a pub in Theydon Bois, Essex, commemorates Jack Rann, a highwayman who was tried and acquitted six times for highway robbery before finally being convicted and hanged in 1774. The 24-year-old was said to have danced a jig before being executed at Tyburn. There are at least twenty-six more pubs across Britain called simply The Highwayman.

Smugglers are another favourite when it comes to pub names. As well as generic names such as The Smugglers, specific boot-leggers are recalled at places like Gulliver's Tavern in Kinson, Bournemouth. Isaac Gulliver led a band of fifty smugglers operating along the south coast at the end of the eighteenth century. He once escaped investigating customs men by lying in an open coffin with white powder on his face. Gulliver's wife told the officers that her husband had died. Gulliver later became a respected figure in the local community and died a wealthy man. Like many pubs, the Gulliver's Tavern is supposed to have a secret tunnel used by the smugglers to avoid detection.

Of course most smugglers and highwaymen were actually hardened criminals, but society seems to be less squeamish about toasting these ne'er-do-wells of yesteryear than plain murderers, even in the case of the world's most infamous and still uniden-tified killer, Jack the Ripper. When The Ten Bells in London's Spitalfields (see page 147) briefly changed its name to Jack the Ripper, on account of the fact that many of his victims drank there in the late 1880s, it was soon changed back again. The moniker had been deemed distasteful.

Less reviled criminals, however, have escaped censure. The Margaret Catchpole in Ipswich pays homage to a remarkable real-life character from the eighteenth century. In the summer of 1797, Catchpole stole a horse and rode it 70 miles to London before being arrested. She then managed to escape from Ipswich jail using a clothes line. She was sentenced to death but this was commuted to transportation for life and Catchpole ended her days in Australia. The Alice Lisle in Ringwood, Hampshire, gets its name from Lady Alice Lisle who sheltered fugitives from the Monmouth Rebellion of 1685. She was beheaded for the 'crime' on 2 September 1685 in Winchester market place opposite what is now the Eclipse Inn, a pub her restless soul is said to haunt.

There are also pubs named after more mythical criminals. Sawney Bean's Howff in Saltcoats, Clyde, is named after the almost certainly fictitious Sawney Bean, who was said to have led a family of cannibal brigands living in Galloway in the 1500s. The Wicked Lady, in Wheathampstead, Hertfordshire, is named after Lady Katherine Ferrers. She was a genuine seventeenth-century aristocrat who, legend has it, turned to highway robbery and died after being shot in an attempted robbery, though there is little evidence to support the stories about her criminal activities.

Some pub names recall specific crimes rather than their perpetrators, though the details of what exactly happened have been lost. The Quiet Woman near Buxton in Derbyshire recalls a landlord's wife who supposedly met a sticky end. The Bucket of Blood in Phillack, Cornwall, got its gruesome name when a former landlord went to the well nearby and found blood when he pulled up the bucket. A corpse of a murdered man was found at the bottom. Other drinking establishments wallow in the execution of criminals, with a host of pubs calling themselves The Gallows. One, on Great Tower Street in London, is called The Hung Drawn And Quartered. It was the penalty in medieval times for those found guilty of high treason to be hanged, disembowelled and then cut up into pieces. There is also The Three Legged Mare in York, which refers to a special gallows which consisted of a wooden triangle supported by pillars that could hang three people at the same time.

But what about those who administer the law and bring the guilty to justice? Surely they deserve to be commemorated on a few pub signs? Sadly, while there are a few pubs named after judges, there are none, it seems, named after policemen. Fictional detective Sherlock Holmes does, however, have his own pub on Northumberland Street in London's West End.

LOCATIONS: *The Nevison's Leap*, Ferrybridge Road, Pontefract, West Yorkshire, WF8 2PG, 01977 702529; *The Nevison Inn*, No. 96 Plank Lane, Leigh, Lancashire, WN7 4QE, 01942 671 394; *Sixteen String Jack*, Coppice Row, Theydon Bois, CM16 7DS, 01992 814920; *Gullivers Tavern*, No. 1492 Wimborne Road, Bournemouth, Dorset, BH11 9AD, 01202 580739; *The Margaret Catchpole*, Cliff Lane, Ipswich IP3 0PQ, 01473 252450; *The Alice Lisle*, Rockford Green, Rockford, Ringwood, Hampshire, BH24 3NA, 01425 474700, alice-lisle-ringwood.co.uk; *The Eclipse Inn*, No. 25 The Square, Winchester, SO23 9EX, 01962 865676, www.eclipseinnwinchester.co.uk;

Sawney Bean's Howff, No. 82 Dockhead Street, Saltcoats, Ayrshire, KA21 5EL, 01294 603342; **The Wicked Lady**, Normansland, Wheathampstead, St Albans, Hertfordshire, AL4 8EL, 01582 832128, www.thewickedladypub.co.uk; **The Quiet Woman**, Earl Sterndale, Buxton, Derbyshire, SK17 0BU, 01298 83211; **Bucket of Blood**, Phillack, Hayle, Cornwall, TR27 5AD, 01736 752378; **The Hung Drawn and Quartered**, Nos 26–27 Great Tower Street, London, EC3R 5AQ, 020 7626 6123, hung-drawn-and-quartered.co.uk; **The Three Legged Mare**, No. 15 High Petergate, York, North Yorkshire, YO1 7EN, 01904 638246, www.york-brewery.co.uk

10

POLICING THE PUB

The link between crime and our national drinking establishments has been giving local and national governments a headache for centuries. Perceived as hotbeds of violence and disorder as well as promoting general drunkenness, alehouses and inns, then pubs and bars, have often been blamed for social ills down the ages, not always with just cause. Since Saxon times there have been countless attempts to regulate and police them, often with little effect.

The first attempts to limit the number of alehouses came as early as the reign of King Edgar in the tenth century who limited villages to one alehouse. In the time of King Aethelred II there was a law passed which decreed that 'In the case of (a) breach of the peace in an alehouse six half marks shall be paid in compensation if a man is slain and twelve ores if no-one is slain.'

During the Middle Ages, alehouses often cropped up in criminal cases of theft and dishonesty, but most of the issues that arose surrounded the selling of short measures. By the Tudor and Stuart period, with a booming number of 'tippling houses' and an increase in the strength of beer, they became more worrisome to the authorities. In many ways alehouses and inns were still seen as essential, because ale or beer still formed an important, nutritious element of the average person's daily diet. But there were increasing concerns that drinking dens were rowdy places that could encourage disturbances and that they fostered indolence and immorality as many sold sexual services along with booze. Alehouses were also seen as breeding grounds for political unrest and dangerous secularism. Justice William Lambarde, writing in the sixteenth century, branded them 'nurseries of naughtiness', while in the 1600s Puritan preacher Robert Harris wrote that they were responsible for 'riot, excess and idleness'.

Alehouses first had to have a licence from 1552, to be granted by local justices of the peace, though inns did not need one until later. During the following 500 years there has been much legislation directed against pubs and drinking, which the writer Nicholas Dorn described as 'a roll-call of crisis points in English history'. In the early 1600s came tough measures designed at punishing drunkenness, while the early eighteenth century saw more legislation in response to the rise of gin fever. Despite being stronger than beer, the latter was taxed and gin was actually cheaper to drink. This gave rise to gin shops, separate from alehouses, and by 1730 there were 7,000 in London alone. There was panic in the upper echelons of society about the effect that spirits were having on the public and it was feared that the gin epidemic would bring about the ruination of the working classes. Commentators like the writer Henry Fielding blamed a rise in crime on excessive gin consumption. The problem was graphically illustrated in William Hogarth's satirical print 'Gin Lane'. The government passed a string of Gin Acts in the mid-eighteenth century which initially caused riots, but as the trade slowly moved to established licensed premises, the gin craze began to wane.

In the early nineteenth century there was a renewed interest in spirit drinking, which saw the rise of 'gin palaces'. The Beer Act of 1830 was an attempt to persuade drinkers to choose beer over spirits and made it easier to open a simple beer house alongside the existing pubs and inns. But it was widely condemned as giving rise to more bad behaviour. One commentator, Sydney Smith, wrote, 'The Beer Act has begun its operations. Everyone is drunk. Those who are not singing are sprawling.' The number of pubs mushroomed by 50 per cent between 1830 and 1880. In 1869 the numbers had grown so much that there were efforts to stem their expansion and eventually the humbler beer houses became assimilated into what we know as pubs today. Nevertheless, at the turn of the twentieth century there were 100,000 licensed premises, twice the number today.

Although they were relaxed in the early nineteenth century, the regulation of hours was also seen as a way of stopping disorder as the Victorian period went on. The most severe restrictions came in during the First World War when pubs were limited to opening at lunchtimes and in the early evenings, regulations that were only significantly loosened in recent times. The relaxation of opening hours in the twenty-first century once again led to a debate about crime and the pub. In 2013 the police reported that twenty-four hour drinking had led to chaos in the early hours, with 400,000 fines dished out for drunk and disorderly behaviour since changes to the law were introduced in 2005.

Despite all these regulations and laws, pubs and hotels have survived as places in which to relax, celebrate and socialise and, for the most part, to the betterment of our culture.

11

CATCH THEM WHILE YOU CAN

The writer Hilaire Belloc once said, 'When you have lost your inns, drown your empty selves – for you will have lost the last of England.' At the time of writing, pubs are closing at the rate of twenty-eight a week and often a lot of history goes along with them. Once lost, pubs rarely reopen, severing a link with our past and the chance to visit places linked to notorious crimes and criminals too. The first murder on a train in Britain, for example, involved a pub which has recently faced closure. On 9 July 1864 Thomas Briggs, a city banker, got on a train at London's Fenchurch Street station bound for north London. At around 10 p.m. he was robbed and thrown out of the train. When he was spotted lying next to the tracks by another train driver near Bow, Briggs was taken to The Mitford Castle pub in Cadogan Terrace where he soon died. The pub later became an Irish pub called Top o' the Morning. A tailor by the name of Franz Müller, who had left his hat behind in the train compartment and was seen wearing Briggs' watch, was eventually arrested in New York after a chase across the Atlantic Ocean. Müller was executed at Newgate Prison on 14 November 1864 amid scenes of drunken disorder in the 50,000 strong crowd.

Another pub with a chequered history stopped trading in 2012, though there is a campaign to have it reopened in the near future. In January 1920, the 53-year-old landlady of the 300-year-old Cross Keys in Lawrence Street, Chelsea, was found in the cellar of the pub, having been murdered. The body of Frances Buxton had been discovered in the early hours of the morning by a policeman who had noticed that the premises were not locked. Frances had been attacked with a bottle and the culprit had even tried to burn the body. Her murder remains unsolved.

The Sun Inn, located in Bedlington, Northumberland, was recently up for sale. It was the scene of a triple murder in 1913 which remains one of the north east's most shocking crimes. John Vickers Amos was licensee of the pub, but on 15 April he argued with the owner over missing money. PC George Mussell was called to the fracas but was shot twice by Amos. Sergeant Barton was also shot and killed when he arrived, as was the wife of the pub's manager. Amos was hanged on 22 July in Newcastle.

While some historic pubs and hotels face closure, others have opened in buildings which were once scenes of major crimes. The Radnorshire Arms Hotel in Presteigne, Powys, a grand Jacobean building, was once the home of Sir Henry Vaughan, who was accused of committing 'unnatural and repugnant acts' in 1754. Before the authorities arrived to arrest him, a mob assembled and Vaughan was lynched in the grounds.

Another hotel with a dark history is the Dunsley Hall Hotel in the Black Country. In 1812, the owner of Dunsley Hall, Benjamin Robins, was shot on his way back from business in Stourbridge. Despite being shot in the spine, Robins managed to get back home, leaving a trail of blood up the staircase. He lived for ten days, long enough to give a description of his assailant, William Howe, who was executed and gibbeted for the crime.

LOCATIONS: *The Radnorshire Arms Hotel*, High Street, Presteigne, Powys, LD8 2BE, 01544 267406, www.radnorshirearmshotel.com; *Dunsley Hall Hotel*, Dunsley Road, Kinver, Stourbridge, West Midlands, DY7 6LU, 01384 877077, www.dunsleyhallhotel.co.uk

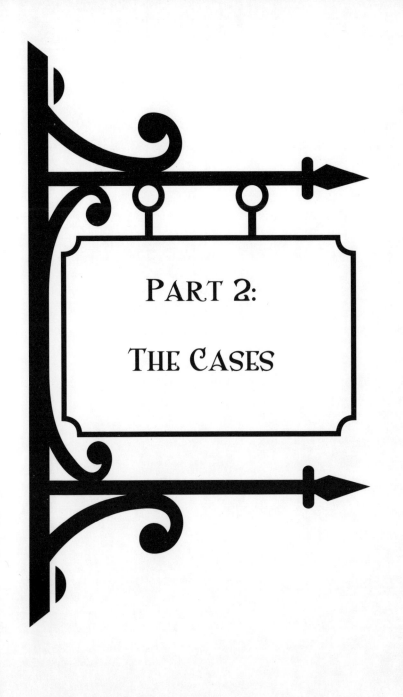

PART 2:

THE CASES

Golden Age of the Scoundrel 1600-1700s

Caught in a Tavern – The Highwayman Who Made the Ladies Swoon, 1670

The Marquis, London; Holt Hotel, Steeple Ashton, Oxfordshire; The Claude Du Vall, Camberley, Surrey; Talbot Inn, Ripley, Surrey; The Bell, Moseley, Surrey

Not many of those hanged at London's notorious Tyburn could expect an epitaph as poetic as that given to the urbane highwayman Claude Du Vall. On 21 January 1670, Du Vall swung from the gallows, despite calls for clemency from some of his wealthier admirers, including Charles II. Judge Sir William Morton had found him guilty of at least six robberies. Du Vall's body was exhibited at the nearby Tangier Tavern for the eager crowd to inspect, before being buried at St Paul's church, Covent Garden. An inscription above his tombstone, though now destroyed, read:

> Here lies DuVall: Reder, if male thou art,
> Look to thy purse; if female, to thy heart.
> Much havoc has he made of both; for all
> Men he made stand, and women he made fall.
>
> The second Conqueror of the Norman race,
> Knights to his arms did yield, and Ladies to
> his face.

The Marquis, on the site of the Hole-in-the-Wall, where highwayman Claude Du Vall was arrested. (© *James Moore*)

Old Tyburn's glory; England's illustrious
thief, Du Vall, the Ladies' Joy; Du Vall, the Ladies'
grief.

Claude was just 27 years old when he met his fate. He had been caught, drunk, at a London inn called The Hole-in-the-Wall, which is today the site of The Marquis pub in Chandos Place near Charing Cross Station. Despite his youth, Du Vall had already built up an image which, in his day, made him as famous as a later highwayman, Dick Turpin. And his career of highway robbery is intertwined with a string of Britain's oldest hostelries and inns.

Born in Domfront, Normandy, Du Vall entered domestic service in Paris and is thought to have attached himself to English aristocrats in exile and then come to England on the restoration of Charles II. But it appears that he soon longed for something more thrilling than his new job as footman to the Duke of Richmond. He soon took to crime, forming a gang which became a menacing presence on the lonely roads out of London. In the seventeenth century the names of both Hounslow Heath and Bagshot Heath (where there is, today, a pub named after Du Vall) were notorious haunts of brigands, and travelling through them sent shivers down

The Bell, Molesey, Surrey, one of the alehouses favoured by Du Vall. (© *James Moore*)

the spines of the well-to-do. Du Vall's preferred inns of refuge, following hold-ups in these areas, included two Surrey inns which still exist, The Talbot at Ripley and The Bell in Molesey.

Du Vall, well-spoken and wearing the attire of an aristocrat, was said never to use violence during his career, though the threat of it must have been there. One of his victims was Squire Roper, Master of the Royal Buckhounds, from whom he managed to get fifty guineas before tying him to a tree. In another story about Du Vall he was said to have turned up in Beaconsfield. There was a summer fair going on in the town and dancing at The Crown Inn where Du Vall sat down and struck up conversation with a farmer who was nursing a drink and had a bag of money at his feet. Du Vall promised to look after it while the farmer went to join the revels. Meanwhile he struck up a deal with one of the grooms at the inn to help him escape. In a cunning wheeze, he asked the groom to dress up a dog in a cowhide, take it up to the roof and then lower it down the chimney on a rope. When the poor animal suddenly arrived in the middle of the room barking and spluttering along with clouds of soot many of the dancers thought the apparition was the devil himself and Du Vall managed to slip away amid the resulting chaos and panic.

Many tales, especially in the years after his death, grew up about Du Vall's gallantry at the point of a gun. He once robbed a coach but on finding that one of his accomplices had purloined a silver baby's bottle he returned the item to the mother, and apologised to her, before fleeing the scene.

The most famous story of all, recorded immediately after Du Vall had been sent to his maker, involved the robbery of a wealthy couple travelling in a coach across Hounslow Heath. The tale goes that on seeing Du Vall and his men approach, the lady immediately took out a flute and began to play. Du Vall was charmed by the music and said to her husband, 'Your lady plays excellently and I make no doubt that she dances well. Will you please to step out of the coach and let me have the honour to dance one courante with her on the heath?'

The man had little choice but to agree and when the dance was over he and his wife were allowed to go on their way. Instead of taking the £400 the pair were carrying, Du Vall only took £100 as 'payment for the entertainment'. Other legends about Du Vall abounded – one stated that he was a secret friend of Nell Gwynn, while another even suggested that he had saved King Charles II's life.

Seductive he may have been, but Du Vall's success worried the authorities and there was soon a large reward on his head. For a time he fled to France. Returning in 1670 he made the mistake of making a spectacle of himself in the Hole-in-the Wall, also known as Mother Maberley's tavern, and was soon locked up in Newgate Prison. As one nineteenth-century author put it, 'He made an unlucky attack, not upon some ill-bred passengers, but upon several bottles of wine.'

There was a chilling postscript to the 'boy's own' style adventures of Du Vall. In the course of his banditry he used local inns as hideouts, including one called The Black Boy in Slough. Another of his favourite haunts was said to be Hopcroft House near Steeple Ashton in Oxfordshire. Here he planned his crimes, spent his loot and wooed the owner's daughter. Indeed his ghost is said to haunt today's Holt Hotel, which stands on the same spot. Nearly exactly a century after Du Vall swung at Tyburn, the landlord and landlady here, a Mr John Spurritt and his wife, were both brutally murdered. The crime was never solved.

LOCATIONS: *The Marquis*, Nos 51–52 Chandos Place, London, WC2N 4HS, 020 7379 0367, www.themarquiscoventgarden.co.uk; *Claude Du Vall*, Nos 77–81 High Street, Town Centre, Camberley, GU15 3RB, 01276 672910; *The Talbot*, High Street, Ripley, Woking, Surrey, GU23 6BB, 01483 225188, thetalbotripley.com; *The Bell*, No. 4 Bell Road, East Molesey, Surrey, KT8 0SS, 020 8941 0400, www.johnbarras.com; *The Holt Hotel*, Oxford Road, Bicester, OX25 5QQ, 01869 340259, www.holthotel.co.uk

WHERE HANGING JUDGE JEFFREYS WAS CAUGHT ... AND CAPTAIN KIDD EXECUTED, 1688 AND 1701

The Town of Ramsgate, The Prospect of Whitby and Captain Kidd, Wapping, London; The George Inn, Norton St Philip, Somerset

George Jeffreys, first Baron Jeffreys of Wem, has gone down in history as brutal and heartless, handing out scores of death sentences during the Bloody Assizes of 1685. Many of the verdicts that Judge Jeffreys passed on the rebels who had taken part in the Monmouth Rebellion of the same year were said to have been given in the surroundings of an old inn, The Antelope in Dorchester, Dorset, which is now part of a shopping arcade. So it was perhaps fitting that when Jeffreys was himself on the wrong end of the law, three years later, the location for his arrest was another hostelry.

Back in the seventeenth century, The Town of Ramsgate in Wapping was known as The Red Cow. It was one of a host of alehouses that lined the shoreline, serving the sailors and tradesmen in the bustling, seedy district. The Red Cow, then in Anchor and Hope Alley, was run by a Mr Porter. And, in December 1688, it had a customer who looked ostensibly like any other member of its regular clientele. He was said to be 'dressed in fur cap a seaman's neckcloth and a rusty coat'. In fact, this was no seafarer but

Jeffreys, who had become the most reviled man in England. Now a desperate fugitive, he had resorted to wearing a disguise as he waited for help to flee the country.

Jeffreys was born a Protestant in 1645, but by the time James II, the Catholic brother of Charles II, had come to the throne in early 1685, he had already worked his way up to Solicitor General and Lord Chief Justice, thanks to James' patronage. Known for his bombastic style in court and ruthless application of the law, Jeffreys presided over some famous cases including that of Titus Oates, a man tried for fabricating a Popish Plot in 1678, whom he had flogged. And when the Duke of Monmouth's rebellion was quashed in July 1685, Jeffreys demonstrated his loyalty to James by leading the prosecution of 1,000 rebels, pursuing the heaviest sentences possible with ruthless vigour. The Bloody Assizes, as they became known, were conducted across the West Country in several locations including Winchester, Taunton, Salisbury, Wells and Dorchester. The case that caused the most outrage was Jeffreys' treatment of 70-year-old Lady Alice Lisle. She was an aristocratic woman who had harboured some of those who had taken part in the rebellion. Although she wasn't directly involved in treason herself, Jeffreys nevertheless pronounced the death sentence, ordering Lady Lisle to be burnt at the stake. Pleas for mercy resulted only in her being granted a beheading instead of a pyre. The execution was carried out at Winchester that September.

Preparing to hear cases in Dorchester, Jeffreys ordered the Oak Room of the Antelope Inn, which was to be the courtroom, hung with scarlet curtains. On the first morning of the terrible proceedings, 5 September, he sent twenty-nine of the thirty who had been accused to be hanged, drawn and quartered. During the course of the assizes, several hundred more people were condemned to death and many others transported overseas. A number of existing inns claim to have been visited by Jeffreys during this process including the ancient George Inn at Norton St Philip in Somerset. Here twelve unfortunate souls executed on the village green. Jeffreys was rewarded for his ruthless efficiency by being given the powerful post of Lord Chancellor. However, in 1688 his fortunes changed almost overnight when James II was forced from power by William of Orange in what became known as the Glorious Revolution.

The king fled the country and Jeffreys, inextricably linked to the old regime, began planning his own escape. On 12 December, as mobs roamed London, he headed to Wapping, and it was while waiting for a passage out of the country on a ship moored nearby that he was apprehended. It was no surprise that he sought refuge in drink while he waited nervously for the craft to be ready. By now Jeffreys, whose vile temper had always been put down to kidney stone trouble, was a confirmed alcoholic.

In one version of the story of his arrest, an old defendant who had once appeared before Jeffreys in court happened to recognise the judge in the alehouse, beneath his sailor's disguise. He then tipped off the authorities. In another, the captain of the ship he was meant to be travelling on gave him away. Either way, constables arrived at the alehouse to find Jeffreys wearing his sailor's outfit while hiding beneath some blankets in a room above the hostelry. He had even shaved off his famously prominent eyebrows in the hope of avoiding capture. They asked the man if he were the Lord Chancellor and Jeffreys, peering from beneath the bedclothes, admitted, 'I am the man.'

Jeffreys was immediately taken to the Lord Mayor's house in a coach, but word soon got out of his arrest and crowds gathered to hurl mud and stones at it as he went past. A terrified Jeffreys broke down and begged to be saved from the mob. He was swiftly thrown into prison at the Tower of London. To the chagrin of many of his victims, the judge did not go to the gallows. Instead he was to die of kidney disease on 18 April 1689.

Just along from the Town of Ramsgate in Wapping was Execution Dock where, for 400 years, pirates were traditionally hanged from a gallows set up near the ebbing waters of the Thames. The felons would first be hanged, then their bodies would be taken down and tied to a post, which was left beside the river until three tides had washed over them. It's claimed that Jeffreys used to watch some of these executions while he relaxed in a local alehouse. One of these was almost certainly the Prospect of Whitby, a pub that has stood by the Wapping foreshore since 1520. It was also frequented by the diarist Samuel Pepys and was originally known as The Pelican, or Devil's Tavern.

The Prospect of Whitby, next to Execution Dock in Wapping. (*Courtesy of the Prospect of Whitby*)

In this era, such public executions were conducted in an alcoholic haze. Not only were the baying crowds fuelled by booze but even the condemned men were allowed to guzzle a final quart of beer at an appointed alehouse before the noose was put round their neck. When it came to pirates, this spectacle would usually occur at the Turk's Head Inn, which used to stand at No. 30 Wapping High Street before succumbing to bombing during the Second World War.

It was at Execution Dock that the famous pirate Captain Kidd would meet his end. Kidd, born in Dundee, Scotland, and in the same year as Jeffreys, first came to prominence as a privateer around the time of the hanging judge's death. At first his exploits raiding French settlements in the Caribbean were sanctioned by the English government and he became a prominent ship-owner based in New York. Then in, 1696, he was given a mission to attack pirates in the Indian Ocean. But Kidd and his ship, the *Adventure Galley*, were soon in difficulties. A third of his crew died from cholera, and his efforts to defeat the buccaneers were floundering. To cover his costs, Kidd ditched his allegiances to the crown and joined the ranks of full-blown pirates himself. At one point his crew became mutinous and, on 30 October 1697, Kidd killed a disobedient gunner called William Moore by bludgeoning him over the head with a heavy iron bucket.

After a series of further escapades in which Kidd and his crew captured a merchant ship called the *Quedagh Merchant*, he was denounced as a pirate by the English government. He was finally arrested in July 1699 when he arrived back in New York, trying to maintain his innocence. Kidd was sent back to England where he was tried at the Old Bailey and found guilty of piracy as well as murdering Moore. Supposedly the treasure Kidd had amassed during his adventures, amounting to some £100,000, was never found.

On 23 May 1701, Kidd was taken from Newgate Gaol to Wapping. There, a little worse for wear, he stood before the crowd and warned other captains to learn from his fate before the noose was put round his neck. Executions were rarely carried out with precision and the first rope used to hang Kidd snapped. Dragged out of the mud, the 56-year-old was hanged again – this time successfully. Dragged out again, Kidd was hanged a second time, this time successfully. His body was then taken to hang in a gibbet at Tilbury Point where it remained for several years. Today there is a modern pub bearing his name, The Captain Kidd, located between the Prospect of Whitby and the Town of Ramsgate.

LOCATION: *The Town of Ramsgate*, No. 62 Wapping High Street, London, E1W 2PN, 020 7481 8000, www.townoframsgate.co.uk; *The George Inn*, High Street, Bath, Somerset, BA2 7LH, 01373 834224, www.georgeinnnsp. co.uk; *The Prospect of Whitby*, No. 57 Wapping Wall, Wapping, London, E1W 3SH, 020 7481 1095, www.taylor-walker.co.uk. *Captain Kidd*, No. 108 Wapping High Street, London, E1W 2NE, 020 7480 5759

KILLED AS HE KNELT TO TOAST
A QUEEN, 1714

The George, Stamford, Lincolnshire

The George at Stamford is one of the oldest inns in the country, believed to date back to AD 947. The ancient hostelry, now a hotel, is set upon the old Great North Road and has served everyone from pilgrims to royalty during its illustrious history. The current building dates back to 1597 when the inn was rebuilt by Lord Burghley. His coat of arms can still be seen over the front entrance and the stone mullioned lattice windows in the upper storey on the north side of The George still date to Elizabethan times.

By the eighteenth century, The George had achieved a reputation as a comfortable resting place for travellers making their way up and down the busy north-south route. It was during this time that it got the famous gallows sign bearing its name that still extends across the whole road outside. At a time when highwaymen were still a peril, it provided both an advertisement and warning that only the best guests were wanted. During this era, forty stagecoaches passed through Stamford every day and The George was their main stopping point.

Over the centuries The George has seen its fair share of drama and given its age it was inevitable that one day tragedy would strike, though it is, perhaps, surprising that it has been the scene of only one murder. The sudden and shocking demise of Mr Bolton was no run-of-the-mill killing. It reflected the political unrest which gripped Britain in the early years of the eighteenth century.

When the last Stuart monarch, Queen Anne, died in August 1714, she passed away without a direct heir. George I was a mere 52nd in line to the throne, but he succeeded because he was the only Protestant. Under the provisions of the 1701 Act of Settlement he became king, being crowned in October 1714. Almost immediately, however, George was faced with the threat of a Jacobite uprising. James Edward Stuart, son of James II and nicknamed the 'Old Pretender', laid claim to the throne, and there was widespread sympathy for him, not just in Scotland but throughout England too, particularly in the north.

The George, Stamford, Lincolnshire, where a murder was committed in 1714. (*Courtesy of The George Hotel*)

Many of Stamford's citizens were supporters of the Jacobites, and after Queen Anne's passing there was unrest in the town. Being a symbol of the Hanoverian claim, a Presbyterian chapel was burned down despite the efforts of the mayor to intervene. Keen to quash rebellion, a troop of dragoons was stationed in Stamford which, given its situation on the road to Scotland where the rebellion against George was gathering pace, was also highly strategic.

At the time a William Wildman ran the George, but a more humble tap room in the building was rented to a Mr Bolton. This served ale to locals as well as staff at the inn. Bolton was known to have Jacobite sympathies but he might have done better to keep them to himself with cavalrymen loyal to King George camped out in the town. It was occasionally the unusual custom of Jacobites to drink to the memory of Queen Anne by kneeling with their legs bared. On one night, Bolton was found taking part in this ritual in the tap room by a member of the dragoons.

Without warning, the enraged soldier pulled out his sword and plunged it directly into Bolton's heart. Death was instant.

Word quickly spread of what had happened and a mob surrounded The George demanding justice. An 1822 history of Stamford, written by the radical journalist John Drakard, recounts the scene: 'An innumerable concourse of people immediately surrounded the inn, armed with all sorts of domestic weapons: they broke all the windows and threatened the utter demolition of the house unless the delinquent was given up.' Surely helped by his fellow soldiers, the terrified culprit appears to have outwitted those demanding justice and escaped out of the back of the inn.

The following year a full-scale Jacobite uprising was defeated, and with the country now at peace, there seems to have been little appetite to track down Bolton's murderer. Nobody was ever convicted of the crime, and by 1746 the Jacobite bid to win the throne finally died too with the defeat of Charles Edward Stuart, the Young Pretender, at the Battle of Culloden. Interestingly, in the year preceding George II's son, the Duke of Cumberland, had stayed at The George before masterminding that victory over the Scots.

LOCATION: *The George Hotel*, No. 71 High Street St Martin's, Stamford, Lincolnshire, PE9 2LB, 01780 750750, www.georgehotelofstamford.com

DICK TURPIN – A LIFE AND DEATH IN TAVERNS, 1739

The Bluebell Inn, Hempstead, Essex; The Blue Boar, York; The Beverley Arms Hotel, Beverley, Yorkshire; Three Houses Inn, Sandal Magna, Wakefield, Yorkshire; Ferry Inn, Brough, North Humberside; Green Dragon, Welton, North Humberside; White Hart, Drury Lane, London; O'Neills', Leytonstone, East London

On Saturday 7 April 1739, the body of Dick Turpin was laid out in the Blue Boar tavern on York's Castlegate. The 33-year-old had been executed at Knavesmire, where the city's racecourse is today, and was buried the next day – though his corpse had to be reburied after it was dug up by grave robbers and eventually turned up in the garden of a local surgeon. The original Blue Boar closed in 1775. But a modern pub nearby, previously known as The Little John, has recently changed its name to the Blue Boar in memory of the event. Such is the draw of Turpin that, across the land, there is no shortage of pubs laying claim to a link with the famous highwayman. Indeed there are several named after him, including one in York not far from the sight of his hanging. There are over 100 more that have Turpin stories associated with them. Many of these tales are no doubt apocryphal. But the fact that so many pubs and hotels claim an attachment to Turpin is testament to our romantic vision of a man whose actual life is shrouded in myth.

The truth is that Turpin was a cunning horse thief, a callous murderer and a man who was either so dispirited or arrogant by the time he was finally caught that he did not even attempt to escape. Much of the legend of Turpin, involving the frock-coated gentleman highwayman holding up rich folk whilst riding trusty Black Bess, has come down to us through the fictionalised account in Harrison Ainsworth's 1834 novel, *Rockwood*. Indeed the most famous tale about Turpin – his supposed 150-mile ride to York to establish an alibi – was in fact not carried out by Turpin at all. This nigh on impossible feat was originally attached to another highwayman called John Nevison half a century earlier. In 1676 'Swift Nick' committed a robbery in Kent and was said to have ridden to York in time to play a game of bowls with the city's Lord Mayor that very evening. When he was arrested and tried for the crime, the Lord Mayor supported his alibi and Nevison was acquitted. In the end Nevison, who operated mainly from the Talbot Inn at Newark, was no luckier than Turpin. On 6 March 1684 he was arrested at the Three Houses Inn at Sandal Magna near Wakefield in Yorkshire, now in a slightly different location to the original inn. He was tried for killing Darcy Fletcher, a constable who had earlier tried to arrest him, and was hanged two months later in York.

What is certain about Richard Turpin is that he had humble beginnings. He was born in September 1705, the son of a man who was both an innkeeper and butcher in Hempstead, Essex. His father ran the sixteenth-century Blue Bell, which, during the

The Bluebell Inn, Hempstead, Essex, where highwayman Dick Turpin is believed to have been born. (*Courtesy of the Bluebell Inn*)

course of its history, became the Rose and Crown and has now reverted back to being called The Bluebell Inn. Dick, who initially took up his father's trade as a butcher, soon became involved with the Gregory Gang, a group of deer poachers in Essex. His career as a thief appears to have begun in 1734, not primarily as a highway robber, but as a burglar in the county, carrying out raids on the homes of the well-to-do with his gang. Their victims were often brutally beaten and the gang would meet at taverns in and around London to plan attacks, share out their booty and fence their ill-gotten gains. The White Hart in Drury Lane is believed to have been one of their haunts.

In February 1735, three of the gang finally came a cropper when the same horses they had used in an earlier robbery were noticed outside an alehouse called The Punch Bowl in King Street, Bloomsbury. A parish constable was called and the trio were caught. One of them, a 15-year-old boy called John Wheeler, betrayed his fellow criminals, and while Turpin remained at large, a description of the now notorious villain was circulated. He was described thus:

Richard Turpin, a butcher by trade, is a tall fresh coloured man, very much marked with the small pox. About 26 years of age, about 5ft 9in high, lived some time ago in Whitechapel and did lately lodge somewhere about Millbank, Westminster. Wears a blue grey coat and a natural wig.

It was at this point that Turpin turned his attention to holding up stagecoaches and travellers. He teamed up with a series of other highwaymen, always managing to evade capture. Then, in May 1737, he and an accomplice called Matthew King stole a horse belonging to Joseph Major near Waltham Forest to the north of London. Major distributed descriptions of the man, whom he named as Turpin, to local inns. Richard Bayes, keeper of The Green Man, now an O'Neill's pub in Leytonstone, helped him track the horse to a pub called the Red Lion in Whitechapel, East London, where there was a gun battle and King was killed. Again Turpin escaped, this time to a hideout in Epping Forest. He was, however, spotted by a gamekeeper called Thomas Morris. When challenged, Turpin drew his pistol and shot Morris down. Turpin

Turpin shot Thomas Morris at Epping Forest in Essex in 1737 but was later hanged for horse stealing, not murder. (*Courtesy of Wellcome Library, London*)

was now a murderer as well as a thief, and a £200 bounty was offered for his capture.

Turpin fled first to Long Sutton in Lincolnshire and then to Yorkshire, stealing horses and selling them on. He initially based himself at the Ferry Inn at Brough, on the Humber, which still exists today. Posing as John Palmer, Turpin managed to make himself a respected member of the community, though William Harris, the innkeeper at the Ferry, was clearly suspicious of his activities and would later give evidence about his guest's mysterious trips south to bring back horses. Then Turpin made a silly mistake. On 2 October 1738, after going on a hunting trip with some local gentry, a tipsy Turpin shot a man's prize cock in the street and threatened to shoot another man who reprimanded him. The incident was reported to the local justices, and when Turpin refused to put up bail he was taken into custody. Some accounts have the arrest happening at The Green Dragon in Welton. Still unaware of his true identity, the authorities ordered that Palmer be taken to the House of Correction in Beverley until the matter could be settled. He was accompanied by a single parish constable and his stolen horse was stabled at the Blue Bell Inn, since rebuilt as the Beverley Arms Hotel.

Making enquiries into how the well-dressed but seemingly penniless Palmer actually made a living, the justices discovered that he was already wanted in nearby Lincolnshire for sheep stealing and horse theft. Turpin was taken to prison in York. Languishing in his cell, he wrote a letter, under the name of Palmer, to his brother-in-law back in the village of Hempstead, asking him to vouch for his character. However, the relative refused to pay for the postage and the letter was returned to James Smith, the man who ran the local post office. He also happened to be Turpin's former schoolmaster and now recognised his handwriting. Travelling to York, he identified Palmer as Turpin, who was soon put on trial. On 22 March 1739 he was convicted on two charges of horse theft, which was, until 1832, a capital offence. He was not tried for the earlier murder of Morris.

If much of Turpin's real-life exploits had, in truth, been rather tawdry, he nevertheless displayed a swagger on his way to the gallows that befitted his future reputation for glamour. After buying new clothes and shoes, he bowed to crowds from an open cart on his way to the scaffold where he happily chatted to his executioner. He then 'threw himself off the ladder and expired in about five minutes'.

Those captivated by the legend of Turpin might want to investigate pubs with a shakier claim to a link with the criminal. The seventeenth-century Anchor in Shepperton, Surrey, is certainly old enough, and here an eighteenth-century pistol which bore the inscription 'Dick's Friend' is said to have been found in the rafters during renovation work. Whether Turpin really was here or at The Spaniards Inn at Hampstead, The Rose and Crown in Enfield, The London Apprentice at Isleworth, The George at Buckden or The Bell at Stilton is probably impossible to prove or disprove. Yet after a couple of ales at any of these historic hostelries it's easy to imagine yourself in Turpin's world, as you relax in the kind of surroundings with which he would have been familiar.

LOCATIONS: **Blue Boar**, No. 5 Castlegate, York, North Yorkshire, YO1 9RN, 01904 593209; **Three Houses Inn**, No. 379 Barnsley Rd, Wakefield, West Yorkshire, WF2 6HW, www.thethreehouses.co.uk; **Bluebell Inn**, High Street, Hempstead, Saffron Walden, CB10 2PD, 01799 599199, www.thebluebellinn.co.uk; **White Hart**, No. 191 Drury Lane, London, WC2B 5QD, 020 7242 2317, www.whitehartdrurylane.co.uk; **O'Neill's**, No. 762 High Road, London E11 3AW, 020 8536 4039, www.oneills.co.uk/leytonstone; **Ferry Inn**, Station Rd, Brough, North Humberside HU15 1DY, 01482 667340; **The Green Dragon**, Welton, HU15 1NB, 01482 666700, www.greendragonpubwelton.co.uk; **The Beverley Arms Hotel**, No. 25 North Bar Within, Beverley, East Riding of Yorkshire, HU17 8DD, 01482 869241, thebeverleyarms.co.uk

BOOZY BOOTLEGGERS ON THE RAMPAGE, 1735-49

Oak and Ivy, Hawkhurst, Kent; The Star and Eagle Hotel, Goudhurst, Kent; The Mermaid Inn and Olde Bell, Rye, Sussex

Today the eighteenth-century era of smuggling conjures up a world of daring moonlight deeds where loveable rogues manage to outwit customs officers in thrilling adventures. The reality of

the time was that many smugglers were determined villains, prepared to commit bloody murder at the drop of a hat. One group
of brutal bootleggers, called the Hawkhurst Gang, were as ruthless
and dangerous as any modern criminal organisation, and exercised
a vice-like grip on the local communities in which they operated.
This eighteenth-century mafia-style outfit, which at the height of
its strength could count on the support of 500 armed men, was
not unique. But the Hawkhurst Gang would become notable for
the sheer audacity with which it operated and the level of violence
that its members were prepared to dish out.

First referred to as the 'Holkhourst Genge' in 1735, the outfit
was originally based in Hawkhurst, Kent. Within a few years its
tentacles had spread from Kent to Dorset. The gang's leaders rev-
elled in nicknames like 'Blacktooth' and 'Poison', and many of their
operations were seriously large-scale affairs, involving large boats
called cutters and up to 500 pack horses to transport goods inland.

Scores of taverns and inns were inextricably linked to the
activities of the gang, who used them as hideouts and bases from
which to conduct their activities or simply as places to water their
horses and receive refreshment. Sometimes the landlords and
landladies were in league with the smugglers at other times they
co-operated with them under duress. According to an account
from an ostler at the George inn at Lydd, Kent, up to forty of the
gang would lodge there for three or four days waiting for a cutter
which was carrying their goods to come in. In 1745, displaying
their self-confidence, some of the gang rode through the Sussex
town of Lewes brandishing their pistols before stopping off for
a drink at an alehouse called the White Horse, where they proceeded to complain about the service.

The Oak and Ivy alehouse in Hawkhurst was used as the gang's
headquarters, but members were also regulars at the Star and
Eagle in Goudhurst as well as The Mermaid Inn at Rye, a historic
half-timbered inn dating back to 1420. Inside it retains the dark,
wood-panelled rooms in which visitors can imagine the gang
openly congregating. They kept their loaded pistols on the tables
in case of trouble. Legend has it that there was a tunnel between
the Mermaid and another nearby inn called the Olde Bell in case
of raids by customs officers. However, such was the strength of

the Hawkhurst Gang that the authorities could rarely summon up the manpower or indeed the will to intervene. When they did, bloodshed inevitably ensued. In 1740, for example, revenue officer Thomas Carswell and a party of soldiers seized some smuggled tea and were on their way to Hastings when they were attacked by members of the gang, fuelled by brandy. Carswell was killed.

There were some setbacks for the gang. While many people resented paying taxes on goods and didn't really see the smugglers as criminals, others became incensed by the increasing arrogance and brutality of those involved. In April 1747, a local militia was formed in Goudhurst to defend the town against threats from the gang. In a confrontation between the two groups, some of the smugglers were killed. Yet, in August of the same year, the inhabitants of Rye were terrorised by the Hawkhurst Gang who fired off their guns in front of the Red Lion and then carried off an innocent young man called James Marshall. He was never seen again.

It wasn't just rum and brandy that were included in the smugglers' booty; the gang also smuggled tea, which was heavily taxed, across the Channel. When a boat carrying some of the gang's contraband tea was intercepted and stored at the Customs House in Poole, Dorset, a group of thirty angry members had the gall to try and wrestle it back. At 2 a.m. on 8 October 1747 they smashed their way into the building with crowbars and hammers and managed to recover the whole consignment.

It was following this incident that some of the most violent episodes in the gang's history occurred. One of those who had taken part in the raid on the Customs House, John Diamond, gave a bag of tea to a shoemaker friend called Daniel Chater while celebrating in Fordingbridge, Hampshire. Shortly afterwards, Diamond was captured in Chichester and the fact of his relationship with Chater became known to the authorities. In February 1748, Chater was summoned to Sussex to identify Diamond, and a customs officer called William Galley was given the job of getting him there. However, en route the pair were spotted at a pub in Rowlands Castle, Hampshire, called The White Hart. The landlady, Elizabeth Payne, whose sons were smugglers, kept the duo occupied with rum while members of the gang were alerted. They took the pair to another alehouse called The Red Lion

The Bloody and Inhuman SMUGGLERS throwing down
Stones &c. on the expiring Body of DANIEL CHATER;
whom they had flung into Lady Holt-Well.

A print showing members
of the Hawkhurst Gang
murdering Daniel Chater.
(*Courtesy of Wellcome
Library, London*)

at Rake, West Sussex. Then, having horsewhipped Galley to the
point of unconsciousness, they buried him alive. Deciding that
Chater was now too much of a risk, they threw the unfortunate
man down a well and proceeded to drop large stones on top of
him to make sure he was dead. In another incident, a particularly
vicious gang member called Jeremiah Curtis led an interrogation
of farm labourer Richard Hawkins at a former inn called the Dog
and Partridge at Slindon Common, West Sussex. Hawkins was
suspected of stealing two bags of tea. He was whipped and beaten
before his lifeless body was callously dumped in a pond.

These murders were the final straw for the government.
A crackdown on the gang was led by the Duke of Richmond.
The gang's first leader, Arthur Gray, was hanged at Tyburn in April
1948. The next leader, Thomas Kingsmill, didn't last long – going
to the gallows a year later. By 1750, there had been thirty-five
executions of prominent gang members, their bodies exhibited

in gibbets across southern counties. Ten more convicted smugglers expired in jail. One of the men responsible for the murder of Galley and Chater, William Jackson, died of a heart attack the night before he was due to be executed. By 1751, the Hawkhurst Gang's reign of terror was effectively brought to an end.

LOCATIONS: *Oak and Ivy*, Rye Road, Hawkhurst, Kent, TN18 5DB, 01580 753293, www.theoakandivy.co.uk; *The Mermaid Inn*, Mermaid Street, Rye, East Sussex, TN31 7EY, 01797 223065, www.mermaidinn.com; *Ye Olde Bell*, No. 33 The Mint, Rye, East Sussex, TN31 7EN, www.yeoldebellrye.co.uk; *Star and Eagle Hotel*, High Street, Goudhurst, Kent TN17 1AL, 01580 211512, www.starandeagle.com

MURDERED WITH A 'LOVE POTION', 1751

Little Angel, Remenham, Berkshire
As she gazed over the bridge from the alehouse that she ran at Henley-on-Thames, on the Berkshire side of the river, landlady Mary Davis was presented with a curious spectacle. She saw a woman she recognised, Mary Blandy, hurrying across the bridge towards her. Not far behind came a simmering mob hurling insults.

At the later trial that would see Blandy accused of murder, Mrs Davis recalled how she immediately went to ask Mary what was the matter and where she was going. Mary told her that the body of her father, who had just died, was about to be opened up for a post-mortem in the family home and that she could not bear to be in the house. Knowing her slightly, and fearing for her safety, Mrs Davis invited Mary to go into her pub, which was called the Angel. The reason that Mary had attracted such vitriol from the pursuing crowd was that many of the townsfolk were already convinced that she was responsible for poisoning her own father.

Mary had been born in 1720 into a middle class family, the only child of Anne and Francis, a well-to-do lawyer and town clerk. When she came of age, Francis let it be known that there was a £10,000 dowry waiting for the man who would marry her. Unsurprisingly this brought a number of suitors and, as it turned out, one particular prize rogue.

The Little Angel, Henley-on-Thames, where murderess Mary Blandy ordered a pint of wine. (*Courtesy of The Little Angel*)

Captain William Henry Cranstoun, the son of a Scottish peer, had met Mary in 1746 whilst he was recruiting soldiers in the district. She was 26 years old; he was some twenty years older. But, since he was from 'good' aristocratic stock, the Blandys felt that Cranstoun was an ideal match for their daughter and he became their house guest. Some time later, however, they made a shocking discovery. Cranstoun was still married, having wed a woman called Anne Murray in Scotland. The couple even had two children. Cranstoun attempted to have his first marriage annulled, but to no avail. And Francis soon banned Mary from having anything to do with the scoundrel, let alone marry him. Cranstoun went back to Scotland.

Yet he was not going to give up on Mary, or her dowry, that easily. In spring 1751, he sent Mary some powders. According to Mary he had claimed that they were meant as a 'love potion' that would miraculously change her father's mind about the union. By this time, Mary's mother had already died. And over the next few weeks, Mary dutifully started administering them to her father's food and drink.

As Mary almost certainly knew, there was no love potion. The powders were, in fact, arsenic and unsurprisingly Francis Blandy soon became seriously ill, as did some of his servants who had eaten his leftovers. When doctors were called they soon realised what was afoot, the servants having revealed that they had seen Mary adding the powders to the food. She was told by one physician that she might be accused of murder if he died. The careless Mary was then also seen trying to burn the powders, as well as letters she had been sent by Cranstoun.

On 14 August 1751, Francis died. But not before, it was alleged, Mary had begged his forgiveness, which he, amazingly, had given. Understanding that he had been poisoned, but clearly believing that Cranstoun was solely to blame, he said, 'Poor lovesick girl, what will not a woman do for the man she loves.'

By the time of her father's death, Mary had already been placed under house arrest. But the next morning, finding the door unguarded, she had managed to slip out for a walk and then came to find herself outside the Angel, today known as The Little Angel. Gossip about what was going on at the Blandys' was already rife and, once she was spotted out, angry locals followed her, venting their fury.

Astonishingly, once inside the Angel, with the door shut against the mob, Mary calmly ordered a 'pint of wine and toast'. Presently she turned to a customer called Mr Lane and said to him, 'Sir, you look like a gentleman – what do you think they will do to me?' He replied that if she were guilty she would suffer according to the law. Mary was then said to have stamped her foot on the ground and, presumably referring to Cranstoun, exclaimed, 'Oh that damned villain!' She then paused before saying, 'But why do I blame him? I am more to blame myself, for it was I gave it him and know the consequence.'

Mary was soon escorted home. The next day an inquest found that she should indeed face trial for murder. The petite, middle class spinster was then taken to Oxford jail where she became something of a celebrity. Despite being clamped in leg irons, she was fed well and even allowed to take tea with guests. Mary had been allowed to take a trunk full of clothes with her, and a servant called Mrs Dean even stayed with her in the prison.

MISS MOLLY BLANDY
who with her own & her Sweethearts Contrivance did Barbarously and Inhumanly Poison her own Father for his Estate

Mary Blandy, who was
accused of poisoning
her own father.
(*Courtesy of Wellcome
Library, London*)

There are many excuses used by murderers for their crimes.
But at her trial for parricide, held on 3 March 1752, Mary maintained that she had not known what the powders she was giving
her father actually were, with the implication that Cranstoun
alone was to blame. He was certainly equally culpable. But the
idea that a mature, well-educated woman such as Mary was
naïve enough to think that she was administering some kind of
potion rather than poison is fanciful. And the jury in the case
thought so too, swiftly passing a verdict of guilty. On 6 April 1752
Mary was hanged outside Oxford Castle gaol in front of a huge
crowd. Despite her guilt, there was no doubting that she went
to her death with humility. Mounting the scaffold, she asked her
executioners, 'Gentlemen don't hang me high, for the sake of
decency.' Mary then covered her own face with a handkerchief
before the hangman did his work. The politician Horace Walpole

MISS BLANDY *at the place of Execution near Oxford, attended by the Revd. Mr. Swinton*

When Blandy went to the gallows in 1752 she pleaded, 'Don't hang me high, for the sake of decency.' (*Courtesy of Wellcome Library, London*)

commented, 'Miss Blandy died with a coolness of courage that is astounding.'

Meanwhile, the much less brave Cranstoun had fled to France, escaping the authorities. But there was some justice when he promptly died himself, apparently in agony, later the same year. After her execution Mary's body was brought back to Henley and buried next to her father at the parish church. But her ghost is still said to haunt the Little Angel – where she runs upstairs and slams doors.

LOCATION: *The Little Angel*, Remenham Lane, Henley-on-Thames, Berkshire, RG9 2LS, 01491 411008, www.thelittleangel.co.uk

From Georgian Dramas to Victorian Scandals 1800s

The Chilling Case of Tom Otter, 1805

The Sun Inn, Saxilby, Lincolnshire

There is a legend that when the battered body of Mary Kirkham was found in a ditch it was taken to the nearby Sun Inn at Saxilby, Lincolnshire, a pub which stands amid the windswept fens beside the Fosdyke Canal. As the corpse was carried into the hostelry some of her blood spilled on to the steps. According to the tale, in the years that followed the bloodstains refused to disappear however much the steps were scrubbed. But rather than Mary's ghost it is the spectre of her murderer, Tom Otter, who is still said to lurk at the pub.

Otter was a stout, handsome 28-year-old labourer from Treswell, Nottinghamshire, who worked on the region's rivers and dykes. He met 24-year-old Mary from North Hykeham, Lincolnshire, while he was working in Lincoln and the pair began an affair. Soon Mary fell pregnant with her lover's child and named Otter as the father. When this fact became known to the authorities Otter was told he must marry Mary or potentially face imprisonment. At this stage, Otter appears to have kept secret the fact that he was already married to another woman, with a child, from Southwell, Nottinghamshire, and agreed to the marriage. Otter was using the surname Temporel – his mother's maiden name – perhaps to cover the fact that he already had another wife.

On Sunday 3 November 1805, Otter was taken in a cart, accompanied by two parish constables, for his impromptu wedding at the church at South Hykeham. Otter said his vows while the constables watched to make sure he didn't abscond. When the nuptials were over, the couple made their way to Saxilby near Lincoln where they called at the Sun Inn in the early evening for refreshments. After they left, Otter took Mary about a mile further and into a field near a spot called Drinsey Nook where he told his new spouse, by now about eight months pregnant, to sit down and rest. Otter immediately went to a nearby hedge and pulled a large stake from the ground. Then, advancing on Mary, he violently struck her over the head with it. She was killed instantly. John Dunkerley, a man who had been drinking earlier at the Sun Inn, had actually seen the murder according to an account he gave later, on his deathbed. On his way home to the village of Doddington he had fallen asleep near Drinsey Nook and woken to see Otter and Mary approach the spot. According to Dunkerley's story, he had lain unseen and heard Otter telling Mary to sit down and rest before he watched him come back and hit her with the stake. Dunkerley said the attack sounded like someone was hitting a turnip. Too scared to help and too embarrassed about not intervening, the man failed to come forward at the time.

Mary's body was found in the field the following morning. Her head had been beaten to a pulp. The murder weapon was found discarded about 40yds from the body. Otter was quickly identified as the most likely culprit and was recognised in Lincoln just a few days after the killing. He was arrested by a constable at the city's Packhorse Inn. An inquest, conducted at the Sun Inn on 5 November, found that Otter should answer for the murder and he was committed to Lincoln Castle jail, awaiting trial. Following the inquest, Mary was buried in St Botolph's church in Saxilby.

At his five-hour trial, which took place on 12 March 1806 at the Lincoln Assizes, Otter offered no defence. The jury listened to the testimony of twenty witnesses and, despite the circumstantial nature of the evidence, took just a few minutes to find him guilty.

Tom Otter was executed in Lincoln on 14 March and the judge ordered his body to be gibbeted in an iron cage on Saxilby Moor as a warning. Few tears were shed for Otter, a brutal individual who was once said to have cut the eyes out of a living ass. Five years after his gibbet was first erected, the *Stamford Mercury* reported that Otter's skeleton was still there, complete with a bird's nest in the jaw of his skull. In fact the gibbet remained in situ until 1850 when it blew down in a storm. By then the story of the murder had achieved mythical status and the crime gave its name to several spots in the locality including Tom Otter Lane, Tom Otter Bridge and Gibbet Wood.

As well as the blood on the steps of The Sun there were plenty of other creepy legends that became attached to the murder, which mostly originated in a semi-fictional account written in the 1850s by Thomas Miller. Of these, the most chilling was the story that, after the murder, the hedge stake used to murder Mary was said to disappear from wherever it was being kept on every anniversary of her death. Each time it would be found lying back at the lonely spot of her demise. According to local tradition it was eventually taken to the Bishop of Lincoln who exorcised it.

LOCATION: *The Sun Inn*, Bridge Street, Saxilby, LN1 2PZ, 01522 702326

THE STRANGE CASE OF THE ODDINGLEY MURDERS, 1806

The Fir Tree Inn, Dunhampstead, Worcstershire; The Talbot, Worcester
Visitors to the Fir Tree Inn in the tranquil Worcestershire countryside may be surprised to find The Murderers Bar, commemorating a double killing from the early nineteenth century with a link to the pub. The confession of a farmer called Thomas Clewes, who would later become the landlord of the inn, was key to the cracking the case. Yet, thanks to a legal quirk, neither Clewes nor his co-conspirators would end up behind bars.

At 5 p.m. on 24 June 1806, a shot rang out in the village of Oddingley followed by a pitiful cry of 'murder, murder!' Two butchers, John Lench and Thomas Giles, who were passing, rushed to the spot where they found the Reverend George Parker, the village parson, lying in a meadow. He had been shot in the side and his clothes smouldered, set alight from some of the wadding from the shot that hit him. The right side of his head had also been smashed in. It was later described by Lench as 'all of a mooze'.

The pair almost managed to grab the man who had fired the shot but he dropped the bag he was holding and fled. Giles gave pursuit, but backed off when the short individual, wearing a dark blue greatcoat, turned and threatened to shoot him too. His description of the culprit soon made an odd-jobbing labourer and carpenter called Richard Heming the chief suspect. He had been seen behaving strangely by villagers in the preceding months and had a reputation locally as something of a rogue.

In the absence of a formal police force, efforts to find Heming were led by a local justice of the peace, the Reverend Reginald Pyndar. Heming was seen in the hours after the murder at an inn called The Virgin Tavern near Worcester. However, despite a large reward of 50 guineas being offered for his capture, Heming seemed then to have vanished. Some said that he had fled to America. Yet there was other gossip too. Many believed that a group of farmers, led by a Captain Samuel Evans, who had some-times employed Heming, had conspired to have George Parker killed. He and the likes of another local farmer, Thomas Clewes, could often be found in pubs like the Speed the Plough, damning Parker in drink. They hated the hefty tithes, taxes on their goods, that were due to Parker. Indeed Parker, knowing of their hatred, was so concerned for his safety that he never walked through Oddingley alone after dark.

Despite the rumours, there was nothing concrete to link the farmers to the murder and as the months and years went by, the grizzly episode faded from memory. For a full twenty-four years the crime remained unsolved. Then, on 21 January 1830, there was a surprising development. The new tenant at Netherwood Farm, formerly owned by Thomas Clewes, had ordered an old barn to be pulled down. Charles Burton was the man employed to do the work, and whilst digging a trench he hit something hard. He had uncovered a skeleton complete with leather shoes and a carpen-ter's rule. Burton was in fact Heming's brother-in-law. He quickly put two and two together and set off to find a local magistrate.

On 25 January an inquest was convened at The Talbot Inn, Worcester. Locals at Oddingley were banned from the jury in case they were implicated in the crime. The evidence presented suggested that the skeleton bore similarities to the description of Heming – and he was known to carry a carpenter's rule. Burton said that he believed the shoes he had found were Heming's. Another witness, Susan Surman, swore that back in 1806 on the morning of the murder she had heard Clewes saying to someone who was with him that he 'should be glad to find a dead parson' when he came home from Bromsgrove Fair.

Gradually more evidence emerged including the fact that Evans had once been overheard saying of Parker, 'There is no more harm in shooting him than a mad dog.' Thomas Clewes had also been seen drinking with Heming at a pub in Droitwich before the murder. Clewes, who had himself been attending the inquest, was arrested and thrown in prison.

Once behind bars, Clewes soon confessed to having witnessed the death of Heming, who had been paid £50 by the farmers to kill Parker. He said that on the day after Parker's murder, Captain Evans had asked if Heming could hide in his barn at Netherwood Farm and he reluctantly consented. That night he, Evans, another farmer called George Banks and James Taylor, a farrier, went to the barn. Clewes claimed that Taylor then smashed in Heming's skull with a blood stick – an instrument usually used to let blood from horses. Heming, it seems, had been killed in case he spilled the beans about who had ordered Parker's murder, though Clewes claimed not to have known that Evans and Taylor were going to go as far as killing him.

In March 1830, Clewes, Banks and another farmer, John Barnett, who had helped bankroll the deed, appeared before the Worcester Assizes, Evans and Taylor now having passed away. They could not be tried for their part in the murder of Parker because as the law then stood, the 'principal' culprit, Heming, was now dead. Instead they were charged with the murder of Heming. Clewes' legal team argued that as his confession was the basis for the charges, it should also be taken as fact that he had not taken part in Heming's murder or known Taylor would kill him as he had stated. A confused jury at first found Clewes guilty 'as accessory after the fact', but the judge told them that this verdict could not be recorded as it was not the charge of aiding and abetting murder which Clewes faced. The jury returned to find Clewes not guilty and he was acquitted along with Banks and Barnett.

When the news got out, some villagers in Oddingley broke into the church and rang the bells to celebrate. But Oddingley's reputation suffered. The case made the national press and the place became synonymous with evil, its ditches said to 'run red with blood' every time it rained. But at The Fir Tree, the landlord is more sanguine about the events which brought this rural backwater notoriety. A sign in the pub's car park reads, 'Every old inn has a story to tell but none as gruesome as the Oddingley murders.'

LOCATION: **The Fir Tree Inn**, Trench Lane, Dunhampstead, Droitwich, Worcestershire, WR9 7JX, 01905 774094, www.thefirtreeinn.co.uk; **The Talbot**, No. 8 Barbourne Road, Worcester, WR1 1HT, 01905 723 744, www.johnbarras.com

SHOT BY SMUGGLERS AND LEFT FOR DEAD, 1821

The Ship Inn, Herne Bay, Kent
Smuggling was still rife around the Kent coast in the early years of the nineteenth century and men in the so-called 'preventive service', charged with catching them, had their work cut out trying to stop the organised gangs that, more often than not, outwitted their pursuers. Around this time about a quarter of all the boats used for smuggling in Britain were based in Kent and Sussex. Hundreds of men were involved in smuggling and local communities tended to stay tight-lipped about their activities for fear of reprisal. It was hard but vital for the authorities to catch the smugglers in the actual act if successful convictions were going to be made.

One of the most successful groups in the region at this time was known as the North Kent Gang, operating between the River Medway and the town of Ramsgate. These were hardened criminals who were quite prepared to take on the officers of the law, often attacking customs officers who got in their way. On one occasion, when some of their number were captured and put in Faversham jail, the gang launched a bold raid on the building, successfully setting their comrades free.

On the night of Monday 23 April 1821, many members of the gang had been drinking heavily in Herne Bay, a town then notorious as a hub for their nefarious practices. They were awaiting the arrival of a boat carrying contraband. At around 3 a.m. on the morning of the 24th between forty and sixty smugglers could be found busily unloading tubs of spirits on the beach directly opposite the Ship Inn.

Sydenham Snow was an enthusiastic 24-year-old midshipman from a sloop called the *Severn*, part of a blockade that had recently been beefed up with the task of crushing the illicit trade. On the night in question he had been patrolling the beach along with a handful of other 'blockade men' when they stumbled upon the crime taking place. Hopelessly outnumbered, the brave, if headstrong, Snow is said to have rushed forward in an attempt to capture the smuggler's boat itself. He let off his own gun, but it misfired. He then drew his cutlass but was swiftly gunned down by the smugglers. Unperturbed, they continued unloading their valuable cargo before making off inland with the hoard. Shortly afterwards, Snow was found by one of his men lying close to the water's edge with blood coming from his mouth. He had been shot at such close range that there were burns marks on his jacket. Snow was still alive but told his comrades, 'I am a dead man.'

Thomas Norris, the landlord of the Ship, had woken with a start when he had heard the gunfire. He later recalled:

I got out of bed, looked out of the window, and saw a number of people on the beach, and a boat on the shore – there seemed to be 20 or 30 men; they appeared in motion from the boat up the road, and appeared to be carrying something. I saw no cart or horse – I could not tell what they were carrying – they passed on, and soon after I heard a person mourning on the beach, and heard him say, 'Lord, have mercy on me!' and in the course of a little time four of the men belonging to the preventive service came into the road; I called to them, and Mr Snow was brought to my house … He was first taken into my bar by four of his men, and then into the parlour; he requested a clergyman to pray with him, and I sent for Mr Dornford, who came; I also sent for a medical man …

A naval surgeon, Joseph Galloway, arrived to attend to Snow and found that he had been shot in his right thigh and his right shoulder. He removed the bullet, but there was apparently little Galloway could do to save Snow's life. His was clearly a slow, painful death. He finally expired, still at the inn, at 8 a.m. on the Friday.

However, Snow had lived long enough to give a description of some of the men in the gang. On the basis of this and information from members of the gang who had turned king's evidence, five of them, including the leader of the party, James West, and the aptly named William Beer, were subsequently brought in. Their trial was held at the Old Bailey that June, having been transferred to London to avoid the possibility of corruption locally. As it was, military assistance had been needed to make the arrests.

But the trial was a shambles, with some witnesses being found to be unreliable and others swearing to the good character of the accused men. The judge ended up acquitting all the defendants. However, the gang's days were numbered: Snow's murder spurred the blockade men to pursue them even harder. Four of its leaders were later executed on Penenden Heath near Maidstone and fifteen others were transported to Australia. Though one officer in the blockade was later to claim that Snow's actual killer was 'still living in 1839, boasting of his exploit, in a parish near Herne Bay'. Snow was buried with full military honours and his own grave can still be seen in Herne churchyard. The headstone reads simply, 'In memory of Sydney Sydenham Snow, who died 21 April 1821, in the 24th year of his age.'

LOCATION: *The Ship Inn*, No. 17 Central Parade, Herne Bay, Kent, CT6 5HT, www.theshiphernebay.com

THE RED BARN MURDER, 1827

The George Inn, Colchester; The Cock Inn, Polstead, Suffolk

In the spring of 1828, a hurriedly convened inquest into the death of a young woman opened at the Cock Inn, a low beamed, cosy hostelry in the sleepy rural village of Polstead in Suffolk. The badly decomposed body of Maria Marten had been found by her own father, a mole-catcher, buried in a lonely barn nearby. Maria, it seemed, had been shot; she had possibly been stabbed and strangled too. The corpse, inspected by a doctor at the Cock, was formally identified by her sister, Ann, from the colour of her hair and a gap in her teeth. Crucially there was a green handkerchief tied around the victim's neck.

The handkerchief pointed towards the likely culprit: William Corder, her former lover who had moved out of the area the year before. Two years earlier, William Corder, the 24-year-old son of a farmer, had started courting Maria, 26, who had already conducted several affairs and given birth to more than one illegitimate child. They would meet on Corder's land in a barn roofed with red tiles. In 1827, Maria gave birth to his child, but the child appears to have died in mysterious circumstances.

Nicknamed Foxey at school, Corder already had form. He'd once fraudulently sold his father's pigs and was known to have forged cheques too. Maria was impatient that Corder should marry her and in May 1827 Corder seems to have agreed. Convincing Maria that the parish constables were aiming to prosecute her for bearing bastard children, Corder told her to meet him at the Red Barn one night wearing men's clothing. The plan was that they would then elope to Ipswich. There the couple argued and Corder shot Maria dead. After hurriedly burying Maria's body, he returned to run his farm. When asked where Maria was he said that she had had move to Great Yarmouth out of shame. Then, in the September of 1827, Corder suddenly left the village. Later he wrote to Maria's family, telling them that all was well and that he and Maria were now living happily together on the Isle of Wight.

Then in April 1828, back in Polstead, Maria's stepmother, Anne, started having some strange dreams. Three nights in a row she

The Cock, Polstead, Suffolk where the inquest into Maria Marten's death was held. (*Courtesy of The Cock*)

dreamt that Maria was dead and had been buried beneath the Red Barn. Eventually she dispatched her husband to start digging there, where he made the gruesome discovery of Maria's body in its shallow grave, inside a sack.

After the inquest at The Cock the local constable, a Mr Ayres, and a detective from London, James Lea, teamed up to find Corder. They eventually discovered him living, not on the Isle of Wight but in Ealing, West London. In the meantime he'd married another woman, Mary Moore, having brazenly advertised for a wife in the pages of *The Times*. And when, on 22 April, Ayres and Lea tracked Corder to the boarding house he was now running, Corder was in the middle of happily boiling some eggs, seemingly without a care in the world. However, during a search of the property the constables found a pair of pistols, one of which was assumed to be the murder weapon. There was also a passport from the French ambassador, seemingly evidence that he was planning to quit the country.

By the time Corder was being taken back to Suffolk to be tried at the Shire Hall in Bury St Edmunds, the case had already become a national sensation. Corder was returned to Bury via Colchester. Here Ayres tried to have Corder shut up in the local prison for the night, but the governor demanded to see a warrant specifying his commitment to a particular gaol. When Ayres couldn't produce it he refused and so Corder spent the night in the George Inn with one arm tied to a bedpost and the other tied to the constable.

Corder's trial began on 7 August and lasted two days. Corder protested his innocence and there was some confusion about just how Maria had died – she had been strangled, shot and possibly stabbed with a sharp instrument. Corder's defence was that, although he had met Maria at the Red Barn, he had then left, heard a gunshot and returned to find one of his own pistols lying by the body.

None of this could save Corder, who was quickly found guilty. Finally, on the night before he met his fate, Corder confessed to shooting Maria in the eye, but claimed it had been an accident. Up to 20,000 spectators turned out to see his execution by hanging, conducted in the pouring rain on 11 August. Another 5,000 queued up to see his slit-open body in the Shire Hall.

Even after death, Corder's ignominy didn't end. His body was dissected and his skin used to bind a book about the trial which is still held at the Moyses Hall Museum in Bury St Edmunds along with his scalp, death mask and his pistols. Maria wasn't able to rest in peace either – her own gravestone was destroyed by ghoulish souvenir hunters who chipped pieces off as keepsakes. Even the scene of the murder, the Red Barn, was chopped up and turned into souvenir snuffboxes and toothpicks.

In the years that followed, the Red Barn Murder inspired ballads and a popular play that was still being performed right up until the 1890s. Elements of the real-life case remained puzzling, however. Much suspicion fell upon Maria's stepmother's 'dreams'. It seemed highly fortuitous that they had led her to the very spot where Maria's body lay. There were rumours that she herself had been conducting an affair with Corder and had been somehow involved in her own stepdaughter's untimely death.

LOCATIONS: *The Cock Inn*, The Green, Polstead, Suffolk, CO6 5AL, 01206 263150; *The George Inn*, Colchester, No. 116 High Street, Colchester, Essex, CO1 1TD, 01206 578494, www.bespokehotels.com

WHERE BODYSNATCHERS BURKE AND HARE FOUND THEIR VICTIMS, 1827–28

The White Hart Inn, The Last Drop and Maggie Dickson's, Grassmarket, Edinburgh

The city of Edinburgh likes to celebrate the more macabre aspects of its history with a drink. And so visitors to Scotland's capital will find The Last Drop, a pub which derives its name from the fact that the Grassmarket, where it is located, was once the venue for public executions. The last man hanged here was a robber called James Andrew, in 1784. Another pub nearby, Maggie Dickson's, commemorates a woman who cheated the hangman at the same spot. She was a fish hawker who became pregnant by an innkeeper's son. She tried to conceal her pregnancy and was then suspected of infanticide. Hanged at the Grassmarket in 1724, her body was taken down and put in a coffin, then sent to her home town of Musselburgh where she was due to be buried. But the noose had not done its job properly. On the way, those transporting the coffin were astonished to hear knocking from inside. Maggie was still alive and had come round after her ordeal. Under law she could not be hanged twice. So she was set free and went on to live another forty years.

Chief among the hostelries that are able to boast a link to the darker side of Edinburgh's past is The White Hart, also on the Grassmarket. The pub dates back to 1516 and was already an institution – frequented by the likes of poet Robert Burns – by the time that it started serving two shady customers, William Burke and William Hare. The pair would become infamous for the murderous plots they hatched and carried out in Edinburgh's taverns and inns.

Both Irish immigrants, Burke and Hare had initially come to Scotland to work on the canals, but both settled in Edinburgh's West Port. Soon Burke and his mistress, Helen McDougal, were living at the lodging house run by Hare's wife, Margaret. Money was tight. Then, in November 1827, an old pensioner called Donald, who was staying at the house, died of natural causes, owing Hare £4 in rent. He and his friend came up with a wheeze to make up the loss. They filled his coffin with bark and then sold the body for a tidy profit of £7 10s to an assistant of Dr Robert Knox, a well-known anatomy lecturer at Edinburgh University, dragging it to his house in a tea chest.

In the early part of the nineteenth century, medical science was developing fast, but there were not enough cadavers for the necessary dissections at medical schools. Until 1832 only the bodies of executed criminals were fair game. With surgeons keen to get their hands on fresh bodies, few questions were asked about the sources of many of those that ended up in their lecture theatres. Grave robbing for corpses became widespread.

Having made such easy ready cash (the sum equates to several hundred pounds in today's money), Burke and Hare soon realised they were on to a good money-spinner if only they could get their hands on some more bodies. Grave robbing was hard work and dangerous, with no guarantee as to the quality of the body that was recovered. It was now that they settled on the idea of murdering people and selling on their freshly killed corpses.

First, the drink-addled duo did away with another elderly and ailing lodger called Joseph, plying him with whisky until he passed out. They then covered his nose and mouth until he expired.

Smothering their victims whilst holding them down and compressing their chests would become Burke and Hare's preferred method of killing, a modus operandi that left few marks on the corpse, just the way the surgeons liked their bodies. Plus, it left no obvious evidence of murder.

Becoming bolder, Burke and Hare now began trawling the drinking dens of Edinburgh, like The White Hart, looking for likely victims. The ideal candidates would be old, homeless or immigrants, people who would not be missed if they suddenly disappeared. On 11 February 1828, they befriended elderly salt pedlar Abigail Simpson at a pub, got her drunk and then lured her back to the lodging house where they again smothered her. This time they got £10 for their trouble. Burke and Hare soon got cocky – more victims swiftly followed, including a prostitute called Mary Paterson. When her body turned up for dissection at the university, some of the students recognised her. But Knox dismissed their concerns.

WILLIAM BURKE.
(From a Sketch taken in Court.)

WILLIAM HARE.
(From a Sketch taken in Court)

William Burke, who was eventually
hanged for his part in a string of murders.
(*Courtesy of Wellcome Library, London*)

William Hare managed to avoid the
noose, despite his role in the killings.
(*Courtesy of Wellcome Library, London*)

Burke and Hare – with their partners very much in on the act – continued to supply bodies, often brazenly dragging them in tea chests or barrels through the streets of the capital.

Victims included a beggar called Effie as well as another old woman and her 12-year-old grandson. A washerwoman called Mrs Ostler suddenly went missing, as did Margaret's own cousin, Ann McDougal. Another local prostitute, Mary Haldane, and her daughter Peggy also succumbed, along with others.

As the year wore on, Burke and Hare were becoming rich on the proceeds of their crimes, which raised suspicions, but they were also becoming rather careless in their choice of victims. That October they lured an 18-year-old man called James Wilson back to their lair, then overpowered and killed him. He was a well-known local character nicknamed Daft Jamie, and when his body arrived on Dr Knox's dissection table he was immediately recognised. The surgeon denied his identity.

Halloween was a fitting date for the last of Burke and Hare's crimes and the one that would lead to their downfall. That morning, Burke was drinking whisky in his local tavern when an

Irish woman called Mary Docherty walked in. Burke bought her a drink, claiming to be a relative, and persuaded her to accompany him home for more carousing. After she had been murdered, her body was stuffed under a bed until it could be transported to Dr Knox. However, two lodgers at the house, Ann and James Gray, became suspicious when they were warned away from a bed by Burke. Then, when he was out of sight, they examined the bed after all and, to their horror, discovered Docherty's corpse. The couple went to the police, refusing a bribe from Helen McDougal to keep quiet. Although Burke and Hare had managed to get rid of the body by the time police arrived it was later found at Dr Knox's office in a tea chest. James Gray identified the body as the one he had seen at the lodging house, and Burke and Hare were finally arrested.

In total, during their killing spree Burke and Hare had done away with sixteen people both at Hare's lodging house and at another property of Burke's. However, prosecutors were hampered by the fact that there was a lack of evidence as to the exact cause of death in the case of Docherty and the possibility that

EXECUTION of the notorious WILLIAM BURKE the murderer, who supplied Dr KNOX with subjects.

Execution of Burke.
From a Contemporary Print.

The execution of William Burke in 1829 at Edinburgh's Lawnmarket from a contemporary print. (*Courtesy of Wellcome Library, London*)

Burke and Hare might both get off scot free if they simply blamed each other in court.

Eventually William Hare was persuaded to rat on his partner and was given immunity from prosecution. While Burke went to the gallows for murder on 28 January 1829, Hare was soon released and was last spotted in Carlisle that year before disappearing without a trace. McDougal had gone on trial for murder alongside Burke, but the case against her was found not proven. Dr Knox escaped prosecution entirely, even though he must have had strong suspicions about the source of such a ready supply of unmutilated bodies. However, his reputation was left in tatters and he moved to London. In the two centuries since the Burke and Hare murders, the White Hart's reputation, however, has gone from strength to strength. In a city of a thousand ghost stories it is also considered Edinburgh's most haunted bar. One particular ghoul said to frequent The White Hart is the ghost of a woman wearing a red dress. Legend has it that she was a prostitute who once frequented the pub – though there is no mention as to whether she may have been one of Burke and Hare's unfortunate victims.

LOCATIONS: *The Last Drop*, Nos 74–78 Grassmarket, Edinburgh, Midlothian, EH1 2JR, 0131 225 4851, www.nicholsonspubs.co.uk; *Maggie Dickson's*, No. 92 Grassmarket, Old Town, Edinburgh, EH1 2JR, 0131 225 6601; *The White Hart*, No. 34 Grassmarket, Edinburgh, Midlothian, EH1 2JU, 0131 226 2806, www.whitehart-edinburgh.co.uk

A DECAPITATED LANDLADY AND A CONFESSION AT THE BAR, 1833

The Bull, Streatley, Berkshire; The Bear and The Blue Boar, Wantage, Oxfordshire

At around 6 a.m. on 31 August 1833, 12-year-old James Pullen woke up and came downstairs at the White Hart in Wantage, looking for his 40-year-old stepmother, Ann, who ran the alehouse. As he went into the parlour, the boy made a gruesome discovery – the decapitated body of Ann, whose severed head was resting by her feet, next to the fireplace. Shortly afterwards a boy delivering milk arrived and ran to find the local constable, Thomas Jackson. On entering the pub in Newbury Street, Jackson found the room 'deluged with blood', some of it spattered up the walls. The pocket of the widow's clothes had been tampered with and her purse was missing. A doctor, Henry Ormond, who was called to examine the body, concluded that Ann, whose head still had its cap tied about her chin, appeared to have been decapitated with a single blow to her neck.

A suspect was quickly identified. He was 19-year-old agricultural labourer George King from the village of Cumnor. He had been seen at the White Hart early on the Friday evening in question and subsequently behaving 'excitably' at the Blue Boar inn, situated opposite the White Hart.

That Saturday morning, after Ann's body was found, a search was made for King. He was found at work cutting beans in a field outside town. He was using his bean hook, a scythe like tool. In King's pocket Constable Jackson found 12s 6d and, crucially, a crooked sixpence. His coat, which was covered in bloodstains, was also found in the field.

An inquest was hurriedly held that afternoon at The Bear which was 'crowded to suffocation' with townsfolk wanting to see what would happen next. King was brought before the coroner and admitted to being a witness to the murder of Ann Pullen but accused another individual, called Edward Grant, of actually carrying out the crime. There was a search, but no one of that name could be found in the town, yet King was able to describe in accurate detail the bloody scene at the White Hart, which only helped to point the finger.

King then suddenly changed his story, switching the target for blame to another man, Charles Merriott, known as 'the French lad', a man with whom he'd been drinking at the Blue Boar late on the Friday night and had afterwards slept next to in a hay loft behind it. The coroner's jury didn't believe him. A verdict of wilful murder was recorded and King was sent to Reading gaol to await a full trial. It wasn't until 28 February 1834 that he was brought up before the assizes in Reading where he pleaded not guilty. In the dock he was described as a 'very heavy looking, clumsy young man' who showed no trace of emotion throughout the proceedings.

The Bull, Streatley, where George King confessed to murder. (© *James Moore*)

Witnesses were brought forward to show that Ann had owned a 'lucky' crooked sixpence just like the one found on King's person. The landlord of the Blue Boar, William Betteridge, told how King had arrived at the pub just before 10 p.m. with his coat over his arm, despite the fact that it was pouring with rain outside. He had asked for a bed but appeared confused when told he was more likely to get one at the White Hart, where of course the defence alleged he had just come from, leaving Ann's mutilated body.

Key to the prosecution's case, however, was a confession that King had apparently made, in front of witnesses, during the journey from Wantage to Reading in the days immediately after the murder. On the way the two men charged with transporting him, Constable Thomas Jackson and James Jones, had decided to stop at the Bull Inn at Streatley – situated halfway to their destination – for refreshment and to feed their horses.

By the early nineteenth century the Bull was already an ancient place, dating back to the 1400s. It had its own gruesome legend about a monk and a nun who had been executed in 1440 for having an illicit relationship and been buried in the pub's garden.

Taken inside this cosy hostelry, King spotted a picture of a woman on the wall. Jackson told the court:

> When we got as far as Streatley we stopped to bait our horses at the Bull. The prisoner went to a picture there and he smiled. He said: 'She turned her eyes like that picture when her head was off'. Then he turned his own eyes like it.

King's story was that on the evening of 30 August he had come from the Squirrel pub in Wantage to the White Hart, and Pullen had cooked him a rasher of bacon. Afterwards he had asked if there was a bed for the night (a witness to this claimed he had propositioned Ann and that she told him that she would hit him with a poker if he tried anything on).

Ann's two children had been sent to bed at around 9 p.m. and at the time the murder was committed there appears to have been no one else in the bar room. No one knows exactly what occurred between the pair but King's version was that he had been sitting at a table with his cup and the tool of his trade, the bean hook, resting on it when he had suddenly felt the urge to lash out.

The constable claimed to have only intended to hit Ann with the back of the bean hook, but to his surprise its sharp blade had sliced the head clean off her body in a manner, later described by one newspaper reporter as an act as 'adroit as a person with a scimitar'.

As the judge summed up the gruesome details of the case the court room descended into chaos as one woman fainted. It took some time to restore order, but only minutes for the jury to find King guilty. Then, a black cap having been placed upon his head, Justice Patteson ordered King to be hanged.

On the following Monday, 3 March, King faced the noose at Reading Gaol. As was tradition, his body was then buried within the prison walls. Ann Pullen was buried in Wantage graveyard, the basic, sorry facts of her demise recorded for posterity in the church's burial register. The White Hart, where she was murdered, later became The Packhorse, but is no longer a pub. However, The Bull in Streatley where King made his confession can still be found, as can the Bear Inn, now the Bear Hotel, where the inquest into the desperate deed was conducted.

LOCATIONS: **The Blue Boar**, No. 4 Newbury St, Wantage, OX12 8BS, 01235 763209; **The Bear Hotel**, www.thebearwantage.co.uk; **The Bull**, Reading Road, Streatley, West Berkshire, RG8 9JJ, 01491 872392, www. marstonspubs.co.uk

THE MURDER OF JONATHAN MAY, 1835

The White Hart Hotel, Moretonhampstead, Devon

Finding an old map on the wall of a pub or hotel is nothing remarkable. However, there is one hanging in the lounge of the White Hart Hotel in Moretonhampstead that is more interesting than most. For this detailed, early nineteenth-century plan of the town was drawn especially to help the jury in a murder trial. In the summer of 1836, two men stood accused of brutally robbing and killing a man called Jonathan May just outside the town. The fact that the map has since been preserved at the White Hart is fitting, since it was here that May had taken his last refreshment before being attacked.

Back in the July of 1836, Moretonhampstead, set on the edge of eerie Dartmoor, was abuzz with the sounds of the annual summer fair. Along with the usual livestock market, the streets were lined with stalls and there was plenty of carousing. During the three-day event the small rural community also attracted a clutch of strangers and one or two criminals too, who would mingle with the crowds hoping to find easy pickings. On the map at the White Hart there are some ten pubs marked in the town and during the fair these would have been full of raucous revellers and visitors taking lodgings.

On Thursday 16 July, Jonathan May rode into town, stabling his horse at The White Hart. May was a 48-year-old bachelor farmer from Dunsford a few miles away. He had a good day – selling his animals for a tidy £80. That evening he went to see a local tanner who owed him some money. Then, between 7 and 8 p.m. he visited a shoemaker's shop to pay a bill. It was time for some refreshment and a contented May headed for the best place in town, The White Hart, which still looks as grand today as it did in the 1830s. The inn, built in 1639, had a proud history and had

The White Hart Hotel in Moretonhampstead, Devon, where Jonathan May supped before his murder. (*Courtesy of Julia Wherrell*)

once been used as a local courthouse. Perhaps May showed too much of the money he had made at the fair, but having enjoyed a good dinner, washed down with a little ale, he was soon on his way. The landlord, Samuel Cann, recalled, 'He left about 10 p.m. at night on horseback. He was then perfectly sober.' Shortly afterwards a tollhouse keeper spoke to May as he left the town.

About an hour and a half later Nicholas Taverner and his family, who had left Moretonhampstead on foot, found a horse without its rider. Taverner took the horse back to town where he discovered that it belonged to May. He then went back off down the Exeter road to search for him. He found May lying on his back near a spot called Jacob's Well. When Taverner lifted May's head 'blood came bubbling out of his nose and mouth'. It didn't look like the man had been dragged along the road as he might have if the horse had bolted. Suspiciously, his pockets had been turned out too. Taverner cried out 'Murder!' and then went back to Moretonhampstead to alert a doctor and fetch a cart to carry May back. He took the farmer to the White Hart where he was placed in a bed. Two doctors attended May, who had a wound over his left eye, three more on the upper part of the head, two on the back of the head and another by his left ear. Despite attempts to revive him, May never regained consciousness and died at 9 p.m. on the Friday.

A post-mortem found that May had suffered a fractured skull, and the two doctors agreed that the head injuries which killed him were unlikely to have been caused by a fall. They were consistent with being assaulted with a stick or having been kicked. Indeed, that morning a bloodied stick was found in a hedge near the spot where May had been found. Though he had clearly been the victim of a robbery, little was missing from May's body apart from his watch and also a pocket book, which was later retrieved from a field. In the same field the tracks of two people were also found leading away from the scene. A coroner's inquest held at The White Hart recorded a verdict of wilful murder.

Suspicion was soon directed towards a local labourer called George Avery, a man who had been sacked by May and had turned to wrestling to earn money. He had narrowly escaped a different murder charge, but had been convicted of an assault. Avery was promptly arrested along with his lover, Elizabeth Harris, and several others who were thought to be accomplices. However, although Avery was definitely at the fair on the night of the murder, he was released when witnesses placed him in his lodgings at the time the killing had occurred. The others were released too.

The following spring a man who went by the names of both Thomas Oliver and Thomas Infield, as well as the nickname Buckingham Joe, was in Dorchester Gaol awaiting trial for another robbery when he boasted about 'the job' he had done on a Devonshire farmer, along with another man whom he referred to as 'Turpin'. The prison chaplain came to hear of this admission and, knowing of the May case, passed on the information to the authorities. May's watch was subsequently found at Buckingham Joe's lodgings.

There was a well-known young ruffian in the south east called Edmund Galley who happened to go by the nickname of Turpin. He was known to cause trouble at fairs. Galley was soon picked up for vagrancy and then accused of May's murder too, effectively on the basis of his nickname. He denied ever having been in Devon, adding that he had been at the races in Reigate, Surrey, on

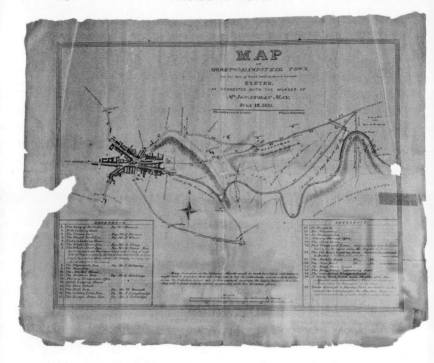

A plan of Moretonhampstead used in the trial, which now hangs on a wall inside the
White Hart. (*Courtesy of Julia Wherrell*)

the day May was murdered, though he later claimed to have been
at a fair in Dartford in Kent.

The trial of Buckingham Joe and Edmund Galley took place in
Exeter on 28 July 1836. A raft of witnesses were brought forward
to say that they recognised the pair as having been at the fair in
Moretonhampstead and acting suspiciously before and after
the murder, but the accounts were conflicting. The case hinged
around the testimony of Elizabeth Harris, Avery's former lover.
She testified that she had seen the two men now in the dock dis-
cussing robbing farmers in Moretonhampstead during the fair.
Astonishingly she then claimed to have seen them commit the
actual murder too. They had, she said, pulled May off his horse and
then attacked him with a stick and kicked him. Harris said she had
not told this story before because she was scared of retribution.

Now she was in gaol for another offence and waiting to be transported. It should be noted that in giving her evidence she hoped to get a pardon. George Avery was brought before the court to say that Harris had actually been in bed with him at around the time of the murder. Then, another witness stated that Galley was not the man she had seen with Oliver and an accomplice at the Lamb Inn on the road to Exeter. Confusingly, another put Galley in the White Hart playing pub games during the fair. Galley, who had no defence counsel during the trial, continued vehemently to protest his innocence and maintained that he had never been to Devon.

The jury took just sixteen minutes to find both defendants guilty of murder. But as the judge, Mr Justice Williams, was reaching for his black cap to pronounce the death sentence, Galley again cried out that he was innocent. Buckingham Joe then suddenly made an extraordinary outburst, admitting, 'I did it.' Then, pointing to Galley, he said, 'The man that was with me was a man no more like that man than that candle.' Although Justice Williams still directed both men to be executed, he ordered further investigations while they awaited the noose. Quizzed by investigators, Galley eventually managed to remember some of the men that he had met at Dartford on 16 July. They were contacted by letter and all confirmed that he had been there and not in Moretonhampstead on the day in question. While Buckingham Joe went to the gallows on 12 August 1836, Galley was granted a stay of execution. In the end, though more witnesses were produced to prove his alibi, Galley was not given an immediate pardon. Instead his sentence was changed to transportation for life. He arrived in Australia in 1839 where he made a new life for himself. However, he continued to plead his innocence and back in Britain his case was kept alive by campaigners. Galley was eventually granted a pardon in 1879. Although he was given the opportunity of returning to his homeland with compensation he decided to remain in Australia where he now had a family. He died there in 1885.

LOCATION: *White Hart Hotel*, The Square, Moretonhampstead, Newton Abbot, Devon, TQ13 8NF, 01647 440500, www.whitehartdartmoor.co.uk

Killing 'The Devil', 1843

The Ship Inn, Cobham, Kent

At 6 p.m. on the evening of 28 August 1843, a four-wheeled chaise pulled up at The Ship Inn, a historic watering hole in Cobham, Kent. Two men got out of the carriage, Richard Dadd, a 24-year-old artist, and his father, Robert. The pair knew The Ship well, for they had made reviving visits to the sixteenth-century inn together in the past. Robert asked the waiter, John Adams, whom he knew, to arrange some accommodation for them. Although there were no rooms available at The Ship, beds were found for the duo in some nearby cottages. A little later the waiter served Richard some biscuits and cheese while Robert ordered some broiled ham and porter. Staff observed that his son's manner was very sullen.

After the meal, Richard proposed to his father that they go for a walk, but Robert said he was too tired and ordered a whisky. At about 9.30 p.m., Richard again asked his father if he would step out with him for a stroll. This time Robert agreed and they set off on a path through Cobham Park, a large country estate nearby. They were returning towards the village and passing a chalk pit called Paddock's Hole when Robert turned his back on Richard in order to relieve himself. It was at this moment, at around 11p.m., that Dadd set upon his father. First he tried to slit Robert's throat with a razor, but he failed to deliver a fatal wound. Then Dadd pulled out a sailor's knife, stabbing his father in the chest.

Robert's dead body was discovered the next morning by a passing butcher, Charles Lyster, who was on his way to market. The corpse was brought back down to the village where it was placed in a building at the rear of The Ship. Suspicion soon fell on Dadd Junior as he had not returned to the Ship the night before. The only trace of the culprit was two bloody handprints on the top rung of a stile near the scene of Robert's murder.

Richard Dadd was born in 1817 at Chatham in Kent. The fourth of seven children, from a young age he showed a considerable talent as an artist. His father, Robert, was a chemist, while his mother died when Richard was just 7 years old. In 1834, Robert

moved the family to London to take up a new job as a carver
and gilder, and by the age of 20, Dadd's artistic skills saw him
admitted to the prestigious Royal Academy of Arts, where he
soon established a considerable reputation, mixing with some of
the leading artists of his generation. In July 1842 he was asked by
his patron, the solicitor Sir Thomas Phillips from Newport, to
accompany him as a draughtsman on a Grand Tour to Europe and
the Middle East. During the trip, which took in Germany, Italy,
Greece, Turkey and Syria, Dadd produced a sheaf of excellent
watercolours and drawings. Yet during a journey down the River
Nile in Egypt he began to exhibit strange symptoms, becoming increasingly violent and delusional; he was convinced that
he was being pursued by devils. He attacked Sir Thomas and, as
the party made their way through Rome, even considered trying
to assassinate the Pope. At first it was thought that he was suffering from sunstroke but after Dadd returned to England in May
1843 his behaviour became increasingly erratic. He shut himself
up in his studio and lived on little but hard-boiled eggs and ale. In
the coming months he painted portraits of his friends but would
add the chilling detail to each of a red gash across their throats.
On 26 August, a Dr Alexander Sutherland at St Luke's Asylum
declared that he was mentally unstable and potentially dangerous.
He recommended that Dadd be confined.

Robert Dadd, however, was clearly very fond of his son and
offered to care for him rather than see him committed to an
institution where he might languish for the rest of his life. Dadd
suggested to his father that they should go to the country so he
could 'unburden his mind'. So, on the 28th, the pair set off to enjoy
the rural charms of Cobham and the surrounding countryside, an
area which Dadd the younger knew well from his youth. It was all
a ruse. Dadd was now convinced that his father was the devil. The
Egyptian God Osiris had 'ordered' him to kill this imposter.

After the murder, Dadd made for The Crown at Rochester.
Here he hurriedly washed his hands before leaving in a carriage.
As the vehicle passed The Star he threw a bloodied towel he had
used to wipe his hands over a hedge. Dadd was heading for Dover
by way of The George at Sittingbourne. Crossing the English
Channel in a small hired boat, he then travelled on to Paris. His

intention was to find and kill more 'devils'. Among his targets was Emperor Franz Ferdinand I of Austria. But while travelling on a stagecoach near Fontainebleau in September he unsuccessfully attempted to cut the throat of another passenger. He was restrained and quickly arrested. Dadd admitted to French police that he had killed his father and was put in a local asylum before being taken back to England in July 1844 to face trial.

Dadd appeared at Maidstone Assizes in August that year where he was swiftly found unfit to plead and committed to Bethlem Hospital in Southwark, better known as Bedlam. He was almost certainly suffering from paranoid schizophrenia – at least two of his siblings also suffered from mental conditions. Dadd was later moved to Broadmoor asylum when it opened in 1863. Ironically, during his incarceration, he was encouraged to continue with his painting and completed some of his finest works during this period of his life, including his most famous masterpiece, *The Fairy Feller's Masterstroke*. Dadd died on 7 January 1886. The chalk pit in Cobham Park, where the murder was committed, is now known as Dadd's Hole.

LOCATION: *The Ship Inn*, No. 14 The Street, Cobham, Gravesend, Kent, DA12 3BN, 01474 814 326, www.johnbarras.com; *The Crown*, No. 2 High Street, Rochester, ME1 1PT, 01634 814874, www.thecrownrochester.co.uk

POISONED BY DOCTOR DEATH, 1855

The Shrew and The Albion, Rugeley, Staffordshire; Lamb & Flag, Little Haywood, Staffordshire; Cross Keys Hotel, Hednesford, Staffordshire
The murderous Dr Harold Shipman, who preyed on his own unfortunate patients, is reckoned to have done away with 250 people over two decades. Finally convicted of murder in 2000, he was Britain's worst serial killer and eventually hanged himself in his prison cell. The nineteenth century had its own doctor death, William Palmer, who is believed to have killed as many as fifteen people during his lifetime, including his own wife and children. The apparently genial Shipman concealed his criminal character beneath a veil of charm which helped him get away with his secret killing spree. And it

appears that Palmer was also invested with an outward affability that enabled him to avoid detection for some years.

Palmer was born on 6 August 1824 in Rugeley, the son of Sarah and Joseph, a timber merchant. At the age of 17 he became a chemist's assistant in Liverpool but was soon in trouble, sacked on suspicion of stealing money. He attempted to regain respectability by studying medicine, landing a role as a student at Stafford Infirmary where he first became interested in poisons, then went to London where he qualified as a doctor in 1846. Palmer returned to Rugeley to practise, renting a house in Market Street. Around this time he would often call for drink at The Lamb and Flag in Little Haywood, a village nearby. It was here that he met what many believe to have been his first victim, George Abley. Palmer, who established a reputation as a womanizer as well as a murderer, was besotted with George's attractive wife and one night challenged him to a brandy-drinking contest. An hour later George fell ill. He died in his bed later that evening. His death was officially put down to natural causes. Later there were whispers that Palmer had tampered with Abley's brandy.

On 7 October 1847, Palmer married 20-year-old Anne Thornton, the illegitimate daughter of Colonel William Brookes, who had owned the Noah's Ark inn at Stafford. Before its closure in 2013, this pub was renamed both The Surgery and Palmers thanks to its link to the desperate doctor. Despite what should have been a lucrative profession, Palmer was always short of cash, often losing heavily by gambling on horse races. Anne was a good prospect in this regard. Her mother Mary, who had been housekeeper and mistress to Brookes, had inherited £8,000 when he died. In 1849 she came to stay with her daughter and her husband but died two weeks later, aged 50. The cause of her death was recorded as 'apoplexy'. The timing of her demise seemed, in retrospect, suspicious to say the least. Palmer was said to have been disappointed with the size of Anne's eventual inheritance.

During the years that followed, Palmer and Anne had five children, only one of which would survive. The rest succumbed to mysterious convulsions. The suggestion is that a financially embarrassed Palmer, seeing the youngsters as an extra expense that he could ill afford, poisoned them all.

In 1850 Palmer went to Chester Races with a brewer called Leonard Bladen to whom he owed money. Bladen had a lucky day, scooping a sizeable sum, and returned as a guest to Palmer's house in Rugeley. On 10 May, Bladen fell ill and died, in agony, at the house. His death certificate reported that he died of a hip injury and an abscess. But when his wife arrived she was surprised to find that none of Bladen's winnings were on his body.

By 1854, Palmer was heavily in debt to the tune of at least £23,000 and took out a life insurance policy on his wife for £13,000. By that September Anne had swiftly died, aged just 27. This time the official cause of death was cholera. Palmer claimed the cash but continued to be hounded by creditors. In early 1855, he took out another policy, this time on his alcoholic brother, Walter. Soon he was dead too, but this time the insurance company smelled a rat, refusing to pay out. Palmer, who had virtually given up medicine to concentrate on gambling by this stage, was also being blackmailed by a former mistress.

At this time Palmer lived opposite the Talbot Arms in Market Street, Rugeley, Staffordshire, which had been a coaching inn since around 1700. The Talbot later became The Crown, then The Shrewsbury Arms. Today it is called The Shrew. In the 1850s it was probably the best accommodation that Rugeley had to offer, though a contemporary account described it as looking like an 'aged gaol'. It was here that, on Wednesday 15 November, a friend of Palmer, John Parsons Cook, booked a room. In the two preceding days, Cook and Palmer had been to the races at Shrewsbury. Cook had won a hefty £3,000, while Palmer had, as usual, backed a loser. Cook celebrated his win with Palmer at the Raven Inn, Shrewsbury, where he complained that the brandy had 'burnt his throat'. Tellingly, Palmer had been seen in the pantry pouring some fluid from a small bottle into a tumbler.

Two days later, at the Talbot, the friends shared coffee in Cook's room. Cook vomited and became seriously ill. Later the same day, Palmer sent for some broth from the Albion pub nearby, which Palmer poured into a cup in his kitchen and sent over to Cook at the Talbot. On the following day, when some more broth for Cook was brought over on Palmer's instruction the Talbot's chambermaid, Elizabeth Mills, tasted it and was violently sick.

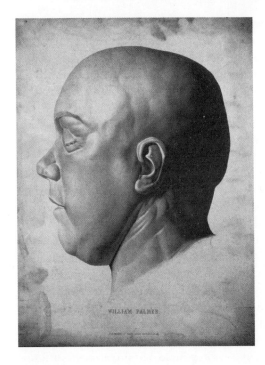

WILLIAM PALMER.

The death mask of serial killer William Palmer. (*Courtesy of Wellcome Library, London*)

Cook briefly recovered while Palmer obligingly went to collect Cook's outstanding betting proceeds for him. He also secretly bought some strychnine. The following night a servant at the Talbot found Cook violently screaming and writhing in his bed. Rushing over, Palmer gave him some pills. Cook, aged just 28, died at 1 a.m. on 21 November.

Two days later, Cook's stepfather, William Stevens, arrived and became suspicious when he saw the stiffness of the body. He was also puzzled that Cook had seemed perfectly healthy when he'd seen them earlier in the month. Palmer told Stevens that Cook, whose betting books had suddenly gone missing, owed him money. Stevens demanded a post-mortem which was conducted on 26 November at the Talbot in shambolic circumstances. One of the two medical students who were given the task was drunk. Incredibly Palmer, already rumoured to be Cook's killer, was present too and 'bumped' into one of the students who was removing the contents of Cook's stomach so that they spilled.

He then tried to tamper with the jar the remains were kept in. Samples from the post-mortem were sent to an eminent toxicologist and, although they weren't satisfactory, he formed the opinion that Cook had been poisoned. Meanwhile, Palmer did himself no favours by attempting to bribe the coroner of the inquest that followed, and the jury's verdict was that 'The deceased died of poison wilfully administered to him by William Palmer.'

The doctor was duly arrested, but due to the public frenzy surrounding the case locally, it was felt Palmer would not be able to get a fair trial in Staffordshire. An Act of Parliament was hurriedly passed, allowing the case to be heard at the Old Bailey in London. Before the trial, which began on 14 May 1856, Ann Palmer's body was exhumed and found to contain traces of the poison antimony. Palmer maintained his innocence at the twelve-day trial. Much of the evidence was circumstantial and it never became clear exactly whether it was strychnine that had killed Cook or a combination of poisons. But his symptoms and Palmer's strange behaviour at the time, as testified to by a raft of witnesses, was enough for the jury to convict him of murder.

Palmer was hanged on 14 June 1856 outside Stafford Gaol, in front of a crowd of 30,000 people. So infamous was Palmer – dubbed the 'Prince of Poisoners' in the press – that he even got his own waxwork at London's Madame Tussaud's. It remained on exhibit to the public for the next 127 years. Tales relating to Palmer's supposed criminal activities flourished too – including the suggestion that he had once poisoned a navvy at The Cross Keys in Hednesford. One of the Palmer case's more curious legacies is that it's thought to have given rise to the expression 'What's your poison?' when enquiring what alcoholic drink someone wants. The question is still popular in bar rooms across the land to this day.

LOCATIONS: **Lamb and Flag**, Main Road, Little Haywood, Staffordshire, ST18 0TU; **The Shrew**, Market Street, Rugeley, Staffordshire, WS15 2JJ; **Albion**, No. 17 Albion Street, Rugeley, Staffordshire, WS15 2BY, 01889 358416; **Cross Keys Hotel**, No. 42 Hill Street, Hednesford, Cannock, WS12 2DN, 01543 879534

Two Sisters Murdered by a Soldier, 1856

Valiant Sailor, Folkestone, Kent

The Valiant Sailor pub is situated above the romantic white cliffs between Folkestone and Dover near a place called Steddy Hole. First opened in 1780, it was called the Jolly Sailor until 1822. But in 1856 it was the scene of a double murder committed by a spurned soldier. Serbian-born Dedea Redanies was serving in the British army but had become consumed with jealousy after falling for a local girl who, it seems, was not quite as besotted with him. Unrequited love often leads people to extremes, but in Redanies' case it drove him to kill not only the woman he loved but her unfortunate sister too.

Aged just 26, Redanies already had plenty of experience of death. He was a decorated soldier who had spent time in the Austro-Hungarian army before travelling to Switzerland and signing up with the British Swiss Legion, one of the regiments of foreign troops recruited to help fight the Crimean War. During the conflict he had been stationed at Dover Castle where, able to speak both German and Italian, he worked as an interpreter.

It was on an evening out to the theatre that Redanies met Caroline Back, 18, and her sister Maria, 16, who lived in Dover with their parents, John and Mary. Before long, Redanies was courting Caroline and had become friends with her family, regularly bringing his dirty laundry round to clean. Soon Redanies was posted for a short time to Aldershot in Hampshire. It appears that during this period, pretty Caroline's affection for the dashing soldier diminished. When Redanies returned he asked to see the love letters he had written her but Caroline mistakenly included one from another admirer instead. A furious Redanies became convinced, wrongly, that Caroline was seeing an artilleryman in Woolwich. He also believed that she had misled him about being pregnant with his child, a ruse, so it was said, that the youngster had come up with to scare him off!

On Saturday 2 August, Redanies bought a dagger from a shop in Snargate Street in Dover. That evening he went to ask

Mary Back if he could take her daughter Caroline for a walk to Folkestone the following Sunday morning. She agreed as long as her sister Maria went along too. At the astonishingly early hour of 3.30 a.m. the trio set off in their Sunday best. Caroline and Mary were wearing smart black capes, bonnets and gloves while Redanies was wearing full uniform. At 5 a.m. Redanies was seen walking arm in arm with the pair in the village of Capel-le-Ferne, not far from the Valiant Sailor. A few minutes later, according to his own account, Redanies asked the girls to sit down on some grass to rest but they apparently refused because it was too damp. He then asked Caroline to lead the way on. As she set off he then plunged his new dagger directly into Maria's heart. Caroline, seeing her sister fall to the floor dead, collapsed sobbing. Redanies said he then bent down to kiss her. When Caroline tried to grab the knife, Redanies repeatedly stabbed her too and then fled.

At 8 a.m. that Sunday a carpenter called Thomas Gurling was trying to find a safe way down to the beach when he stumbled across the bloodied, dead bodies of the two girls, lying about 15yds apart. Racing to the Valiant Sailor nearby he told the landlord, Richard Kitham, of his discovery and the pair went back to the scene. Kitham then rushed off to fetch the police in Folkestone and the bodies were removed to a nearby cottage. A doctor, William Bateman, was also called. As well as three wounds to her chest, Caroline had suffered cuts to her left hand where she had tried to parry the blows. Maria had been stabbed four times, also in the chest. Both of the girls, identified that morning by Mary Back, were still wearing their gloves and bonnets but their black capes were missing. Chillingly, their mother told police that she had dreamed that morning that Redanies would murder the girls and that their bodies would be found on the beach.

Redanies clearly regretted his moment of madness. The next day he called at a shop to buy some envelopes, writing paper and a pen. He then sat down and composed two letters, both in German. One was to his company commander and the other was sent to Mary Back:

Dearest Mother Back—On the first lines, I pray to forgive me the awful accident to the unlucky Dedea Redanies which I committed upon my very dear Caroline and Maria Back yesterday morning at five o'clock. Scarcely I am able to write, by heartbreak for my ever memorable Caroline and Mary Ann. The cause of my deed is: 1. As I heard that Caroline is not in the family way, as I first believed. 2. Because Caroline intends to go to Woolwich. 3. Because I cannot stay with my very dear Caroline, it made my heart so scattered that I put into my mind at last that Caroline rather may die from my hands than to allow Caroline's love being bestowed upon others. However, I did not intend to murder also Mary Ann, her sister; but not having other opportunity, and as she was in my way, I could not do otherwise – I must stab her too.

At 4 p.m. that day a police constable spotted a man acting suspiciously on the road to Canterbury. It was Redanies, still carrying the capes of the two girls. He immediately tried to stab himself, before throwing the dagger to the ground. Redanies was badly injured but later recovered in hospital.

Redanies' trial for murder began on 16 December 1856, where he pleaded guilty and was quickly convicted and sentenced to death. His execution, carried out by William Calcraft, took place in Maidstone on New Year's Day 1857 and was witnessed by a crowd of 5,000 people. Tragically, a man called James Anderson was killed by accident when he fell whilst helping to take down the scaffold.

LOCATION: *Valiant Sailor*, New Dover Road, Capel-le-Ferne, Folkestone, Kent, CT18 7JJ, 01303 252 401, www.valiantsailor.com

THE MURDER OF 'SWEET FANNY ADAMS', 1867

The George and The Swan, Alton, Hampshire
At 7 p.m. on Saturday, 24 August 1867, Frederick Baker walked into The Swan in Alton High Street with a fellow clerk, Maurice Biddle. The pair worked together at William Clement's solicitors firm across the road. It was clear to Maurice that Baker, who had

been in and out of the office that day, had already been drinking. Baker related how, whilst out for a walk that afternoon, a woman had accused him of taking away a child and said, 'if the child is lost or murdered I shall be blamed for it.' Baker then told Maurice that he might leave town on the Monday. After a boot boy overheard Baker's plans and said he was also leaving Alton on the Monday, Baker suggested they could both leave together. When it was suggested that Baker might have difficulty getting another job he replied, 'I could go as a butcher.'

Baker's odd statement at the bar took on a spine-chilling significance when Maurice later heard the rumours that Baker was indeed suspected of murdering an 8-year-old girl, Fanny Adams, whose body had just been found. Rushing to find Baker again he challenged him, saying, 'They say you have murdered a child.' Baker answered, 'Never mind, it is a bad job for me then.' At 9 p.m. the 29-year-old was arrested back at his place of work by Superintendent William Cheyney and marched to the police station. Word of the terrible deed – and the identity of the man suspected of perpetrating it – had already spread through the town and a baying crowd had assembled. Two days later, Baker's office diary would be found. The entry for 24 August read simply: 'Killed a young girl. It was fine and hot.'

Young Fanny had left her home in Tanhouse Lane at 1.30 p.m. on the 24th to play in a meadow with her sister Lizzie and a friend called Minnie Warner. Here they encountered a man wearing a black coat, light waistcoat and trousers who gave them some halfpennies. He then asked Fanny to go into a hop field with him, while he gave the other two some more money and told them to go off and buy some sweets. Fanny took her money but was reluctant to go with Baker. He then scooped the child up in his arms and disappeared with her among the hop poles. Although she was out of sight of the other children, they could hear Fanny crying.

At 5 p.m., Minnie and Lizzie returned home from playing without Fanny. They told a neighbour, Mrs Gardiner, what had happened. Mrs Gardiner immediately raised the alarm with Fanny's mother, Harriet, and the two rushed up the lane to the spot where she was last seen. As they did so, they encountered a man coming the other way. Suspecting foul play, Mrs Gardiner said, 'What have you done with the child?' The man, who seemed utterly composed, told them that he had indeed given some children a few pennies but that he had left them all unharmed. While he didn't offer up his name he did tell the name of the solicitors' firm where he worked – Clement's.

At 7 p.m. a search party was formed and Fanny's dead body was found a little later in the hop field. Her head and legs had been cut off and her eyes gouged out. There were many other hideous injuries and body parts were scattered over a wide area. She had also been disembowelled. Poor Harriet Adams ran to the cricket pitch at the Butts to tell her husband, George, the terrible news, before collapsing with grief. An equally devastated George had to be restrained from taking his own revenge on whoever the culprit might be with a shotgun. Meanwhile Fanny's remains were taken to the Leather Bottle tavern in Amery Street (which later became a restaurant) and then to the police station.

When Superintendent Cheyney heard the description of the man who had last been seen with Fanny, he immediately thought of Baker and headed to his office. Upon his arrest, Baker maintained that he was innocent. However, there were traces of blood on his shirt and trousers and some of the clothes he had been wearing were found to be wet as if they had been washed. Two small knives were also found in his possession. A local painter later found a large stone in the hop field with blood and hair stuck to it. This would turn out to have been the murder weapon.

The inquest into Fanny's death was opened at The Dukes Head Inn. This grade II listed pub has since been through several name changes and is now called The George. Here the jury had the unpleasant task of viewing Fanny's remains. A handcuffed Baker, who appeared before the coroner, repeated that he had not killed the girl, but the jury quickly returned its verdict of wilful murder against him for the 'slaying of Fanny Adams'. Feeling was running so high that by now a lynch mob had assembled outside the pub. In the end the prisoner was smuggled out of the Duke's Head via a back exit, but Baker was still forced to run to the prison surrounded by policemen for his protection.

Baker was tried at Winchester Assizes that December, where he pleaded insanity. The court heard that a cousin of Baker's had been in Bedlam asylum in London and that the prisoner himself, it was said, had once tried to commit suicide. In Baker's defence, it was also pointed out that the small knives found on Baker were surely too small to have been used to cut up Fanny's body.

Neither the argument that Baker was mad nor the fact that there was not enough evidence to link him to Fanny's terrible fate was enough to convince the jury of his innocence. They took just fifteen minutes to find him guilty. At 8 a.m. on Christmas Eve – four months after the crime – some 5,000 people assembled at Winchester's county prison to see Baker hanged. It was the last public hanging there.

It turned out that, following his conviction, Baker had written to Fanny's parents expressing sorrow for what he had done. He had murdered her, he said, when she began to cry. He had done it 'in an unguarded hour and not with malice aforethought'. Baker maintained to the end that he had not sexually assaulted their daughter, though he had so badly mutilated her body that it was impossible for surgeons to be sure.

The case shocked the whole nation and newspapers described the murder as unparalleled in its brutality. It also had a curious legacy for the English language. It gave rise to the use of the phrase 'Sweet Fanny Adams' to mean 'sweet nothing', which is still heard today. This came from the dark humour of sailors, who moaned about the new meagre tins of mutton that they were issued with for sea voyages from 1869.

LOCATIONS: *The George*, formerly the Dukes Head Inn, Butts Road, Alton, Hampshire GU34 1LH, 01420 82331, www.thegeorgealton.co.uk; *The Swan Hotel*, High Street, Alton, Hampshire GU34 1AT, 01420 83777, www.oldenglishinns.co.uk

WAS JACK THE RIPPER ONCE ARRESTED AT A PUB? 1873

Burton Bridge Inn, Burton-on-Trent

Few criminals could have used as many aliases as Michael Ostrog if, indeed, that was his real name. The shadowy figure was known to have used at least twenty different monikers during a bizarre career of misdemeanours. They included Bertrand Ashley, Stanistan Sublinsky, John Sobieski, Claude Clayton, Max Grief Gosslar, Ashley Nabokoff, Knuth Ostin and, perhaps most exotic of all, Mutters Ostrogoc. But the question that has faced crime historians for more than 100 years is whether this elusive eccentric should also be branded Jack the Ripper.

Sir Melville Macnaghten, chief constable of the Metropolitan Police in the 1890s, certainly believed that Ostrog fitted the profile of the notorious serial killer who is believed to have viciously murdered at least five women in the Whitechapel area of London in 1888. In February 1894, Macnaghten produced a handwritten memorandum on the Ripper case in response to newspaper claims that a man called Thomas Cutbush was the culprit. Although not involved in the original Ripper investigation, Macnaghten named three suspects who he felt were more likely to be the murderer. These were Montague John Druitt, a barrister turned teacher who committed suicide in late 1888; Aaron Kosminski, a Polish Jew who lived in Whitechapel and was committed to an asylum in 1891; and Michael Ostrog. In the document Macnaghten described Ostrog as follows:

> … a mad Russian Doctor and a convict and a homicidal maniac. This man was said to have been habitually cruel to women and for a long time was known to have carried about with him surgical knives and other instruments; his antecedents (criminal records) were of the very worst and his whereabouts at the time of the Whitechapel murders could never be satisfactorily accounted for.

The details of Ostrog's life are sketchy. Possibly born in 1835 in Warsaw, Poland, Ostrog claimed both to have been a doctor and to have served in the Russian army or navy. What is certain is that he was educated and eloquent, as well as an expert con man and thief. Ostrog first came to the attention of the authorities in 1863 when he was to be found in Oxford passing himself off as a German student called Max Grief Gosslar. He was convicted of pilfering items from the university's colleges and given ten months' hard labour.

Michael Ostrog, a man of Polish descent, who has been suspected of being Jack the Ripper. (*Author's collection*)

The following year he popped up in Bishop's Stortford, Hertfordshire, this time posing as an impoverished Polish count on the run. In February he was convicted of more offences in Cambridge and given a three-month sentence. By July 1864 he was in Tunbridge Wells, Kent, this time pretending to be the son of the King of Poland, selling hard luck stories to anyone who would listen in order to get cash. Ostrog came a cropper in Devon in December that year when he was found guilty of fraud and imprisoned for another eight months.

In 1866, Ostrog turned up in Kent again where he stole a watch among other items. That July, in Maidstone, he was handed down a sentence of seven years, the judge being aware of his former convictions. Just three months after his release in 1873, however, he was at Woolwich Barracks in London somehow talking his way into the quarters of an officer and stealing £5 worth of his belongings. Moving on to Windsor in Berkshire he began, in July that year, taking valuables from the rooms at Eton College including a silver cup and some rare books. Knowing the police had his description, Ostrog soon did another runner. But he was not at large for long.

On Sunday, 5 October 1873, Ostrog was tracked down to the modest Fox and Goose Inn, today known as the Burton Bridge Inn, at Burton-on-Trent where he had taken a room. Quite why he had popped up in the town is uncertain, but Ostrog seemed to have a habit of fleeing to random destinations if his nefarious activities generated too much heat in one location.

It was the landlord's son at the inn, John Taylor, who realised that Ostrog matched the description in the newspapers of a man wanted for the thefts at Eton. Superintendent Thomas Oswell of the Staffordshire Constabulary was quickly on the scene and found Ostrog enjoying his dinner at the pub. Worried that Ostrog might turn violent, Oswell threw all the knives and forks out of Ostrog's reach before confronting him with a copy of the *Police Gazette*. Ostrog protested his innocence, claiming to be a Swedish doctor who was visiting the breweries for which the local area was famed, but he was swiftly marched off into custody. Despite his cautious approach, Oswell does not seem to have had Ostrog's pockets checked. Once at the station, his captive suddenly pulled

The Burton Bridge Inn, formerly known as the Fox and Goose, where Michael Ostrog was arrested. (*Courtesy of the Burton Bridge Inn*)

out a loaded, eight-chamber revolver. Ostrog was only prevented from using it when Oswell grabbed his wrist and wrestled the weapon off his prisoner. The next day, Ostrog was taken to Slough for formal identification. In the meantime his behaviour was said to have been so unruly that he had to be handcuffed to one of the larger police officers in the Staffordshire force.

By this time, Ostrog was being referred to in the newspapers as 'one of the most accomplished swindlers of the period', and in January 1874 he was brought in front of the Buckinghamshire Quarter Sessions at Aylesbury. This time Ostrog was sentenced to ten years' penal servitude.

In 1883 he was released 'on licence', but soon his description was being circulated in the pages of the *Police Gazette* again, for failure to report. For four years he disappeared from the records. But in July 1887 he appeared again, this time in London attempting to steal a tankard from a military cadet's room. He was chased across Woolwich Common and apprehended. Before his trial he tried, unsuccessfully, to throw himself under a train. In September 1887 he was sentenced to six months with hard labour. However, this time he was also judged insane and sent to an asylum in Tooting, then in Surrey. Ostrog was let out in March 1888, having apparently 'recovered'.

By 26 October 1888, just at the point when the Ripper outrages had gripped London, the police were apparently desperate to find Ostrog. They put out his description after he 'failed to report' as he was meant to do on a monthly basis, warning that 'Special attention is called to this dangerous man.' There's no doubt that just weeks after the double murder of Elizabeth Stride and Catherine Eddowes on Sunday, 30 September the police had added Ostrog to their list of suspects in the frantic search for the serial killer who was becoming the scourge of London's East End.

But Ostrog was not found and the killing went on. He was finally traced in April 1891 living in London and was once again found insane and committed to an asylum. He was soon out and committing more thefts. In 1900 he was given five years for stealing a microscope. Following his release from Parkhurst in 1904 he vanished for good and his death certificate has never emerged.

So is there any chance that he was indeed the Ripper? Unless the police had more information about Ostrog than came to light in court, his criminal history of theft and deceit does not seem to support Macnagthen's assertion that he was habitually cruel to women. But he certainly had the capacity for violence as his reaction to arrest at the Fox and Goose showed. He is also known to have made easy attachments with women, deploying his considerable charm to win them over. His alleged background as a doctor was also interesting as the Ripper appeared to have had a good level of surgical and anatomical knowledge, given the way in which the bodies of his victims has been mutilated.

Though Ostrog was a deeply troubled man, he was clearly clever. Yet he was not talented enough to avoid the clutches of the law, which had frequently caught up with him. Could he really have been disturbed enough to go on a sudden killing spree, and so astute at deception so successfully to cover his tracks? It seems unlikely. There is also the suggestion that Ostrog, who was in his 50s and stood at 5ft 11in, did not match the portraits of witnesses who had supposedly seen the Ripper – describing a younger, shorter man.

Despite this, for decades Ostrog was held to be a plausible Ripper suspect. Yet recent research suggests that at the time of the Ripper murders in 1888 he was actually in prison in France, serving a two-year sentence for theft. Ostrog was convicted on 14 November 1888 using the name Stanislas Lubinski. Crucially he had been arrested in July. It is therefore highly improbable that he could have been in England in the intervening months murdering prostitutes in London. While he probably wasn't the Ripper, Ostrog was certainly one of the more colourful criminals of his age. Ironically, it's unlikely that either of the two other individuals mentioned by Macnaghten was the Ripper either. Many believe that Thomas Cutbush was actually a better candidate.

LOCATION: **Burton Bridge Inn**, formerly known as the Fox and Goose, No. 24 Bridge Street, Burton on Trent, Staffordshire, 01283 536 596, www.burtonbridgeinn.co.uk

THE PUZZLING DEATH OF CHARLES BRAVO, 1876

The Bedford, Balham, South London

On the morning of 11 July 1876, a throng of lawyers, reporters and curious onlookers clamoured to be let into the Bedford Hotel in Balham, South London, for a second inquest which was being opened into the death of a barrister who had died locally after writhing in agony over the course of three days. The proceedings, held in the oak-panelled billiard room of the Bedford, were aimed at uncovering just how 31-year-old barrister Charles Bravo had come to be poisoned. The evidence which emerged during the course of the inquest would provide a feeding frenzy for the Victorian press as they realised that they had a scintillating mystery on their hands. What is more, the notorious case remains an intriguing 'whodunit' to this day and just as captivating as it was to a nineteenth-century audience, who lapped up every lurid detail. The Bravo case fascinated the crime writer Agatha Christie, though even the creator of Miss Marple and Hercule Poirot struggled to piece the puzzle together.

At the time of his death, Bravo had been living at a grand, crenelated pile in Bedford Hill, Balham, called The Priory with his new wife, Florence. The couple had been married in December 1875. By all accounts, Bravo was an arrogant bully. He was in debt and had already fathered an illegitimate child. He expected complete obedience from Florence who, it appears, he also beat. Florence, born in 1845, was herself a colourful character. A beautiful heiress, she had already been married to a handsome soldier in the Grenadier Guards before she met Bravo. Her first husband, Captain Alexander Ricardo, was an alcoholic and, when the marriage failed, Florence ended up having an affair with James Gully, an eminent married doctor twice her age. Gully may have made her pregnant and performed an abortion. The relationship certainly saw Florence become estranged from her family.

Ricardo died in 1871 and, four years later, Florence, desperate to re-establish her good name, met and married Bravo. Much to her husband's displeasure, Florence had decided to hold on to

The Priory, Balham, where Charles Bravo died in mysterious circumstances. (© *James Moore*)

her own money after they wed, invoking the Married Women's Property Act of 1870. She's said to have had £40,000 stashed away. Also living at The Priory was Florence's housekeeper and companion Jane Cox, a woman who Bravo resented.

Just four months into the marriage, on the evening of 18 April 1876, Bravo dined with his wife and Jane at around 7.30 p.m. All of them, it later emerged, had been drinking heavily. Bravo later retired to his bedroom – separate from that of Florence's – taking a swig of water from the carafe on the bedside table. Within fifteen minutes he was rolling around in pain and vomiting violently. Over the next three days, as he endured violent stomach pains, a string of doctors were called in to treat him. Though they didn't know exactly what had caused his symptoms they agreed that he must have been given, or taken, poison. Mysteriously, all that Bravo would say was that he had taken some laudanum to ease the pain of toothache. Bravo finally died at 5 a.m. on 21 April, in excruciating agony.

A post-mortem carried out the next day indicated poison but an unsatisfactory inquest, which was held just four days later at the Priory itself, recorded an open verdict. Yet questions about how he had died lingered. Had he taken his own life? Was his death a terrible accident? Or, more likely, had he been murdered?

The police had been slow to get involved, but now something Bravo had said to Mrs Cox in the minutes after he fell ill came out. Initially Mrs Cox had said that Bravo had told her, 'Mrs Cox, I have taken poison … don't tell Florence.' But now she changed her story, saying that he had actually said, 'Mrs Cox I have taken poison for Dr Gully, don't tell Florence!' Things were murkier than they had at first appeared as Florence's personal life came under the spotlight. One of the doctors who had attended Bravo stated that he believed Bravo had not knowingly taken poison. It also transpired that the sacked groom at the house had been in possession of antimony. Bravo's own stepfather hired a private detective and there was a clamour in the press for further investigation.

In a highly unusual move, the Attorney General granted another inquest. It was this second inquest at the Bedford, a cavernous hotel which had been opened in the 1830s, that would make the case such a cause célèbre. Bravo's body was exhumed and a post-mortem demonstrated that he had been poisoned with a large amount of antimony, which causes symptoms similar to arsenic. The inquest was finally held in searingly hot weather. A penny broadsheet called *The Balham Mystery*, published as the case unfolded, set the scene:

> The accommodation presented at the Bedford Hotel is unusually ample. Not only is the inquest room of much larger dimensions than one might expect to find in so comparatively quite a locality but the hotel affords the additional advantage of a series of rooms for separately locating the various classes of witnesses summoned to give evidence as well as others of the jury and the numerous members of the legal profession who are engaged in this remarkable inquiry.

Before the hearing began, one of the jury, made up of seventeen local tradesmen, was asked for his opinion about whether the floor in the room would be able to bear the weight of all the people crowded inside. The large sash windows of the room also had to be shut against the sound of train noise and the din of the crowd lolling outside waiting for juicy titbits.

The Bedford, where the second inquest into Charles Bravo's death was heard.
(© *James Moore*)

As the facts of the case were considered, Florence found herself on the stand under a heavy air of suspicion. Her affair with Dr Gully emerged, a fact which shocked prudish Victorian morals, especially since the doctor was an eminent physician who had treated the likes of Charles Dickens. Florence also claimed that she had suffered two miscarriages while with Bravo, who had forced her to undertake 'unnatural acts'.

But, on 11 August, after thirty-two days of enquiry and cross-examination, the jury was not much closer to discovering the truth. They delivered their verdict as follows:

> We find that Charles Delaunay Turner Bravo did not commit suicide; that he did not meet his death by misadventure; that he was wilfully murdered by the administration of tarter emetic; but there is not sufficient evidence to fix the guilt upon any person or persons.

There would be no formal trial of any of the suspects, but in the 135 years that followed, debate raged about just what did happen to Bravo. Had Florence had enough of Bravo's sexual demands and, scared that a third pregnancy might kill her, decided to get her husband out of the way? Had it actually been Jane Cox who killed Bravo? After all, he was apparently set to dismiss her. Was it George Griffiths, Bravo's groom, who had been let go? When Florence and Charles had first got married he had been overheard saying that Bravo would not 'live for more than four months'. Perhaps the culprit was actually Dr Gully, who still had feelings for Florence – this was Agatha Christie's somewhat outlandish conclusion.

Others believe that there was no murder at all and that Bravo had aimed to poison Florence and ended up killing himself by accident. Others think that Florence had been trying to stop him drinking by giving him regular tartar emetic, which contains antimony. This was an old remedy used to tackle alcoholism by inducing vomiting. Perhaps Florence administered too much to Charles by mistake. All the theories are plausible, yet no conclusive proof to back any of them has ever been found.

There were certainly no winners in the sorry saga. After the inquest, Florence moved away and died of alcohol poisoning just two years later. Dr Gully faced professional ruin. Even Charles Willis who ran The Bedford claimed to be out of pocket thanks to the whole affair. He wrote to the Home Secretary demanding compensation for the damage done to seats, bannisters and brickwork at The Bedford. The Home Secretary is said to have given him short shrift, retorting that he was sure Mr Willis had received ample remuneration from all the food and drink he'd sold during the heady spectacle.

LOCATION: **The Bedford**, formerly the Bedford Hotel, No. 77 Bedford Hill, Balham, SW12 9HD, 020 8682 8940, www.thebedford.co.uk

THE BUTLER DID IT – IN A ROW OVER A PUB, 1876

Dolaucothi Arms, Pumsaint, Carmarthenshire

Henry Tremble was a troubled man. Fired from his job as butler, and seething with anger at his perceived ill treatment, he was out for revenge. And he planned to exact it not only on his former employer but anyone he could blame for his lot in life. On the morning of Saturday, 19 August 1876, Tremble confronted his 76-year-old boss, John Johnes, in the library of his Carmarthenshire country pile and shot him in the lower abdomen. Johnes, a former judge, was found by his maid lying on the floor, with his entrails already spilling out. He told her, 'I've been shot by Tremble in the stomach. I am dying.' Johnes expired an hour later.

After leaving the bloodied body in the library, Tremble had left the room in search of his next intended victim – Johnes' daughter, Charlotte. He found her in the kitchen with the cook. He declared, 'Take that for your persecution of me' before firing off his shotgun from a distance of just a few feet. Charlotte was left badly wounded in the back and leg but was to survive. The cook, Margaret Davies, was also wounded. After threatening other servants, Tremble then went to the kennels and shot each of Johnes' dogs too, before leaving the estate looking for another man against whom he had a grievance.

Tremble, by this time aged 36, had once been on good terms with the Johnes family who lived at Dolaucothi House. Indeed by the time he went on his killing spree he had been employed by them for a total of seventeen years. In a former life he had been the valet of Charlotte's husband, Captain Cookman. When the officer died in 1859 Tremble was kept on by the Johnes family as a stable boy and coachman, finally working his way up to the post of butler. There is evidence that over the years Johnes had considered dismissing Tremble thanks to his surly attitude but had been dissuaded by his daughter who had promised her late husband that he would take care of his servant.

With six children to support, Tremble decided, like many people of his era, to take on another job. At some point he and his wife Martha had also run a pub called the Sexton's Inn at Caio but had been unsuccessful and had to give it up. It was the issue of the tenancy of another hostelry, the Dolaucothi Arms, that was to tip Tremble over the edge and lead to murder. The pub was owned by Johnes and in the summer of 1976 its tenancy had become available. That July, Tremble applied to Johnes for the lease but was turned down. Quite why he was refused isn't clear

– but Tremble's wife, Martha, is said to have had a drink problem, and this may have been the reason. Tremble's home life was an unhappy one. For some reason he harboured feelings of jealousy towards his wife, and his domestic troubles were said to have 'provoked his already irritable nature beyond all bounds'. He once described himself as an Irishman with no friends.

John Johnes was lining up another existing innkeeper, John Davies, who ran the nearby Caio Inn for the role of tenant at the Dolaucothi. This incensed Tremble and he made his fury clear to his boss. Apparently fed up with Tremble's mood swings, Johnes had then fired him. After that, he made veiled threats towards the family, once telling Charlotte and her sister Bertha (who was away at the time of the shooting), 'Now yous are both together I tell yous that as sure as God's in Heaven yous shall repent the injustice you have done me.'

It was on what was meant to be the last day of his employment that Tremble had decided to terminate the lives of his employer and his family.

Following the double shooting at Dolaucothi House, it was to Davies' pub that Tremble now set out, still armed in order to do away with his business rival. On the way, Tremble threatened a local police constable, who went to raise the alarm. But on arriving at the Caio Inn, Tremble found that Davies was not there. Deprived of his target, he went to his home at Myrtle Cottage, Caio and, after a stand-off with police officers, shot himself in the chest instead. He died fifteen minutes later.

There was a strange postscript to the sad tale. Tremble was quietly buried in the local churchyard at Caio. But locals resented having a murderer in their graveyard, especially since Johnes was buried there too, in the family vault. In the dead of night a group of them dug up Tremble's coffin and took it to another village, Llandulais, some miles away, leaving it at the churchyard there instead. When locals there got wind of what had happened, they decided that they would rather not have another village's murderer buried in their churchyard and took the coffin back to Caio, where it was dumped and later reburied.

LOCATION: **Dolaucothi Arms**, Pumsaint, Llanwrda, Carmarthenshire, SA19 8UW, 01558 650237, www.thedolaucothiarms.co.uk

The Violent Life of Charles Peace, 1876

Banner Cross Hotel and Stag's Head, Sheffield, South Yorkshire
Moments before the trapdoor was released and Charles Peace was hanged he begged his executioners for a beverage. 'I should like a drink,' he said, 'Have you a drink to give me?' They were his last words, and he never got the drink. It was a typically rumbustious statement from one of the most intriguing villains of the nineteenth century and one of the most unpleasant characters in the history of crime. Peace was a sly cat burglar, opportunistic thief and a calculating killer. Yet he was also possessed of a strange charm and some extraordinary gifts. He was a master of disguise, an ambitious escape artist as well as being an extremely accomplished musician. Peace, born in Sheffield in 1832, certainly had an unusual upbringing. He was the son of a collier, turned one-legged lion tamer … after an injury. And this circus heritage would define a breathtaking criminal career that saw him roam far and wide across Britain and successfully elude police who were pursuing him for murder.

At the age of 14, Peace was working at a steel mill in Sheffield when he was injured by a red-hot piece of metal that went into his leg, leaving him with a lifelong limp. He supported himself by playing the fiddle in pubs across the city but also took to theft and burglary, spending long stretches as a prisoner during the 1850s and 1860s. During this time he shot at and almost killed a police officer too. He had also found time to get married to a widow called Hannah Ward. In 1866 he was caught burgling another house near Salford and sentenced to another eight years behind bars. He said he had only been caught because he had been drunk on whisky. While in Wakefield Prison for the crime, he made a daring escape attempt, managing to smuggle a makeshift ladder into his cell, saw a hole in the prison ceiling and run along the roof of the building. He was tracked down to the governor's house before he could make good his escape. But he had evaded warders for four hours and even had time to take a bath and change his clothes.

Returning to Sheffield in 1872, Peace set up home with his family again, working as a picture framer. In 1875 they moved to the suburb of Darnall where Peace became obsessed with his buxom neighbour, Katherine Dyson. She was an Irish American who had married her much older husband, Arthur, a civil engineer, in Ohio. Arthur was, by all accounts, a mild-mannered man, but he and Katherine often rowed. Katherine was fond of a drink, and she and Peace struck up what might be described as, at the very least, a romantic friendship. They would drink together, without Arthur, at pubs in the city, including the now demolished Marquis of Waterford on Russell Street. It's likely that Peace also frequented the Kelham Island Tavern nearby, which dates back to 1836 and still stands today. Arthur Dyson soon put his foot down. In June 1876 he threw a visiting card into Peace's yard which read, 'Charles Peace is requested not to interfere with my family.'

Peace wasn't one to back down without a fight. He once said, 'If I make up my mind to a thing I am bound to have it.' He set about on a campaign of harassment, and in July 1876 he tripped up Arthur Dyson in the street, threatening Katherine Dyson with a gun the same evening. A warrant was issued for his arrest but, as he did so often, Peace simply moved towns. This time he went to Hull where his wife ran an 'eating house' while he busied himself with burgling houses in upmarket districts in far-off Manchester. Meanwhile the Dysons had moved to start a new life in another district of Sheffield, Banner Cross. Yet on arrival at their new home on 26 October, a few doors down from the Banner Cross Hotel, one of the first people Katherine Dyson saw was her old drinking partner who cried out, 'I am here to annoy you and I will annoy you wherever you go.'

Things came to a head on the night of 29 November 1876. Peace had spent that afternoon entertaining drinkers at pubs in Ecclesall by playing tunes using a poker, strong piece of string and a stick. At 7.50 p.m. a man matching Peace's description was seen walking in front of the Banner Cross Hotel. Charles Brassington was standing outside the pub underneath a gas lamp when the man asked him if he knew of some strangers who had come to live nearby. He told them that he didn't. The man asked him to look at some letters, but Brassington told him that he couldn't

An illustration of the Banner Cross Hotel, Sheffield, where Charles Peace was seen before committing murder. (*Courtesy of The Banner Cross Hotel*)

read. At 8 p.m. the pair parted with Peace saying that he would make the night a 'warm un' for the 'strangers'.

At around the same time, Katherine Dyson had put her 5-year-old son to bed and went out to a privy which stood beside the terrace where they lived. Peace was watching from a passageway and suddenly sprang in on her, wielding his gun. Mrs Dyson screamed and her husband, who had been reading in the back parlour, rushed out to see what all the commotion was about. Arthur chased after Peace who fired off a shot from his revolver to frighten him. With Dyson still giving pursuit, Peace then shot a second time, this time hitting him in the temple. Katherine Dyson screamed, 'Murder! You villain, you have shot my husband!' Dyson died shortly afterwards. A man who was drinking in the Banner Cross ran out and tried to give pursuit, but he did not catch Peace who later took a train to Hull. The inquest into Dyson's death was held at The Stag's Head on Psalter Lane on 9 December 1876 where enough evidence was produced to name Peace as the likely killer.

Over the coming weeks, Peace managed to evade capture despite a £100 reward on his head. Peace made use of his abilities as showman and actor to alter his appearance, successfully thwarting those looking for him. He would dye his hair, use walnut juice to darken his skin tone and even made a fake arm to hide a missing finger. Wanted posters listed his age as anywhere between 40 and 60, for Peace was said to have an unnerving capacity to change the shape of his face at will.

Before long, Peace was living in Peckham, London, in a house which contained both his real wife and a new girlfriend. He established a new identity for himself as a Mr Thompson. Here he would spend the next two years becoming wealthy by stealing from posh properties in Blackheath. His run of good luck only came to an end in October 1878 when he was caught by a PC Edward Robinson during a burglary. Robinson managed to hold on to Peace despite being shot at five times and injured in the arm. Peace was sentenced to penal servitude for life for the attempted murder of the policeman. While Peace had not revealed his identity, his real name and his criminal past were eventually uncovered thanks to a tip-off. His mistress, 'Mrs Thompson', even tried to claim the reward for his capture.

Peace now faced the prospect of another trial, this time for Dyson's murder. Yet on the train ride from London to Sheffield for a hearing, he contrived to produce more drama, by unsuccessfully trying to escape by jumping from the train.

Appearing before the Leeds Assizes on 4 February 1879, Peace's defence was largely based on the idea that he had been having an affair with Katherine Dyson and that her jealous husband had been killed accidentally during a struggle. Mrs Dyson denied she'd had a relationship with Peace. However, he had dropped letters at the scene of Arthur's shooting which were allegedly from Katherine and appeared to suggest she was very intimate with Peace. She had also been seen drinking with a man in the Stag's Head the night before the shooting. To the amusement of the court, Mrs Dyson could only 'almost' swear that it wasn't Peace. The man she had imbibed with seemed to be much younger.

The jury took just twelve minutes to find Peace guilty and he was sentenced to death. Before his execution Peace, who professed to be a religious man, did express remorse for his crimes. He also admitted to the Reverend Littlewood from his cell that he was responsible for another killing in 1876, that of a policeman in the Whalley Range area of Manchester. Peace said that on 1 August he had fatally shot PC Nicholas Cock when the officer and another constable surprised him during a burglary. He told the clergyman that 'I got away, which was all I wanted.' Another 18-year-old man, William Habron, was already serving a life sentence for that murder. Peace knew this as he had brazenly attended Habron's trial, sitting in the public gallery and saying nothing as the man was convicted for a crime he didn't commit. Habron was thought to have killed Cock because he was always making trouble in a local pub called the Royal Oak and, it was said, had once threatened to kill the policeman. Upon Peace's eventual confession, Habron, who had only avoided execution himself because of his youth, was given a full pardon with compensation.

Charles Peace was finally hanged by William Marwood on 25 February 1879 at Armley Gaol in Leeds – but not before he had complained about the quality of the bacon he had been given for breakfast.

LOCATION: **Banner Cross Hotel**, No. 971 Ecclesall Road, Sheffield, South Yorks, S11 8TN, 0114 2661479, www.thebanner.co.uk; **The Stag's Head**, No. 15 Psalter Lane, Sheffield, S11 8YL, 0114 2550548, www.mystagshead.co.uk

MURDER AT GLENCOE? 1877

Kings House Hotel, Glencoe
Glencoe, in the Scottish Highlands, possesses a majestic, eerie beauty. It is an awe-inspiring valley surrounded by high mountains, yet it is also an unsettling place. For it's difficult to forget that here, in 1692, the terrible slaughter of the Clan MacDonald took place. The massacre occurred after the MacDonalds were deemed to have failed to swear proper allegiance to the new king, William III.

The two storeyed, whitewashed Kings House Hotel, with its distinctive dormer windows, is located in the middle of this remote, wild landscape. It is thought to have been an inn since around 1765 and was built following the Jacobite rebellion of 1745. The idea was to give troops and travellers a staging post through the inhospitable terrain on their way to and from Fort William, further north.

For at least the first 100 years of its existence, conditions were extremely hard for innkeepers and their families. In 1802, James Donaldson, a surveyor of the military road, recorded that the King's House had been for some years in a 'very bad state and has been kept in such a miserable style that the weary traveller, when he arrives there, finds himself destitute of every accommodation either for himself or his horse'. He reported that the roof was leaking and that not one of the inn's windows had a pane of glass in it.

Things had improved somewhat by the 1870s, and the likes of the writer Charles Dickens had even stayed at the inn. But the King's House was still a difficult and lonely place in which to make a living. It was located miles from any other significant habitation and the winters were cruel. Unsurprisingly there were dark tales associated with the place. One former innkeeper was said to have drunk himself to death. And a hawker had once been executed after throwing his wife off the bridge over the River Etive that runs beside the inn.

As the *Edinburgh Evening Telegraph* noted on 30 March 1877, 'News travels slowly from a region where there is no communication by telegraph, railway, post office or coach' from a place it described as 'the most desolate in Scotland'. The newspaper then went on to relate the horrible recent death of the landlady at the hands, it was alleged, of her own husband.

Alexander MacDougall, 43, was described as a man 'of superior education and intelligence' who hailed from Kenmore in Perthshire. He had been a much admired teacher before taking on the £60 annual lease of the King's House from the Earl of Breadalbane in 1870 on a year-to-year basis. He was then recently married to Sophia Jarrett, the daughter of a former keeper of an inn at Dalmally. While Sophia was said to be an amiable young woman, MacDougall, who was thirteen years her senior, soon became 'sullen and of a jealous disposition'. The couple quarrelled continually and MacDougall was known to hit his wife. 'It was

The remote Kings House Hotel in Glencoe, Scotland, where a landlord beat his wife to the point of death. (*Courtesy of Kings House Hotel*)

evident,' reported the *Evening Telegraph*, to 'even those whose stays at the hotel were brief that the domestic arrangements were very inharmonious'. It was said that the atmosphere at Kings House was so bad the couple's young daughter had to be sent away to stay with relatives in Edinburgh. On one occasion Sophia was said to have left the inn and taken refuge in the houses of local shepherds, while in the New Year of 1877 she fled to stay with her brother who had a farm near Killin. Each time, however, Sophia decided to return and give the marriage another chance.

On Monday 12 March there was another scene at the inn between the couple. That morning, along with the MacDougalls, a servant called Mrs Margaret MacDonald and two boys, Donald MacLeish and Alexander MacGregor, were also at the inn. MacDougall had been drinking heavily since the Saturday night and when Mrs MacDonald came in at about 9 a.m. from her duties she saw MacDougall dragging Sophia through the bar. This is where the couple normally slept on a 'bar bed'. Sophia was wearing a 'polka and petticoat' while he was clad only in a shirt. MacDougall angrily ordered Mrs MacDonald out and she went to a local shepherd's house about a mile away.

Meanwhile the two boys went about their work outside the house, returning at 11 a.m. to find the doors to the inn unusually bolted. When they returned at about 4 p.m. and found the place still locked up, they managed to force their way in and were shocked to see Sophia lying on the floor of the lobby. Her face was covered in blood and she was completely naked, a blood-ied chemise lying next to her. They immediately ran to fetch Mrs MacDonald, who returned with the shepherd's wife, a Mrs Cameron. They now found Sophia lying naked in the kitchen where her body had evidently been dragged in the preceding hour. She appeared to have been beaten insensible. The party picked her up and got her into a bed. MacDougall was nowhere to be seen, though he appeared later to ask Mrs MacDonald to clear up some of the blood in the bar.

Although badly knocked about, Sophia was still alive and the next morning, from her bed, she had recovered conscious-ness enough to ask Mrs MacDonald for a clean chemise. Mrs MacDonald noticed that Sophia had bad wounds on her fore-head and legs and that there was dried blood everywhere. Sophia continued to be ill for the next ten days while MacDougall went about his work at the inn as usual. During this time, Mrs Cameron asked Sophia several times about her injuries. She replied, 'If I get better I will leave him altogether.'

Strangely, a doctor was not called until the night of 20 December. The nearest physician lived 13 miles away. By the time he arrived Sophia was slipping in and out of consciousness, her stomach and breast now very swollen. There did not appear to be much he could do for her, but he was able to ask Sophia who had caused her wounds and she named her husband. That night, said Mrs Cameron, MacDougall went to Sophia's bedside, took her hand and asked for her forgiveness, which she gave. By the early hours of Wednesday morning she was dead.

Suspicions now having been raised, a constable then made his way from Dalmally to arrest MacDougall. Meanwhile Sophia's body was taken in a coffin on a cart from King's House and to the churchyard in Dalmally where she was buried. MacDougall was arrested and imprisoned at Inverary while further inves-tigations took place. He was finally brought to Edinburgh for trial at the High Court in July 1877 and accused of mortally wounding Sophia by inflicting wounds with kicks and his fists.

He pleaded not guilty, swearing that Sophia had got her injuries through falls.

Margaret MacDonald deposed (in Gaelic) that she had often seen the deceased with injuries about her face and had recently seen a cut on her forehead and a large bruise on her back. Sophia had told her that MacDougall has caused them. However, she did admit that both MacDougalls were keen on a drink. And one of the boys admitted that Sophia had once fallen out of a window in one of the bedrooms after she had been drinking.

There was disagreement among the doctors that were called to give evidence as to what had actually caused Sophia's death. Two doctors who carried out a post-mortem believed she had died from infections caused by her wounds. But doubt was raised about whether the injuries she had sustained were, in themselves, enough to kill her. Indeed a police surgeon who was called to give his view told the court that he believed Sophia had died from chronic alcoholism, although there was little evidence to suggest that she had a habitual drink problem. Indeed the post-mortem had shown that her internal organs were in good working order. On 16 July MacDougall was found guilty, but not of murder. After fifteen minutes deliberation the jury delivered a verdict of culpable homicide, akin to manslaughter, and sentenced him to ten years' penal servitude.

LOCATION: **King's House Hotel**, Glencoe, Argyll, PH49 4HY, 01855 851259, www.kingshousehotel.co.uk

LAST ORDERS FOR JACK THE RIPPER'S VICTIMS, 1888

The Ten Bells, The Brick Lane Hotel, The White Hart & The Bell, Whitechapel, London
London's East End pubs provided a boozy backdrop to the brutal Jack the Ripper murders, crimes perpetrated in a world where drink flowed as freely as the blood of the killer's victims. Life in the late nineteenth-century district of Whitechapel was hard and often short. Riven with poverty and slums, it seethed with

gangs of thieves and prostitutes and it still mirrored the image of London's darker side conjured up in the works of Charles Dickens a generation earlier. Alcohol was a crutch that kept life tolerable for many. The fact that one of the Ripper's victims, Mary Kelly, was last heard singing, 'Only A Violet I plucked from my mother's grave,' in a tipsy manner was somehow tragically fitting. Indeed, the tragic stories of each of the women who were murdered and then mutilated by the infamous serial killer are peppered with references to local drinking dens, places that were often like second homes. Here the prostitutes, who would become the Ripper's prey, would sometimes tout for trade and often spend what little money they accrued as they mixed with multifarious locals who thronged the bars at all times of day and night.

The shocking string of gruesome murders that gripped the smog-shrouded capital between 1888–1891 remain the most notable unsolved murders of all time. But the environment in which they occurred was one in which violence was commonplace. Fights in the public houses of the East End could break out at any time and there were any number of violent characters. There are even stories of a man in the district at the time with wooden legs who would suddenly smash up pubs when in drink. Murders too were a regular occurrence, with prostitutes often the victims, a fact that has contributed to the enduring puzzle over just which crimes could be linked to a single serial killer.

The murder of Mary Ann Nichols, a woman with dark, greying hair, brown eyes and a small scar on her forehead, is widely regarded as the first of five victims that can almost certainly be ascribed to the Ripper. Mary Ann, better known as Polly, was a formerly married woman who had fallen into prostitution and was almost certainly an alcoholic by the time she was killed, aged 43. At 12.30 a.m. on 31 August 1888 Polly was seen leaving The Frying Pan pub on Brick Lane, returning to her lodgings around the corner in Thrawl Street. However, she was behind on the rent and was turned out. A little drunk, Polly laughed, pointed at a new straw bonnet she was wearing and said, 'I'll soon get my doss money.' At 2.30 a.m., a few hundred yards away, she told a fellow lodger, Ellen Holland, that she'd actually had the money for her bed earlier in the day but had since spent it on drink. As the pair

The Frying Pan pub on Brick Lane, where Polly Nichols drank on the night of her murder, is now a hotel. (© *James Moore*)

parted company, Polly was apparently confident of finding the 4*d* she needed and was last seen walking in an easterly direction along the Whitechapel Road.

Just over an hour later her body was found. It was lying three quarters of a mile away in Buck's Row, which has since been renamed Durward Street. Her skirt had been hitched up and her throat had been cut twice. The lower part of her abdomen had been slashed and violently ripped open with a knife. One large, jagged wound extended from her rib cage to her pelvis.

Police had little to go on, but there was soon speculation in the press that there were links between Mary Ann's murder and that of the deaths of two other prostitutes, Emma Smith and Martha Tabram, earlier that year. Modern researchers have concluded that it is unlikely that those murders had demonstrated the same modus operandi as the Ripper. However, it was at this point that Scotland Yard began investigating the possibility that a serial killer was at large in London, with Inspector Frederick Abberline brought in on the case for the first time.

Suspicion soon fell upon a man called John Pizer, nicknamed Leather Apron. He was a bootmaker of Polish extraction who had a history of mistreating local prostitutes. He was alleged to have held a knife to their throats. Local women told a reporter from the Star newspaper that he was often to be found in The Princess Alice pub on Commercial Street, lurking in the shadows. Pizer was not picked up until after the murder of the next victim, Annie Chapman, but was ruled out when he appeared to have cast-iron alibis for both murders.

Annie's body was found at 6 a.m. on 8 September near the back yard of a house on Hanbury Street in Spitalfields. Her throat was cut and she had been disembowelled – part of her uterus was missing too. Coming just a week after Polly Nichols' death, the two crimes bore a striking resemblance. Annie was a 47-year-old woman who had fallen on hard times and while she made money from doing crochet work and selling flowers, she was also an occasional prostitute. She was described by one witness as being often 'the worse for drink'. Annie's pub of choice was The Britannia on Commercial Street, and it was here, in the days leading up to her death, that she got into a fight over a man with Eliza Cooper.

In the early hours of 8 September she had been unable to find money for her lodgings and had gone out to raise some. One report put her in the Ten Bells on Commercial Street at 5 a.m. when a man put his head round the door and called her out. At 5.30 a.m. she had been seen with a man with a dark complexion who the witness thought looked foreign. He wore a deerstalker hat and dark overcoat. A few minutes later Annie was dead. After her death a different pub, the Prince Albert which stood on the corner of Brushfield and Steward Street, provided police with a possible clue to her killer. An hour and a half after Annie had been murdered, the landlady, a Mrs Fiddymont, had served a man with a half of ale. She was struck by his wild appearance. His shirt was torn and he had blood on his right hand. He was later identified as a Swiss butcher called Jacob Isenschmidt. He was one of a number of suspects followed up by Inspector Abberline and his men. Isenschmidt was taken into custody but while he was being detained the real culprit struck again – killing twice in twenty-four hours.

The Ten Bells in London's Spitalfields where Ripper victim Annie Chapman was seen on the morning of her murder in 1888. (© *James Moore*)

The murders of two more prostitutes, Elizabeth Stride and Catherine Eddowes, on 30 September 1888, unleashed panic on the streets of London. Liz's body was discovered at 1 a.m. in a yard next to a Jewish social club in Berner Street. She had been killed just minutes before Louis Diemschutz stumbled upon her corpse in his horse and cart. Her throat had been cut, though this was her only wound, probably because the killer had been disturbed. Just forty-five minutes later, Catherine's corpse was found in Mitre Square by a patrolling policeman. It was only walking distance away. She had also been killed just a few minutes earlier. This time, as well as being slashed at the throat, her face had been disfigured and her abdomen had been mutilated. Her intestines had been removed as well as a kidney and her uterus.

Liz, 44, who was regularly in trouble for being drunk and disorderly, had been seen drinking at The Queen's Head on Commercial Street with an Elizabeth Tanner at 6.30 p.m. on the evening of her death. She may also have been seen at 11 p.m. that evening in the company of a man with a dark moustache at The Bricklayer's Arms on Settles Street. However, despite lots of people being at the social club that night, no one seemed to have seen Liz's killer.

Catherine Eddowes, 46, had also been drinking on the night of the 29th. In fact she had been found drunk in the road on Aldgate High Street and was taken to a police station to sober up before being released at 1 p.m. The last sighting of her was probably at 1.35 a.m. when she was seen with a man described as having a fair moustache, a peaked cloth cap and red scarf.

Towards the end of September, Scotland Yard, now under intense pressure to find the murderer, received a letter purporting to be from the killer. He signed himself Jack the Ripper. More missives followed, including the infamous 'From Hell' letter, which came with a box that allegedly contained one of the victim's kidneys. The police conducted a huge manhunt involving hundreds of interviews and many arrests but they simply could not come up with a plausible suspect.

A month went past. Then, on Friday 9 November, there was another murder, of a prostitute called Mary Jane Kelly. This killing was the most savage to date. Mary, aged 25, had been killed in her own bed at her lodgings in Miller's Court, Dorset Street – possibly by a client that she already knew. Her body was discovered at 10.45 a.m. on the 9th by a man who had come to collect the rent. Like the other victims, her throat had been slashed and her abdomen had been sliced open. Her organs had been removed and her heart was missing. Mary Jane's breasts had also been cut off, her thighs cut and her face had been obliterated. She wore only a chemise and her other clothes were folded on a chair, though some had been burnt in the fireplace. It was judged that her death must have occurred between 2 a.m. and 8 a.m. that morning.

Much of Kelly's movements during the day before her murder appear to have involved pubs. A tailor called Maurice Lewis claimed to have seen Kelly drinking with friends at a hostelry called The Horn of Plenty on Crispin Street on the evening of the murder. However, the same man also claimed to have seen her at the Britannia at 10 a.m. on 9 November, after the likely time of her death. It's probable that he had confused her with another woman. More convincing was the testimony of Elizabeth Foster, a friend of Mary Jane's, who drank with her in the Ten Bells on the evening of the 8th. Mary Jayne left the pub at 7.05 p.m. Later that evening, at about 11 p.m., she was also spotted drinking in The

Britannia with a well-dressed young man with a dark moustache. Three quarters of an hour later, and by now drunk, Mary Jane was seen by her neighbour Mary Ann Cox going into Miller's Court with a man. She described him as a man in his thirties who had a ginger moustache, was wearing a bowler hat, a long shabby coat and was carrying a pail of beer. Mary Jayne could soon be heard singing a ditty in her room. The singing had stopped when another neighbour, Elizabeth Prater, who had the room above Mary Jane's, went to bed at 1.30 a.m. At 2 a.m. labourer George Hutchinson claimed to have seen Mary Jane walking arm in arm with a man in a dark astrakhan coat outside the Queen's Head on Commercial Street and said he saw them go into Mary Jane's lodgings at Miller's Court. At 4 a.m. Elizabeth Prater woke up and said she heard a faint cry of 'oh murder'. About an hour later she got up and went to the Ten Bells for a glass of rum but saw nothing suspicious. At 5.45 a.m. Mary Ann Cox thought she head the footsteps of a man leaving Miller's court. Confusingly, at around 8.30 a.m., after the time at which surgeons believed she died, Mary Jane was seen again by a Caroline Maxwell complaining of having had too much beer, though this testimony is in doubt because of her poor description of the victim and the fact that she had only met her once or twice before.

Over the next three years, there were more murders linked to the Ripper, but all efforts to find the shadowy serial killer failed. Traditionally only the murders of Nichols, Chapman, Stride, Eddowes and Kelly, known as the 'canonical five', can definitely be identified as having been the work of the same person. Fierce debate still surrounds the true identity of the Ripper, with scores of candidates suggested during more than a century of analysis. Abberline's preferred culprit was a Polish man called Severin Klosowski, otherwise known as George Chapman, who became a publican and went to the gallows in 1903 after killing three women, though in a very different manner (see page 23). He once worked as a barber in the basement of The White Hart on Whitechapel Road, which is also near where the body of a possible early victim, Martha Tabram, was found.

The truth about the Ripper will almost certainly never be known, but millions of people remain fascinated by the mystery and tourists still tour locations related to the murders in London's East End. Many of the pubs associated with the crimes have since disappeared. One, The Frying Pan, which Polly Nichols frequented, is now a hotel. Traces of the original pub have all but gone, though the old name and a crumbling crossed frying pans motif is still discernable on the top of the building. Other existing pubs have more tenuous links to the Ripper story, including The Bell on Middlesex Street where Frances Coles, a later possible victim, drank the night before her death on 13 February 1891.

The Ten Bells, a place where at least two of the victims were known to have drunk, and a place the murderer himself may have known well, was renamed Jack the Ripper in the 1970s. It has now reverted to the name which refers to the peals of bells that ring out from Nicholas Hawksmoor's Christ Church across the road. The Ten Bells retains a brooding Victorian atmosphere complete with murals and original tiles. It is the perfect place in which to ponder the true identity of the Ripper and, above all, remember his unfortunate victims.

LOCATIONS: **Ten Bells**, No. 84 Commercial Street, London E1 6LY, 020 7366 1721, tenbells.com; **The Brick Lane Hotel**, formerly The Frying Pan, www.hotelbricklane.com; **The White Hart**, No. 89 Whitechapel High Street, London, E1 7RA, 020 7247 1546; **The Bell**, No. 50 Middlesex Street, London, E1 7EX, 020 7247 3459, www.thebellpub.co.uk; **The Princess Alice**, No. 40 Commercial Street has recently closed. **The Britannia** was at No. 87 Commercial Street and the **Queen's Head** was at No. 74 Commercial Street but both have since closed. **The Prince Albert** was at No. 21 Brushfield Street and the **Horn of Plenty**, formerly on Crispin Street, has also gone. **The Bricklayer's Arms** was at No. 34 Settles Street and is now a grocery shop.

A FATAL DRINK WITH A SERIAL SADIST, 1891-2

The Wellington Hotel, Waterloo Road, Lambeth, London; Sherlock Holmes, Charing Cross, London

The Wellington likes to claim that the Great Train Robber Buster Edwards used to drink there. It was the nearest watering hole to the flower stall he ran outside Waterloo station after being released from jail in 1975. But eighty years earlier, the Wellington was the scene of a crime committed by a man who was far more dangerous and one whom some believe to have been Jack the Ripper himself.

At 7 p.m. on 13 October 1891, a woman called Constance Linfield noticed Ellen 'Nellie' Donworth in the company of a well-dressed gentleman going arm in arm into an unlit court-yard at the rear of the Wellington, opposite Waterloo Station. Nellie was a 19-year-old prostitute who had left her lodgings at 6 p.m. that evening saying that she was going to meet a man. A few minutes after Constance had seen Nellie with the stranger, a local stallholder called James Styles, who was standing outside the Wellington, saw Nellie staggering as if drunk before suddenly falling down in a heap. Styles ran to her aid. As he helped her up, Nellie told him, 'Someone has given me a drink.'

Writhing in agony Nellie was taken home. Despite the pain, she managed to tell her landlady, 'A tall gentleman with cross eyes, a silk hat, and bushy whiskers gave me a drink twice out of a bottle with white stuff in it.' Within a couple of hours, Nellie was suffering with violent convulsions. A doctor who attended her that evening recognised them as the kind associated with the poison strychnine. By 10 p.m. Nellie was dead. A post-mortem conducted three days later revealed that the doctor's suspicions had been right – she had been poisoned with strychnine. But the police were unable to identify the culprit.

Poor Nellie's rendezvous that night, initially at the nearby York Hotel, had been with Dr Thomas Neill Cream, a serial sadist who had already killed in America and was now embarking on a spate of cruel murders in London. He had been born in Scotland in 1850 and educated at both McGill University in Montreal and St Thomas' Hospital in London before going back to Canada in 1879 where he started practising as a doctor.

There he began performing illegal abortions and was soon linked to the strange deaths of two women. Cream escaped jail due to a lack of evidence, but soon moved to Chicago in the United States. There he started prescribing remedies for epilepsy and in 1881 a man called Daniel Stott died after using one of them. Stott's death was not considered suspicious until Cream

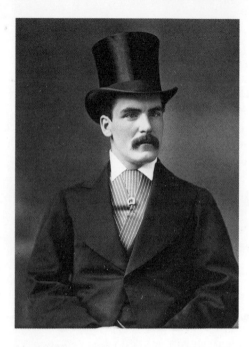

Thomas Neill Cream, a sadistic murderer who went to the gallows for his crimes in 1892. (*Courtesy McCord Museum*)

contacted the coroner to accuse a local pharmacist of poisoning Stott. Stott's body was dug up and found to be full of strychnine. But it was Cream who ended up accused of murder – he had been having an affair with the man's wife. Although convicted of murder and sentenced to life imprisonment, Cream was given clemency after just ten years. It's thought he used his father's inheritance to bribe his way out.

Having created too much heat on the other side of the Atlantic, Cream returned to London in October 1891. He took up lodgings in Lambeth and immediately began preying on the local prostitutes, looking for more victims. He was not just a killer but an attention seeker also. Following the death of Nellie Donworth he wrote a letter to the doctor conducting the inquest demanding money in return for helping to solve the crime, signing it 'A. O'Brien, detective'. He also wrote to an MP, using another pseudonym, accusing him of the murder and threatening blackmail. The letters were passed to the police, but at this stage the authorities had no idea they were dealing with a serial killer.

The Wellington, near Waterloo Station in South London. Nellie Donworth fell ill nearby. (© *James Moore*)

Just a few days after Nellie's death, on 20 October, Cream met another prostitute, 27-year-old Matilda Clover, at the Canterbury Music Hall, and the pair later returned to her lodgings. Another servant at the accommodation, Lucy Rose, reported seeing Matilda come in with a man in a silk hat and a bushy moustache who called himself Fred, and left sometime later that evening. Then, in the middle of the night, the house was awakened by Clover's screams. She was found stretched out across her bed suffering from searing pains and said, 'That man Fred has poisoned me … he gave me some pills.' She died the next morning at 9 a.m. But, having had a history of alcoholism, her death was put down to natural causes.

At the end of October, Cream attempted to poison another prostitute, Lou Harvey. He took her to the Northumberland Arms near Charing Cross, since renamed the Sherlock Holmes. After treating Lou to a glass of wine, he gave her some pills to take, supposedly to improve her complexion, before leaving. But Lou was suspicious and only pretended to take them.

When Cream had gone, she threw them in the river, while he must have assumed she had died. Lou's testimony would later prove vital in convicting Cream.

In April 1892, after a trip back to Canada, Cream struck again, this time killing two prostitutes, Alice Marsh, 21, and Emma Shrivell, 18, whom he'd fed a dinner of Guinness and tinned salmon laced with strychnine. Before they died, again in agony, they also mentioned a man called Fred. It was now clear that a maniac was on the loose and the unknown murderer was branded the 'Lambeth Poisoner' by the newspapers.

During his six month killing spree, Cream continued to draw attention to himself by writing more letters accusing notable doctors and others of being involved in the crimes in a bid to extort more money. But that summer, Cream made a crucial error. He befriended a former New York City detective, John Haynes. The pair discussed the Lambeth Poisoner case but Haynes was surprised when Cream mentioned two names that had not cropped up in the coverage – Matilda Clover and Lou Harvey.

Haynes passed on his concerns to the London police who put Cream under surveillance. They then discovered his conviction for murder in America. Clover's body was exhumed and it was concluded that strychnine, not booze, was the real cause of her death. Detectives also tracked down Lou Harvey who had been lucky enough to survive Cream's clutches – and she identified him.

Cream was charged with murdering Matilda Clover and went on trial in October that year. Convicted in just twelve minutes he was hanged on 15 November at Newgate Prison. According to James Billington, the man who conducted Cream's execution, the vain villain had some shocking final words, saying 'I am Jack the …' as the noose tightened around his neck. No one else present recorded hearing him saying this. Is it possible that Cream was actually Jack the Ripper, responsible for the string of unsolved murders in Whitechapel four years earlier? Records suggest that Cream was in jail in the United States at this time. But he was certainly released early from that sentence in shady circumstances and almost certainly thanks to a bribe. Some have suggested that Cream was not actually in prison in 1888 and that he had gained his freedom earlier through corruption, perhaps even paying for a double to take his place behind bars.

But even if we accept that he was at large during the Ripper murders, Cream's modus operandi appears to have been very different from Jack the Ripper, involving poisoning rather than strangling and mutilation. On balance it seems unlikely that he was the Ripper. Yet Cream was just as much a threat to young women, enjoying the idea of the pain he caused them. And, if correctly reported, his final words were no doubt another sign of his fetish for both mischief as well as murder.

LOCATION: **The Wellington Hotel**, Nos 81–83 Waterloo Road, Waterloo London, SE1 8UD, wellingtonhotelwaterloo.co.uk; **Sherlock Holmes**, Nos 10–11 Northumberland Street, London, WC2N 5DB, 020 7930 2644, www.sherlockholmespub.com

CIDER AND PATRICIDE IN THE COTSWOLDS, 1893

Butchers Arms, Oakridge Lynch and Stirrup Cup, Bisley, Gloucestershire
When the wife of septuagenarian farmer James Wyndham passed away in 1889 he decided to take a new partner by the name of Virtue Mills. It was a name James' son, Frederick, thought highly inappropriate for a woman his own father once described as 'the biggest whore he could find'. Frederick Wyndham believed that his irascible father had sold out on his family by taking up with 41-year-old Virtue and moving her in as a 'housekeeper' when she was still married to another man. He was also incensed that Wyndham senior had thrown his own sisters out of the family home in the process. In September 1893, James had even tried to run down one of them, Susan, in his horse and cart following a row about money she was owed.

Frederick, a fiery bailiff and butcher who himself had five children, had been mistreated by his father as a youngster. He was once tied by his thumbs to a beam and left standing in an attic on his own for twenty-four hours. It was, perhaps, unsurprising that there was not much love lost between them. After James got

The Butchers Arms, Oakridge Lynch, Gloucestershire, where Frederick Wyndham drank cider before murdering his father. (© *James Moore*)

together with Virtue the incensed Frederick would often state publicly that if his father didn't throw 'the whore' out of the house, he would shoot them both.

Despite the family tension, James did allow his son to go game shooting on Twissell's Farm near Oakridge in Gloucestershire where he was the tenant. On 19 October 1893, James set off to do just this with his employer, a coal merchant called William Farrar. But as the day progressed, neither the country air nor the mellow Cotswold landscape would lighten Frederick's mood. Before going hunting, Frederick called at the New Inn at Bisley, a pub now known as The Stirrup Cup and which has existed since 1774. Susan was lodging at the pub and confirmed to Frederick that their father had indeed tried to run her over in a road nearby. Frederick then borrowed a double-barrelled shotgun from the landlord, a Mr Skinner, and the party headed up to Oakridge, stopping for more refreshments at The Butchers Arms. Here Frederick sank another two pints of cider. By the time he and Farrar finally set off for the shoot the 45-year-old was well oiled.

Once on his father's farm, Frederick took out his frustrations on a man called Gilbert Rawle who had been shooting rabbits on the land. Rawle said he had permission to be there from Wyndham senior, but Frederick confiscated Rawle's dead rabbit and told him that if he saw him on the farm again he would throw him into the brook.

At 4 p.m. that afternoon, Frederick spotted his father lifting potatoes with two labourers. Farrar went to speak to James, then Frederick stepped up and an argument soon erupted. Frederick brought up the issue of Virtue Mills and the incident involving Susan. James accused him of being drunk and told him off for bringing up such matters in front of employees. Frederick then told his father about throwing Rawle off his land. James was furious, saying he had indeed given Rawle permission to be there.

It now looked as if the Wyndhams might come to blows and Farrar attempted to step in and separate them. Frederick and James both began to walk away, but then Frederick turned around, bringing up Mills again and shouting out that he would 'shoot the whore'. Soon the pair were advancing on each other again and this time Frederick said, 'I will shoot you.'

He then swiftly put his gun to his shoulder and fired off two rounds. The first tore into James' neck and shoulder, the second into the lower part of his heart. Farrar looked on horrified as James fell to the floor, dying.

Farrar bundled Frederick into the trap which had brought them to the farm and which was parked in a nearby field, setting off for Bisley with the intention of going straight to the police station. He ignored the killer's plea to be given some more cartridges so he could shoot himself. The murder had been witnessed by both a farm worker and a passing woman called Georgina Stephens. Before long, the trap arrived back in Bisley where Frederick went into the New Inn, found Susan and told her, 'I have done it, I have shot my father, I will die for you. He'll drive over you no more.' The landlady, Mrs Skinner, heard what he said and gossip soon spread in the village. Frederick handed back his borrowed gun, then walked to the police station shouting to a growing crowd, 'I have shot my father.' At the station Frederick then told a shocked pair of constables, 'I have been and shot my

The Stirrup Cup, Bisley, which was once the New Inn, where Wyndham borrowed the murder weapon. (© *James Moore*)

father and if he is not dead, I hope he is.' Frederick was locked in a cell while his father's body was recovered from the field and taken to the Butchers Arms. There it was washed and laid out. Two days later the inquest was carried out here too.

Later, at Stroud police station, Fredrick made a signed statement which read, 'I solemnly declare that I shot him. Put two barrels into him. I hope he is dead … and I can die happy in a minute.' At Stroud Magistrates', Virtue Mills gave evidence of the fierce arguments between her lover and his son, to which Frederick shouted, 'Let me get at her for two minutes and I'll tear her limb from limb. I could cut her to pieces. Nothing is too bad for her. She'd better jump in the canal and drown herself.'

At his trial at Gloucester Assizes, which began on 28 November 1893, Frederick continued to show no remorse for killing his father, and his ire continued to be directed towards Virtue Mills. Before sentence was passed – and having been found guilty in two minutes flat – he was asked if had anything to say. He replied simply, 'I should like to kill the woman sir … she was the cause of it all.' Frederick was said to have gone calmly to the gallows on 21 December. Ironically he had, himself, once applied for the job of hangman.

LOCATION: *The Butchers Arms*, Oakridge Lynch, Gloucestershire, 01285 760 371, www.butchersarmsoakridge.com; *The Stirrup Cup*, Cheltenham Road, Bisley, 01452 770007, www.stirrupcupbisley.co.uk

MURDER NIGHT AT THE CAFÉ ROYAL, 1894

The Café Royal Hotel, London

By the 1890s the swanky Café Royal in the heart of 'that part of London which is never asleep' was in its heyday, frequented by the artistic giants of the age such as Oscar Wilde and George Bernard Shaw. Having been set up in 1865 by an ex-pat Parisian, Daniel Nicolas Thevenon, it was the haunt of an eclectic mix of painters, poets and writers who could regularly be found enjoying the heady atmosphere of The Domino Room, with its marble topped tables, plush velvet benches and gilded mirrors. Wilde once became so drunk on absinthe here that he started to hallucinate, imagining that he was in a field of tulips.

Despite its reputation as a trendy place to drink, dine and socialise, the Café Royal's location in lower Regent Street meant it was also cheek by jowl with the less salubrious Soho, an area infamous by the 1890s for harbouring a criminal fraternity that spanned everything from prostitutes to anarchists. It was an area dubbed the 'cosmopolitan home of arson and murder'. And on 6 December 1894 a shocking murder occurred at the Café, violently at odds with its reputation for fun and frivolity. The Café's management appears to have been keen to play down interest in the case lest the sorry saga dent its reputation. Meanwhile the police were left so puzzled by the killing that the investigation was soon put on ice. However, in the run up to that Christmas, the mystery of who killed Marius Martin, the Cafe's burly night porter, became the talk of the town, before just as quickly fading into the pages of history.

French-born Martin was an impressive man, described as having 'enormous muscles'. The 40-year-old stood 6ft 2in tall and weighed in at 18 stone. Sporting a huge handlebar moustache,

The Café Royal as it is today. It was the scene of a murder in 1894 which remains unsolved. (© *James Moore*)

he was a familiar figure at the Café where he had worked for ten years after arriving from his native land without a job. He lived in an apartment above the venue with his wife, Mathilde.

On the night of his death the Café closed as usual at 12.30 a.m. Just after 1 p.m. the cashier, Richard Crossman, counted up that night's takings – a tidy £450 – and placed them in the safe, taking the key with him. At 1.05 a.m. Crossman wished Martin good-night and left the night porter to do his rounds. It was Martin's usual habit to go down to the kitchen at about 2 a.m. for a supper of leftovers. But it was a meal he would never eat.

Shortly before 7 a.m. that morning, Café cellar man Alexandre Delagneau found Martin's body near the building's Glasshouse Street entrance when he went to answer a workman who was knocking at the door. Martin was lying on his back half under one of the tables, near the cashier's office. Delagneau roused Martin's wife before running to the house of a local surgeon, Mr F. W. Axham, who lived further down Glasshouse Street.

When the doctor arrived, he found Martin unconscious but still alive. There was blood across his face and hair which a distraught Mrs Martin had been trying to wash away. The initial reaction of the doctor, given Martin's size, was that he had suffered a fit or stroke and hit his head when falling. It was only when Martin was taken to the nearby Charing Cross Hospital that it was discovered that he had in fact been shot, twice, with a small calibre revolver. The first bullet had struck Martin above the right ear and the second was fired into his left cheek. Sadly doctors could not save him and at 3.45 p.m. he was pronounced dead.

That morning police had made a thorough search of the building but found no weapon. There was a broken pane of glass in the cashier's office but no conclusive evidence that the safe had been tampered with. As well as the Martins, several staff lived over the Café but no one had heard any commotion during the night.

Two days after the crime, *The Times* reported that 'The utmost reticence is shown by the police and by those connected with the Café Royal.' Perhaps this was partly because the police were increasingly baffled by the motive. At first it was assumed that Martin had simply been the unfortunate victim of burglars who wanted to get their hands on the money in the cashier's office. But there didn't seem to have been a break-in as such. While the glass in the cashier's box had been smashed, the safe was untouched and Martin's keys to the building were still in his pocket. Would armed robbers have made so little effort to have taken the money, especially since they would surely have made a detailed study of the arrangements of the building and its night porter's habits prior to the crime. There also appeared to have been little sign of a struggle and nothing had been removed from the premises.

Within days the newspapers and the police were asking if Martin might have known his killer and if the motive had been due to some grudge against the man himself. There was some evidence that Martin had a bad temper and was unpopular for having reported staff for taking food. There was also a suggestion that one of the men's toilets might still have been occupied when the restaurant had closed that night, prompting detectives to believe that the killer or killers could have lain in wait until everyone was gone before pouncing on the victim.

Another intriguing piece of evidence was that during the night the doctor who had attended to Martin had been awakened by the whining of a hansom cab's horse in the street below, which he saw standing near the Glasshouse Street entrance.

Detective Inspector Greet, put in charge of the case, asked for a list of waiters who had been dismissed from their employment at the Café. It emerged that one foreign waiter who occasionally worked there had disappeared on the day of the murder. Greet appears to have been so convinced that this man was the culprit that he even put out a description:

Wanted, on suspicion of murder, a man aged 20; height five feet only, stout build; very dark hair, slight moustache; eyes dark. Dress – short jacket, soft felt brown hat indented on the crown, dark waistcoat, probably buttoned close up to the neck. Has the appearance of an Italian. Probably has a revolver.

A man was duly arrested in Soho but was soon released without charge. After that the trail appears to have gone cold. And despite the police's theory, there was actually nothing concrete to suggest that any of his colleagues was so incensed by Martin that they had a carefully planned murder in mind. At Martin's inquest, on 18 December, a verdict of murder was recorded by 'persons or persons unknown'. Interestingly, the coroner ruled that the reason Martin had left France back in 1884 need not be brought up in court as it was not relevant. But it does beg the question as to just why he had left and whether, in some way, his past could have caught up with him on the morning of 6 December.

For seventeen years the murder at the Café Royal remained unsolved and largely forgotten. Then in February 1911 there was an intriguing sequel to the story when a shabby man went into a police station in Liverpool and shocked officers by saying he wanted to confess to the crime. Frederick Charles Bedford, 53, an unemployed labourer from Exeter, said he had shot Martin and subsequently given the gun to Henry Fowler, a man famously hanged for a murder in London's Muswell Hill in 1896. Although Bedford was charged, the case against him was soon dismissed when police found that his story did not accord with the facts.

Who shot Martin remains a mystery to this day. Perhaps this is why his tortured spectre is said to have been seen lurking in the kitchens in the decades since. Unlike its ill-fated night porter, the Café Royal survived closure in 2008 and has recently opened as a luxury hotel.

LOCATION: *The Café Royal*, No. 68 Regent Street, London, W1B 4DY, 020 7406 3333, www.hotelcaferoyal.com.

WHERE OSCAR WILDE WAS ARRESTED, 1895

The Cadogan Hotel, Knightsbridge, London
In the 1890s the newly opened Cadogan Hotel was home to Lillie Langtry, the famous actress and mistress of the Prince of Wales, a serial philanderer who would later become King Edward VII. Langtry lived at the Cadogan between 1892 and 1897. Of course the scandalous behaviour of this resident remained largely unknown to the wider public. But, at the same time as Langtry inhabited the Cadogan, it also entertained another member of the arts whose personal life would become the subject of national debate. It was in room 53 (now room 118) of the Cadogan, on 5 April 1895, that the writer Oscar Wilde was arrested in dramatic circumstances.

Wilde was world famous for works that included *The Picture of Dorian Gray*, *Salome* and *The Importance of Being Earnest*. Wilde was also married with two sons. But in 1891, aged 38, he began an affair with the 22-year-old Lord Alfred Douglas, nicknamed Bosie. When Douglas' father, the Marquis of Queensbury, found out about the relationship, he was furious.

On 18 February 1895, Queensbury left his card at Wilde's London club, the Albemarle, which read, 'To Oscar Wilde, posing as a sodomite.' Not only was sodomy illegal but, thanks to an 1885 act, 'gross indecency' between two men was effectively illegal too. Wilde seemed intent on suing for libel but his friend Robert Ross

MR. OSCAR WILDE.

A portrait of the playwright Oscar Wilde from the *Illustrated London News*. He was arrested at the Cadogan Hotel in 1895. (*Courtesy of Wellcome Library, London*)

warned against it. When Wilde went for a lunch with the journalist Frank Harris and the playwright George Bernard Shaw at the Café Royal, they too counselled that he should drop the case. But, when Douglas arrived to join them, he urged Wilde to have his day in court. Wilde was persuaded that Douglas was right.

The case began at the Old Bailey on 3 April. As his friends had predicted it turned out to be a horrible mistake, opening up Wilde's private life to scrutiny, with all the lurid details splashed across the newspapers. Queensbury's lawyers dug up witnesses that linked Wilde to homosexual activities and under intense cross-examination Wilde's case soon collapsed. Queensbury was acquitted. The same afternoon a warrant was immediately issued for Wilde's arrest on charges of gross indecency.

Wilde had already been urged to leave the country with haste. Instead he retired to the Cadogan where he vacillated. At 1.45 p.m. Robert Ross brought Wilde the £200 he had asked him to draw on his bank and implored his friend to make for Dover and the continent. Another friend, Reginald Turner, who stayed with him, did the same. But Wilde, still apparently indecisive, eventually said simply, 'The train has gone, it's too late.' Ross left to tell Wilde's wife, Constance, of the situation before returning to the Cadogan where Ross told Wilde that she had hoped he was going abroad.

Wilde simply sat in a chair for several hours drinking hock and seltzer, a kind of white wine spritzer. At 5 p.m. a reporter called Thomas Marlowe, from the *Star*, came to see Wilde but was turned away. However, he did pass on the information that the warrant for Wilde's arrest had now been issued. When Ross told Wilde of this the writer was said to have gone 'very grey in the face'.

Wilde then asked Ross for the money he had got him, before sitting down and saying , 'I shall stay and do my sentence whatever it is.' For the next hour, Wilde sat in silence only occasionally asking where Bosie was. Douglas had left earlier to see the MP George Wyndham, his cousin, to find out if a prosecution was inevitable.

Finally, at 6.20 p.m. a waiter knocked at the door and showed in two detectives, Inspector Richards and Sergeant Allen. One of them said, 'Mr Wilde, I believe?'

'Yes, Yes,' said Wilde, smoking a cigarette by the fireplace.

Richards then said, 'We are police officers and hold a warrant for your arrest on a charge of committing indecent acts.'

Before he left, Oscar was allowed to write a note to Douglas informing him that he was unlikely to get bail. Ross helped a now very tipsy Oscar on with his coat and Wilde was allowed to take a novel called *Aphrodite* with him. The officers then took the writer in a hansom cab to Bow Street police station where he was charged.

On 26 April, Wilde again found himself in court – but this time as the accused. He pleaded not guilty. The trial featured the famous question from the prosecution to Wilde, 'What is the love that dare not speak its name?' Wilde's eloquent response could not save him from an unsatisfactory outcome – the jury failed to reach a verdict. Finally, following another trial, Wilde was convicted. He was sentenced to two years' hard labour, eventually ending up in Reading prison. Once released, both Wide's reputation and health were in tatters and he died in Paris on 30 November 1900. However, in the decades after his death, Wilde's literary reputation continued to grow. His arrest would later inspire a 1937 poem written by John Betjeman.

He sipped at a weak hock and seltzer
As he gazed at the London skies
Through the Nottingham lace of the curtains
Or was it his bees-winged eyes?

Today Wilde is seen as one of the greatest writers in history. And the Cadogan trades on its links with the playwright. Room 118 is now the Oscar Wilde Suite with décor that 'pays homage to the flamboyant playwright'.

LOCATION: **The Cadogan**, No. 75 Sloane Street, Knightsbridge, London, SW1X 9SG, 020 7235 7141, www.cadogan.com

BLUDGEONED TO DEATH WITH A BREWER'S TOOL, 1895

The Gardeners Arms, also known as The Murderers, Norwich, Norfolk
On the morning of 1 June 1895 the sound of screams rent the air at The Gardeners Arms, a pub on Norwich's historic Timber Hill. Then a young woman cried out, 'Murder! Mother!' Hurrying downstairs to the bar, Maria Wilby found her daughter Mildred lying in a pool of blood, bleeding profusely from her head. Though badly injured, Millie, aged just 21, was still alive. She was taken to the nearby Norfolk and Norwich hospital where a doctor dressed her injuries. However, it appears that because of her matted hair – and his own ineptitude – he failed to realise how severe the two wounds to her skull were. Millie was sent home. But, on the Monday, she was back. This time doctors found that the wounds extended into her brain. They attempted to operate but without luck and Mildred died on the Tuesday. Surgeons agreed that even if the full extent of her injuries had been realised sooner it would not have made any difference to her fate. It was a sorry end for a woman who, just three years earlier, must have been on top of the world when she married a dashing cavalryman.

On Whit Monday in June 1892, Mildred had wed Frank Miles. Born in Southampton he had been a cavalryman in the 8th Hussars and had served in India before returning to England

The Gardeners Arms, Norwich, as it looked in around 1915. (*Courtesy of the Gardeners Arms*)

where he was stationed at a barracks in Norwich. Miles left the army on marrying Millie and got a job in a brewery. But from early on the marriage was not a happy one. In June 1895 the couple separated and Millie moved in with her mother. Millie's father died in the January and she began helping out at the busy Gardeners Arms.

But Miles, now living above a different pub, continued to harbour feelings towards Millie. He also believed she had been unfaithful. Despite their estrangement the idea of her with another man was obviously still too much to bear. At 10 p.m. on the evening of Friday 31 May, he had gone to the Gardeners to see Millie, levelling accusations at her. He then threw an earthenware match holder at her, crying, 'I will do for you my lady,' before storming off.

At 9 a.m. the next morning he set out for the pub again, this time armed with an iron 'bung picker' used to draw bungs out of casks in the brewery. Once at the Gardeners he confronted Millie again. This time he flipped, attacking her with the sharp end of the tool. When Millie's mother arrived downstairs at the sound of the commotion, Miles told her, 'I have killed the b★★★★, there she lay!' before leaving the premises. He apparently headed straight for the police station where he confessed to the crime. Miles handed officers the bloodied weapon, saying, 'That is what I did it with, three minutes ago.'

On 7 June, wearing a 'neat blue serge suit', Miles appeared in the dock at Norwich Guildhall charged with the murder of Mildred. At his trial it was said, in his defence, that he had suffered sunstroke while serving in India and that he had suffered extreme provocation thanks to Millie's 'behaviour'. In a climate fuelled by the recent Jack the Ripper murders, the issue of prostitution was very much at the forefront of people's minds and Millie appears to have been portrayed as something of a wanton woman. The actual evidence for this is scant, amounting to the fact that she had been seen laughing and joking with other men.

Miles was found guilty of the brutal murder but the jury had been convinced that he had been distraught over Millie's behaviour. They requested leniency from the judge who passed the death sentence anyway. Miles' execution was set for 3 July. On 14 June, from his cell in Norwich prison, he wrote a penitent letter to his mother saying that he had killed his wife 'when greatly excited and provoked by her conduct towards me' and asked for forgiveness.

From the outset there appears to have been widespread sympathy for the condemned man. And now lawyers, journalists and family rallied round. A petition pleading for clemency, with 15,000 signatures, was sent from his home city of Southampton to the Home Office. It worked. Miles was given a reprieve, with his sentence commuted to life. In 1897, Miles was transferred to Parkhurst prison on the Isle of Wight. He died there eight years later, as an inmate, aged 37. But the case was not to be forgotten. While it is still officially called The Gardeners Arms, the scene of the crime has become best known to locals as simply 'The Murderers'.

LOCATION: *The Gardeners Arms*, Nos 2–8 Timber Hill, Norwich, Norfolk, NR1 3LB, 01603 621 447, www.themurderers.co.uk

A BOXING MENTOR GUNNED DOWN IN HIS OWN BAR, 1895

The Trocadero, Birmingham

Before 1902, today's busy Trocadero pub, with its ornate glazed exterior, was known as the Bodega wine bar. Despite the name change, however, it is said that the watering hole retains the ghost of a landlord who was cruelly murdered here in 1895. To this day, a mysterious presence is said to knock over beer glasses, fling beer mats around and even interfere with the fruit machines. And many regulars and staff believe that the restless soul responsible belongs to Henry James Skinner.

Skinner had been a sergeant in a Guards regiment before taking on the Bodega, a smart hostelry and well-known haunt of actors from the nearby theatre. Now in middle age, he was a popular figure who had previously run a boxing and fencing academy and even, it was said, taught boys swordsmanship at Eton.

At the pub, Skinner employed two brothers, Arthur and Herbert Allen, as barmen. On 3 December 1895, Skinner reprimanded Arthur, who had worked at the bar for nine years, for leaving some bottles open. He slammed his hand down on the bar for emphasis and hit Arthur's hand, perhaps by mistake, as he did so. A scuffle ensued in which Arthur slapped Skinner in the face. Herbert, fearing for his brother, had tried to stop the brawny Skinner returning the gesture by holding him by his coat tails. In the end both of the Allens were sacked on the spot and thrown off the premises. The next day Arthur came back to the pub for his outstanding wages. He apologised and was soon paid, though when he asked for his job back Skinner turned him down. Half an hour later, Herbert turned up asking for his wages too, but was turned away – apparently on account of being drunk – and told to come back the next day.

Herbert became increasingly upset. At just 23 years old and married only a month earlier, he was now out of a job – one that he had been doing for five years. That day he suddenly brandished a gun in front of his brother Charles saying, 'This is meant for Skinner.'

There was no doubt that Herbert was a troubled man. The Allens also worked as handymen and six months earlier Herbert had fallen from a tree, breaking a jaw and suffering from concussion. It's thought he may have suffered a brain injury which had altered his character. Before the accident he had been described as light-hearted but afterwards was always found to be gloomy. Herbert had already tried to commit suicide at least once, having flung himself in front of a train that summer. Interestingly, his family also had a history of mental health problems. One of his brothers had already shot himself and both his father and another brother had attempted to do away with themselves too.

At 9 a.m. on Thursday 5 December Herbert called again at the Bodega and was given the wages he was owed. At noon, Herbert and Arthur returned to the bar together where they found Skinner on the doorstep. Realising there was now no chance of getting his job back, Arthur told Skinner that he had taken out a summons for assault against him, before walking off. Herbert, already worse for wear, went inside to collect some building tools he'd left there and asked bar manager Dave Andrews for a brandy while he was at it. Andrews asked Skinner, who had now come back inside the bar, if it was okay and although Skinner agreed, Andrews decided to refuse Herbert after all. Skinner then said to Herbert that maybe it wasn't such a good idea for him to have a drink after all – telling him about the summons that Arthur had taken out and turning his back.

Herbert suddenly pulled his revolver from his overcoat and shouted, 'Mr Skinner!' As Skinner turned he then fired off two shots across the busy bar towards the landlord who was standing just feet away from him. One of them hit Skinner in the heart, another burying itself in the wainscoting. The bullets were later found to be of a bulldog pattern type – capable of felling an ox at close quarters.

At the sound of the gunfire, a quick-thinking Andrews had leapt over the bar and wrestled Herbert to the floor. Herbert shouted, 'Loose me Dave, or I'll shoot you,' but soon Andrews had managed to grab the gun off him. Meanwhile, a PC Owens who happened to be across the road and had heard the shots, rushed into the bar too. Herbert was soon in custody but Skinner was already dead, having uttered only a simple 'oh' before slumping to the floor.

Herbert Allen was brought up in front of the Birmingham Assizes in March 1896. The jury found him guilty of murder but recommended mercy. Yet Allen himself made an extraordinary statement in which he begged to be put to death. He said that it was with 'the greatest anguish that now I have taken the life of a fellow creature' and claimed that if he was not given the death sentence he would strangle himself 'at the first opportunity'. Initially he got his wish. The judge sentenced him to be hanged on 7 April at Winson Green Gaol. However, just days before the sentence was due to be carried out, Herbert was given a reprieve by the Home Secretary. He spent the rest of his days behind bars. Given his state of mind, it was perhaps the worst punishment he could have received.

LOCATION: *The Trocadero*, Temple Street, Birmingham, B2 5BG, 0121 643 6107, www.thetrocaderobirmingham.co.uk

Murder Most Modern 1900s

A Landlord Who Killed His Wife, 1900

The Marlborough Pub and Theatre, Brighton

The marriage of Thomas and Lucy Packham, landlord and land-lady of the Marlborough Hotel in Princes Street, Brighton, was not a happy one from the outset. Packham, who was often drunk in his own pub, was a cruel husband who subjected both his wife and children to verbal and physical abuse, as a number of witnesses would later attest. The couple were married in 1888 and took over at the Marlborough in 1895. The pub's live-in housekeeper, Bertha Virgo, said that Lucy herself was also intemperate and that this led to her making mistakes in the hotel when taking orders. The pair often rowed and Mrs Virgo was forced to step in and stop Packham hitting his wife on more than one occasion. For some reason, when Lucy looked smart and tidy, Packham was said to have objected and torn off her clothes. He also regularly threat-ened his wife in public. Lucy's father, a butcher called Edward, said he had often complained about his son-in-law's treatment of his daughter, which had begun just a week into their union. Thomas, who kept a revolver in his bedroom, had once tried to cut Lucy's throat. Edward often told Lucy to leave her husband but she wouldn't for the sake of the couple's three children.

At around midnight on Thursday 1 March 1900, PC Mullins was passing the Marlborough when he heard a row going on inside between a man and a woman. He heard the woman begging, 'Don't, Tom', then the man shouting, 'You're a lazy woman!' She replied, 'I know I am.' An hour later, he returned with a colleague, PC Puttick, who heard the man inside the

The Marlborough, Brighton, where Lucy Packham was found dead in the bar. (*Courtesy of The Marlborough*)

Marlborough saying, 'I'll kill you.' He recognised the voices – he had heard the Packhams quarrelling many times before. Puttick then heard a thud. This was almost certainly Lucy's body hitting the floor as she was killed. Puttick knocked at the door, but when no one came he left, assuming the altercation was now over.

The Marlborough's potman, Joseph Miles, who also lived in, found the Packhams arguing before he went to bed. As he came out of the kitchen and went up, he saw Lucy on the floor by the foot of the stairs and Packham saying, 'Will you get up – do you want to get up?' Miles did nothing to intervene – he had seen it all before. The last thing he heard was Packham saying to Lucy, 'I forgive you.'

At about 4 p.m., Packham knocked on the door of Mrs Virgo's room and said, 'It's me, Mr Packham. Will you come down, the wife is either dead or dying.' Lucy was lying at the back of the bar, her head on some broken bottles with her feet pointing towards the beer pumps. Mrs Virgo said that a still drunk Packham knelt over her badly bruised body and kept repeating, 'Lucy, oh, do come back

Lucy.' Yet it was clear to Mrs Virgo that Lucy was already dead. She went to wake Miles and he was sent to get the family physician, Dr Ross, who confirmed that Lucy was indeed beyond help. The doctor challenged Packham as to whether he was responsible and found him barely coherent. Packham did, however, deny striking Lucy and then said, 'I shan't be long after her.'

No one had actually seen anyone assault the 32-year-old, but to the coroner's jury the case seemed pretty straightforward. Lucy's inquest, which was held at the Marlborough itself, heard that she had died of a cerebral haemorrhage caused by either a fall or a heavy blow. Her body had been covered in bruises and there was a cut on her lip. Her injuries certainly suggested that she had been beaten up. After three hours a verdict of wilful murder was returned against 34-year-old Packham.

Yet when Thomas Packham's full trial began on 30 June at the Sussex Assizes in Lewes, he had the fortune to be represented by the barrister Edward Marshall Hall who would become famed for his skills in defending those accused of the highest crimes. Hall managed to persuade an all-male jury that both of the Packhams had been drunk and that his client hadn't actually meant to kill Lucy, despite his apparent history of abuse. The jury took just 22 minutes to decide that Packham was guilty only of manslaughter. They even recommended mercy for the prisoner. Packham was sentenced to just four years' penal servitude. The crime is still remembered at the Marlborough where, in recent years, it was possible to buy a Lucy Packham cocktail made in her honour.

LOCATION: **Marlborough Pub & Theatre**, No. 4 Prince's Street, Brighton, East Sussex, BN2 1RD, 01273 570028, www.drinkinbrighton.co.uk/marlborough

THE MERSTHAM TUNNEL MYSTERY, 1905

The Feathers Hotel, Merstham, Surrey
Just before 11 p.m. on the evening of 24 September 1905, William Peacock, a railway inspector, headed into Surrey's Merstham

Tunnel on the London to Brighton line. He was with a gang of workers dispatched to undertake some repairs. When Peacock was about 400yds inside the tunnel, the beam of his lamp picked out the form of a human figure lying beside the track. It turned out to be the body of a badly mutilated young woman. He ran to inform police. The body was removed from the tunnel and taken to the Feathers Hotel on Merstham High Street where it was placed in a locked stable at the rear of the building.

At first it appeared to be a simple, if tragic, case of suicide. A local doctor, Henry Crickett, was called to examine the dead woman. The corpse was still warm, indicating that she had died about an hour before. Dr Crickett found that the features of the woman were virtually unrecognisable. She had a fractured skull and one of her legs had been almost severed from her body at the thigh. There were also bruises and scratches on her body, arms and face indicating that she may have been involved in a struggle. A white silk scarf had also been rammed down the victim's throat. Meanwhile, an examination of soot marks on the tunnel's wall made it clear that the woman had either fallen or been pushed out of a railway carriage rather than having wandered in on foot and been run down by a train. No railway ticket, money or papers could be found on the deceased woman to suggest who she was. However, her underwear bore a laundry number which read '245'. This was the vital clue that police needed. When it was published in newspaper reports the next day, a man called Robert Money, a farmer from Kingston Hill, came forward. He was brought down to Merstham and identified the dead woman as his sister, Mary Sophia Money. She was a 22-year-old bookkeeper at a dairy located at No. 245 Lavender Hill, Clapham, where she also lived.

An inquest was opened on 26 September at the Feathers, there being no local mortuary. Here Robert Money told the court that he felt that several men had been pursuing Mary romantically, but this evidence was hazy and the men that Money had specifically mentioned were soon ruled out by police as having cast iron alibis, although one did admit to knowing her and having given her a ring found on her body.

Slowly more came to light about Mary's movements on the last day of her life.

Emma Hone, a woman who had worked with Mary, remembered that she had left their lodgings at 7 p.m. to go for 'a little walk' but had not returned. This was unusual. Interestingly, Emma stated that, to her knowledge, Mary had no regular boyfriends. Mary had just been paid and had a purse on her full of cash on the evening she went out. This was never found. Mary left the premises without a jacket, indicating that she didn't expect to be going far. She was, however, wearing a white scarf. The last definite sighting of Mary was at a sweet shop at Clapham Junction station where she bought some chocolates and mentioned that she was on her way to Victoria station. It seemed clear that she had a rendezvous with someone. Had that someone suggested an impromptu train ride?

There were only a few trains that passed through the tunnel around the estimated time of death. A guard, who had been on the 9.33 p.m. train from Charing Cross, remembered seeing a young woman matching Mary's description on the train travelling in a first-class compartment. She had been with a young man. They had been sitting close to each other at South Croydon, but when the train arrived at Redhill on the other side of the tunnel, only the man, described as thin, with a moustache and wearing a bowler hat, got off the train. By this time the woman seemed to have disappeared. Sadly this man was never traced. Meanwhile a signalman at Purley Oaks, situated before the tunnel, thought he had seen a woman and man struggling on the 9.13 p.m. train from London Bridge. Confusing things further, a man on another train, this time one travelling towards London, saw a woman matching Mary's description in a nearby compartment. He heard a carriage door being slammed twice as the train went through the tunnel. Whichever train Mary was on, she – and any companion – would have had to change trains at London Bridge or East Croydon. It was an odd journey to take given that Mary was always home by 11 p.m.

Faced with this puzzle the police investigation soon ran into the sand. Officers conducted more than a hundred interviews and several experiments with train carriages in the Merstham tunnel. Yet no obvious suspect could be identified. At a final hearing into her death, which took place on 16 October, the jury recorded a vague verdict – saying that although Mary had met her death through severe injuries caused by a train, the evidence was insufficient even to show whether she had fallen or had been pushed from the carriage.

Many tantalising questions were left unanswered. Had Mary simply been the victim of a robbery? And if there was another motive, had she been killed by someone she knew well or simply a passing acquaintance? Where had she been going at that time on a Sunday evening? Was it, as some suggested, because merely travelling in a first class compartment would have given her and a companion some much needed privacy?

Over the next seven years, the case faded from the public consciousness and police shelved their enquiries. Then, in 1912, a shocking murder took place in Sussex involving Mary's brother. It transpired that Robert Money, who had given up farming for property development, had been leading a bizarre double life. At first he had lived with a woman called Florence Paler in Clapham with whom he'd had two children. He then left her and somehow managed to marry her sister Edith, with whom he had another child, all apparently without either woman knowing what was going on. Robert was clearly a fantasist who had been using a string of aliases and passing himself off as a former soldier.

In August, using the name of Robert Hicks Murray, he took a house in Eastbourne where he lured both of his families. Here, on the 19th, he shot them all before turning the gun on himself too. Then he set fire to the house. All died except for Florence who escaped the inferno and survived a wound to her neck.

For a while there was doubt whether the man calling himself Murray was actually Money. Another of his sisters, however, confirmed it from samples of handwriting. The tragedy certainly seemed an incredible coincidence, and it left many asking the obvious question – could Money have somehow been involved in Mary's death too? Adding to the mystery was an interview given at the time by James Brice, a former superintendent of the Surrey Constabulary who had been involved in the original investigation into Mary Money's death. He now revealed that Mary had been a gambler and in his opinion she had killed herself because her stock was short with her employer. She was worried sick that they would find out. This conclusion seems at odds with the other known facts and it should be said that there was some criticism of the 1905 police investigation at the time. The police had also admitted that Robert Money had misled them about aspects concerning the Merstham Tunnel tragedy. Furthermore there was no suggestion that Mary had appeared depressed before her death. Indeed the last person to see her said she had been laughing. Nor does all this explain the scarf found in Maria's throat. Given her lack of reputation for seeing male friends it seems much more likely that, rather than her own money problems, Robert Money was her problem. Crucially no satisfactory account of his movements on the night of Mary's death has emerged. Given his disregard for life, he has to be the likely culprit in Mary's death. Yet the case remains as baffling as it did in the Edwardian age when it left even Sir Arthur Conan Doyle, the creator of the great detective Sherlock Holmes, scratching his head.

LOCATION: **The Feathers Hotel**, No. 42 High Street, Merstham, Redhill, Surrey, RH1 3EA, 01737 645643, www.thefeathersmerstham.co.uk

THE PUB, THE POSTCARD AND AN INVITATION TO MURDER? 1907

The Grand Union, Camden Town; The Rocket, Euston; The Water Rats, King's Cross; Swan Hotel, Bedford

'Dear Phyllis. Will you meet me at the bar of the Eagle at Camden Town, 8.30 tonight, Wednesday.' So read the letter, which was signed 'Bert'. The recipient was a young woman called Emily Dimmock who lived in London's Camden Town and was better known to the string of men she entertained as Phyllis. On 11 September 1907, at the arranged time, 22-year-old Emily headed for the Eagle, a pub which is today part of the Grand Union bar chain. She told her landlady, Mrs Stocks, that she wouldn't be long and left with her hair still in curlers. The next morning Emily's common law husband, who worked nightshifts, found Emily dead at their lodgings. Her throat had been slit. The Camden Town Murder, as it became known, would lead to one of

The Grand Union was once The Eagle, where suspected murderer Robert Wood was seen with victim Emily Dimmock on the night of her death. (© *James Moore*)

the most sensational court cases of the century as a talented commercial artist attempted to clear his name.

Emily was born in the village of Standon, near Ware, in Hertfordshire and her family may well have been lodging at The Bell in the village, while other reports suggest that her father ran the Red Lion there. Her parents moved regularly in search of work, and at one time Emily was employed as a chambermaid in the Swan Hotel in Bedford. Aged 17 she was working in service in Finchley, North London. By 1905, Emily had drifted to the Kings Cross area of London, where she lodged for some time at a brothel before moving in with a man called Bertram Shaw, 19, who became her common law husband. They lived at No. 29 St Paul's Road in Camden, a road which is now called Agar Grove. Bertram was a railway chef and worked away most nights on trains going north from St Pancras. He would leave home at 4.15 p.m. and return at 11.30 a.m. the following day. During these nocturnal absences Emily, who enjoyed a night on the tiles, saw a string of men without her partner's knowledge. She sometimes brought them back to St Paul's Road and occasionally they paid her for her company. Emily was often to be found in the Rising Sun, a Victorian pub at No. 120 Euston Road, now called The Rocket. She also frequented The Pindar of Wakefield in Gray's Inn Road, which is now a music venue called The Water Rats.

On Thursday 12 September 1907, at around midday, Bertram arrived home to find his mother, who had come to visit, waiting in the passage. Unusually, the couple's rooms in the house were locked. Bertram borrowed a key from the landlady. On entering he was horrified to find Emily's lifeless body on the bed. Her throat had been cut so deeply that her head had been almost completely severed. There was blood everywhere in the bedroom and the lodgings had also been ransacked. The killer had obviously washed their hands in the room's sink too. Intriguingly Emily's beloved postcard collection had been scattered around the room. Had the killer been looking for something that could incriminate them?

A few items were missing, including a silver watch, a cigarette case and keys to the rooms, while a post-mortem showed Emily's death to have been between 3 a.m. and 6 a.m. that morning. There were no cuts or bruises on the body to indicate a struggle and police concluded that Emily must have been killed while asleep. The examining surgeon said that there was no way the victim could have inflicted the wound herself. He also identified that in the hours before her death, Emily had consumed a meal involving bread and potatoes and probably been drinking stout.

Bertram had been in Sheffield that night and his alibi was rock solid. Emily appeared to have invited someone else back to their rooms that evening and police began to piece together Emily's movements in the days before the crime. They discovered that on the Sunday, Monday and Tuesday nights she had slept with a ship's cook called Robert Roberts, who she had met at The Rising Sun. He told police that on the morning of Wednesday 11th she had shown him a postcard which read, 'Phillis darling. If it pleases you to meet me at 8.15 at the (then a picture of a rising sun) Yours to a cinder. Alice.' The rising sun was taken to mean The Rising Sun on the Euston Road. Roberts told police that Emily had also shown him a letter that she had just received – the

The Rising Sun pub on Euston Road. It was at the heart of the Camden Town Murder mystery and is now called The Rocket. (© *James Moore*)

one inviting her to the Eagle – and commented on how similar the handwriting was. Police found the charred remains of this letter in the fire-grate of the room where Emily had died, though they only had Roberts' word to go on in terms of its full wording. Roberts told them that he had seen Emily burn it, presumably in case it might alert Bertram to her 'other life'. The cook himself was ruled out as a suspect when it transpired that he had an alibi for the night of the murder. He had been drinking at The Rising Sun before retiring with a woman called May Campbell.

Two weeks later, while clearing out his belongings from No. 29 St Paul's Road, Bertram Shaw found the 'Rising Sun' postcard. Deemed a vital clue in the hunt for Emily's killer, it was reproduced in several newspapers in the hope that someone would recognise the handwriting. A woman called Ruby Young did – it was that of her former boyfriend, a young artist called Robert Wood. Then Wood contacted Ruby by telegram and asked her to provide him with an alibi for the evening, which she agreed to do. Wood's plan soon unravelled. Ruby couldn't keep the secret, telling a friend who passed it on to a journalist and hence the police too, who soon tracked Wood down. He admitted to Inspector Arthur Neil that he had first met Emily on 6 September at the Eagle and that he had written the 'Rising Sun' postcard to her in the pub at the time. Emily, it seems, had asked him not to sign his real name in order that Bertram's suspicions shouldn't be aroused. However, Wood denied having sent Emily any letters. Meanwhile, police had found a man called Robert McCowan who had seen a man matching Wood's description coming out of No. 29 St Paul's Road at 4.55 a.m. on the morning of Emily's death. Wood was arrested and charged with murder.

His trial began at the Old Bailey on 10 December 1907.

Robert Roberts gave evidence, which was corroborated by others, that Wood had been in The Rising Sun on the night of 9 September when he, Roberts, had left with Emily. A bookseller said that on the evening of the 11th he had enjoyed a drink with Emily and Wood in the Eagle. He already knew Wood and had bumped into him by chance in the pub that evening. It seemed that Wood was the last person to be seen with the victim while she was alive. Another witness, who knew Emily Dimmock when she was probably working as a prostitute, reported seeing her several times with Wood, indicating that the accused had actually known her for fifteen months.

Things looked bleak for Wood but he had the good fortune to be represented by the dashing Edward Marshall Hall QC, who had already established a name for himself for his dramatic style in court and brilliant cross-examination skills.

While Wood's frantic efforts to get a false alibi from Ruby Young looked damning, Marshall Hall explained them away, saying that his client was merely worried at how it looked, having been with the victim on that evening so late. He said that Wood hadn't wanted his father to know he had been visiting prostitutes. And why, he asked, if Wood knew what time Emily had been murdered, had he only asked Ruby to vouch for him until 10 p.m.?

A resident of St Paul's Road, William Westcott, was also produced to say that he had seen McCowan in the otherwise quiet road at the same time that the latter had reported seeing Wood. It was suggested that, in the dim light, Westcott could actually have been the man McCowan had seen, not Wood.

Finally Wood, who had been busily sketching in court, himself gave evidence on his own behalf – the first defendant to do so in a murder trial. Asked directly if he had killed Emily, he said, rather pompously, 'Of course, not. I mean it is ridiculous.' He swore that he had left Emily in the Eagle at around 11 p.m. and that he had then gone straight to his father's home. A neighbour, who was in his garden at the time, said that he had seen Wood coming home at around midnight.

The judge ordered the jury to acquit Wood, saying that the prosecution had not proved their case. It took them just fifteen minutes to find Wood not guilty and so the murder remained officially unsolved.

A couple of years after the trial, the impressionist artist Walter Sickert took up the theme of The Camden Town Murder for a set of paintings which showed a clothed man and a woman on a bed. The American crime writer Patricia Cornwell has suggested that Emily's real murderer was actually Sickert himself – and that his paintings could not have been done without intimate knowledge of the crime scene. She is also one of those claiming that Sickert was Jack the Ripper. Whether Sickert was the Ripper or not, the length of time between the Whitechapel murders of 1888 and Emily Dimmock's death in 1907, plus the fact that her murder did not involve the same sort of mutilation, makes this theory highly questionable.

LOCATION: *The Grand Union* (formerly the Eagle), Nos 102–104 Camden Road, NW1 9EA, 020 7485 4530, www.grandunionbars.com/venue/camden; *The Swan Hotel*, The Embankment, Bedford, MK40 1RW, 01234 346565, www.bedfordswanhotel.co.uk; *The Rocket* (formerly The Rising Sun), No. 120 Euston Road, London, NW1 2AL, www.therocketeustonroad.co.uk; *The Water Rats* (formerly the Pindar of Wakefield), No. 328 Grays Inn Rd, London, WC1X 8BZ, 020 7209 8747

MURDER OF A SWEETHEART, 1914

The Goddard Arms, Swindon, Wiltshire
By the time Walter James White arrived at the Goddard Arms Hotel in Swindon, with murder in mind, the inn had already been trading for at least two centuries. It had seen a lot – includ-

ing the coming of the railway in 1840, acting as a makeshift ticket office before a proper station was built. But the historic hotel was about to play host to its most scandalous event. In early 1914 a tragic chain of events unfolded which was to destroy the lives of White and his sweetheart, Frances Priscilla Hunter, and leave the community shattered.

Frances was born in the nearby town of Devizes, the daughter of a labourer, and worked as a maid at the Goddard Arms in Swindon's Old Town. White was the son of a railway labourer and worked as a painter and decorator. In Autumn 1913, the pair started seeing each other and became engaged. A few months into their relationship the couple decided to visit Frances' brothers who were working away at Gilfach in Glamorgan, South Wales. However, when they arrived, the landlady at the lodging house where they were staying, a Mrs Blewitt, refused to allow Frances in. It turned out that Mrs Blewitt had known Frances when she was in service in Wales and had some information about her character. Later she wrote to White telling him that there was something he ought to know. A worried White returned to Mrs Blewitt's lodging house to see what she had to say. She revealed to him that Frances had previously run away with a married collier. Frances had lived 'in sin' for three months.

This news enraged 22-year-old White who was consumed with jealousy and anger at discovering that the woman he thought was pure and chaste had conducted an affair with another man. He later said, 'That very much upset me, I couldn't stand the strain.' In fact White was so furious that he decided to take revenge: 'I loved the poor girl dearly, but she deceived me, so I thought I would finish it to prevent further trouble.' While in Wales he bought a revolver. Then, on 29 April, he wrote some letters before heading to Frances' workplace, arriving at 6 p.m.

Inside the Goddard Arms he found the 23-year-old and asked to see her privately. The pair went to the staff room and then to the hotel yard. Ten minutes later gunshots were heard.

According to White's statement to police he had confronted Frances over Mrs Blewitt's claims. He said, 'I asked her if it was right. She confessed she had disgraced me and hoped God would forgive her. I told her she would never deceive anybody else as

The Goddard Arms, Swindon, Wiltshire, where Frances Priscilla Hunter was murdered in 1914. (© *James Moore*)

I was going to kill her.' Frances then said, 'For God's sake do it, then!' before kissing White goodbye. He explained, 'I then shot her and waited for somebody to come.'

The victim was found dying in a coalhouse at the back of the hotel. There were two bullet wounds in her face. White was standing over Frances' body with the gun still in his hand. He said, 'Now justice will be done.' A policeman and doctor were called, but Frances was said to have died within minutes.

Upon White's arrest, several letters were found on him which indicated that the crime had been premeditated. In one of them he spoke of how 'I have been ruined by my sweetheart.' To the girl's father, Richard, he wrote, 'You ought to have a bullet put through you, instead of Frances. You are as much to blame as she is. You have killed two lives with the price of your silence.'

On 28 May the case was brought before the Wiltshire Assizes. White's defence team argued that he was in a perturbed state of mind when he found out that his idol was not what she seemed. The jury didn't buy the excuse. White was found guilty but with a plea for mercy on account of his youth. White was nevertheless given the death sentence and on hearing his sentence was said to have been in a 'state of collapse'. He practically had to be carried out of the dock. A petition to the Home Secretary for a reprieve fell on deaf ears and in the end White appeared to welcome his fate. In a letter written from his prison cell he said, 'I would have chosen death. I shall go like a soldier and a man … Remember me, but not my shame.' White was hanged on 15 June 1914 at Winchester prison. Before he died, White sent a bunch of flowers to Frances' funeral with an inscription that read, 'I kissed her good-bye. Earth's troubles are over; for her heaven will be best.'

Interestingly, the crime echoed one that had occurred in another Swindon pub eleven years earlier. On 18 September 1903 Esther Swinford, a 19-year-old barmaid at The Ship on Westcott Place, was shot. On that occasion the killer had been a spurned lover. Edward Richard Palmer was furious that Esther had broken off their engagement after she had discovered how he'd frittered away some of her hard-earned wages. On the evening of the murder, 24-year-old Palmer had walked into The Ship, ordered a bottle of Bass, then fired his revolver, shooting Esther through the heart. When the landlord appeared in the bar he told him, 'I done it, I loved the girl.'

At his trial, Palmer's defence tried to suggest that there had been some impropriety on the part of Esther, a claim which was dismissed by the prosecution. Palmer was hanged at Devizes prison on 17 November 1903. The pub where the killing took place has since closed but a memorial to Esther, paid for by locals touched by her death, can still be seen at the town's Radnor Street Cemetery.

LOCATION: **The Goddard Arms**, No. 1 High Street, Swindon, SN1 3EG, 01793 619090, www.goddardarms.co.uk

A LANDLORD MURDERED IN HIS BED, 1921

The Swan Inn, Talke, Staffordshire
The Swan Inn is located in a prominent position at the top of a hill in the sleepy community of Talke, Staffordshire, originally known as 'Talk o' th' Hill'. Along with a smattering of other pubs

in the village, The Swan has been open since before 1800. The Swan served not only the locals but also traffic ferrying north and south between the Potteries and the industrial towns of Lancashire. In 1921, the landlord of the pub was 54-year-old Walter Hulse who ran the hostelry with his wife, Mary, and their two teenage children. Walter also ran a 40-acre farm and had a milk business.

On the evening of Thursday, 1 December, Mary Hulse had locked up the Swan as usual and was in bed upstairs at the pub when, at 3.45 a.m., she felt something brush her hand. She thought it was a mouse and barely opened her eyes. A few moments later Walter sat bolt upright, crying out, 'Hello, who's there?' Someone was moving around in the darkness of the room. Suddenly a shot rang out and Walter fell back, dead. He had been hit full in the face and his brains blown out. As Mary lay beside him, utterly terrified, she heard the murderer running down the stairs and slamming the door on his way out. Drenched in her husband's blood, she screamed for help and as she did so one man's name came into her head: James Edward Linney. She had, she felt, recognised the departing footsteps as his. How did she know? Linney walked with a limp.

Linney was a 39-year-old father of one. Until a week before the murder, he had been employed by Walter to do odd jobs and look after his cows. He had also lived at The Swan until February 1921 when he'd got married. Linney therefore knew his way around the passageways of the old, gaslit pub and where the gun and cartridges with which Walter was killed were stored. Indeed he had been allowed to use it on several occasions. Linney was also known to have a grudge against Walter who, he alleged, owed him money for work he'd done. However, if Linney was the murderer, he certainly behaved calmly on the morning after the killing. He was one of the village folk who assembled outside The Swan watching the comings and goings of the police during that day.

Detectives found that the hotel cashbox, containing £30, was still on a chair in the Hulses' bedroom where it was always kept at night. There were no useful fingerprints but the window of the pub's snug at the rear of the building was found unlatched and there was dirt on the sill. This, said Mary, was often used by

Linney as a way of entering the locked building when he had come home late during the time he was living there. The double-barrelled sporting gun with which Walter had been shot was found at the bottom of the pub's stairs. When the police went to Linney's house that morning, his wife, Ruby, maintained that he had been with her all night.

At 7 p.m. on the Saturday evening, Inspector Williams and PC Jones went to arrest Linney at his home, about 50yds from The Swan. He walked with a limp and was very deaf, so the inspector wrote down the usual caution on a piece of paper and handed it to him. He was subsequently charged with murder in Newcastle-under-Lyme. Linney found it difficult to follow the proceedings at the magistrates' court, at one point saying, 'I am as deaf as a stone wall.'

In the legal proceedings that followed throughout that December, a picture emerged of a disgruntled man. Local labourer Martin Payton told how Linney had recently threatened to put a fork through his former boss, and even Linney's own niece said that in the week of the murder he vowed to 'have his whack out of' Walter before the weekend. A miner told how, three months before the killing, he had heard Linney threatening to shoot his employer after he was stopped 5s.

Constable Jones gave evidence that he had passed Linney's house on the morning of the murder and saw a bright light in his window. In a search of Linney's home, nothing had been found. But at 7.30 a.m. on the Friday the accused had also been seen by two witnesses acting furtively in a field behind his house. He had asked George Ollerhead, 'What is the matter with the boss?' Looking under a stone behind the house on the Monday morning, Jones found two spent cartridge cases concealed there. They matched the unused ones found in a kitchen drawer at The Swan. A Mrs Burnip, who lived next door to Linney, told how he had complained to her on the day before the murder that he had no money or food.

At Linney's trial, held at the Stafford Assizes in February 1922, Linney pleaded not guilty. He said that Walter Hulse had actually offered to give him his job back on the day before the murder, so he had no motive to kill him. He also maintained that he had not been out on the night in question and had slept downstairs in his house, next to his wife. He did not get up until 4.45 a.m. when he went into his garden. He claimed that the first he knew of the death was when he was told by a neighbour.

Much depended on the alibi given to Linney by his wife, Ruby. She said that on the night in question the couple's baby had been ill and that was why they had all slept downstairs by the fire. She had been awake all night and therefore knew that her husband had been asleep on the floor of their house at the time the murder was supposed to have been committed. She also said that she had watched him go out into the garden that morning, but that he had not tampered with any stones.

During the trial, there was an enquiry from the jury as to whether there had been any life insurance policies on Walter Hulse's life, and it turned out that there had been. The implication here was clearly that Walter's 18-year-old son, also called Walter, might somehow be implicated. On the morning of the murder, after hearing his mother's screams, he had calmly dressed in formal attire, including a tie, before going to find help, which seemed a little strange. But the judge told the jury that there was nothing to suggest that Walter's own family had been involved in the crime. After fifty-five minutes, the jury returned and acquitted Linney. The police never identified any other suspects in the case and the murder remains unsolved.

If Linney thought life back in Talke would carry on as normal, he was much mistaken. Many of the locals still felt that he was guilty and he struggled to find work. In 1927, now with three children, he walked out on his family and was never seen again. Walter Hulse was buried in the graveyard of St Martin's church next to The Swan.

In November 1922 there was a strange postscript to the case when two dressmakers from Talke, Clara Jones, 30, and Alice May Jones, 28, appeared at the Stafford Assizes accused of sending letters demanding money with menaces to poor Mary Hulse. Alice Jones told the court, 'I did it under the spirit of Spiritualism. It was impossible to do otherwise.' She alleged that the dead Mr Hulse had been speaking to her for the 'last six months, and it has ruined my health.' Alice also claimed to know the real identity of the killer – because the dead man had told her. Both women were sentenced to eighteen months' hard labour.

LOCATION: *The Swan Inn*, Swan Bank, Talke, Stoke on Trent, Staffordshire, ST7 1PS, 01782 499 171, www.swan-inn-pub.co.uk

DEATH AT THE SAVOY, 1923

The Savoy Hotel, London

The sumptuous Savoy Hotel on London's Strand was built by the impresario Richard D'Oyly Carte with the proceeds of Gilbert and Sullivan operas. But the hotel, which opened in August 1889, was also the setting for a real life drama that was just as outlandish as anything the D'Oyly Carte Opera Company had staged. The shooting of a 22-year-old Egyptian playboy in 1923 was anything but a mystery. It was plain who had pulled the trigger. But the court case that followed still captivated millions and ended in a surprise verdict.

In its 125-year history, the Savoy has entertained guests as varied and illustrious as Edward VII, Charlie Chaplin and the Beatles. But it has also had its fair share of controversy. In 1895, at Oscar Wilde's trial, male prostitutes testified that the writer had entertained them in room 361 of the hotel. The judge in the case famously observed, 'I know nothing about the Savoy, but I must say that in my view chicken and salad for two at 16 shillings is very high.' Then, in 1918, the actress Billie Carleton was found dead in her Savoy hotel room at the tender age of 22. She had died from a drug overdose.

Yet, among its raft of exotic guests, it would be hard to find residents as wild or eccentric as Egyptian Prince Ali Kamel Fahmy Bey, a 22-year-old millionaire and his sultry French wife, Marguerite. The self-styled prince, actually the son of a wealthy engineer, had a reputation for extravagance and arrogance. Marguerite was ten years his senior. She was an impulsive, beautiful divorcee who had begun an affair with Fahmy in 1922 in Paris, then married him in Egypt.

From the outset, the marriage had been an odd one. She was a former high-class prostitute who may well have had an affair with the future Edward VIII. To wed Fahmy, she had become a Muslim, though he had agreed to let her wear Western-style dress. From the day of their nuptials in December 1922 the couple had battled constantly.

At the beginning of July 1923, along with a chauffeur, secretary, valet and maid, this odd pair travelled to London and checked into a plush suite at the Savoy. But none of its features, which included marbled bathrooms and silk sheets, appeared to lighten the mood of the Fahmys.

The afternoon of 9 July was a heavy, humid one. And at lunch in the Savoy's restaurant the oppressive nature of the Fahmys' relationship was soon on public display. A row broke out, with Marguerite threatening divorce. When the conductor of the orchestra in the restaurant asked Madame Fahmy if she would like anything particular played for her, she retorted, 'My husband is going to kill me in 24 hours and I am not very anxious for music.'

That evening the couple went to see a performance of a play called *The Merry Widow*, a title that would become painfully appropriate. The couple continued to quarrel, this time over Marguerite's plans to go to Paris for an operation on her haemorrhoids. Fahmy wanted her to stay and have the operation in London. At dinner Marguerite picked up a wine bottle and shouted at Fahmy, 'You shut up or I will smash this over your head.' Fahmy replied, 'If you do, I'll do the same to you.'

By the time the couple went up to their suite in the early hours the weather had finally broken – a violent thunderstorm was raging outside. Things also came to a head in suite No. 41 on the hotel's fourth floor. At 2.30 a.m. the night porter, John Beattie, was passing with some luggage. Suddenly Ali Fahmy stormed through the double doors shouting at him, 'Look at my face, look what she has done.' Madame Fahmy came behind him, gesturing at her own face. Neither seemed particularly hurt. But, as Beattie moved on round the corner three shots suddenly rang out and a woman screamed. Beattie ran back to the suite just in time to see Marguerite throwing a smoking gun to the floor. The body of Fahmy was slumped against a wall in the corridor. There was a wound to his temple and his brains were already spilling out. Beattie sent for help. When managers arrived, Marguerite

Marguerite Fahmy, who shot her husband dead in the Savoy Hotel. (© *Getty Images*)

The Savoy Hotel, London, as it is today. (© *James Moore*)

was bending over Fahmy's body, cradling his head and crying, 'Qu'est ce que j'ai fait, mon cher', or, 'What have I done my dear?' Shortly afterwards she turned to one of the stunned hotel staff who had rushed to the scene, saying, 'I've lost my head, I've shot him!' Fahmy died soon after being taken to hospital.

As shocking as the incident was, and as glamorous as the couple were, the case seemed an open and shut one. There was, at least, no doubt that Madame Fahmy had shot her husband. She was duly arrested and charged with murder. An inquest jury returned a verdict of wilful murder and she was committed for a full trial which opened at the Old Bailey on 10 September 1923.

Defence counsel Sir Edward Marshall Hall soon managed to turn the case on its head in a spectacular performance that cashed in on the casual racism of his day. Marshall Hall was the same man who had sensationally got the artist Robert Wood off a charge of murder in 1907 (see page 182). This time he managed to present Marguerite as the victim. He portrayed her as a defence-less white woman who had been treated cruelly by an 'oriental' and highlighted the 'unnatural acts' to which Marguerite had been subjected during their marriage. She had referred to these in a consultation about her haemorrhoids with the Savoy's doctor earlier in the trip. Fahmy, he said, had tried to strangle his wife on the night of his death. She had only grabbed the pistol out of self-defence. It was also claimed that Marguerite had no idea that the Browning semi-automatic pistol which she fired was actually loaded – even though it was her own. She claimed never to have fired a gun before and simply lost her mind when the pistol surprised her by going off. On 14 September, after just an hour's deliberation the jury acquitted Marguerite on the grounds of self-defence. She walked free and lived in Paris until her death in 1971.

LOCATION: *The Savoy Hotel*, Strand, London, WC2R 0EU, 020 7836 4343, www.fairmont.com

THE FOREIGN FLING THAT PROVED FATAL, 1924

The Blue Anchor Hotel, Byfleet, Surrey; The Hotel Russell, Russell Square, London

With his florid moustache, bushy beard and eccentric air, Jean-Pierre Vaquier was not the sort of exotic guest that The Blue Anchor Hotel, in the sleepy town of Byfleet, Surrey, ordinarily attracted. The flamboyant French inventor was ostensibly in the country to peddle a new sausage-making machine. Yet Vaquier's stay at The Blue Anchor would not end up enhancing its reputation as a place to stay. Instead he would stand trial for the murder of its owner. And the sordid details surrounding his crime would shock not only this leafy suburban enclave but the whole nation as a tale of adultery and skulduggery emerged.

By January 1924, the humble red-bricked Blue Anchor had a new landlord, Alfred George Poynter Jones. The 37-year-old First World War veteran had been married to his wife Mabel since 1906 and they had two children together. But the couple's union appears to have run into troubled financial and emotional waters after the war. Alfred was rather too fond of the drink he sold at the hotel. And Mabel ran a local catering business which had gone bust, leaving her facing bankruptcy and suffering from a nervous breakdown.

Mabel's doctor recommended she take a break. And, while Alfred stayed behind to mind The Blue Anchor, Mabel found herself on holiday, all alone in the glamorous resort of Biarritz in south-west France. In her vulnerable state it was perhaps no surprise when she fell for the charms of the 45-year-old Vaquier. He had been a telephonist during the 1914–18 war and was carrying out wireless demonstrations at the Hotel Victoria where she was staying. Despite the fact that he spoke no English and she spoke barely any French they appear to have begun a relationship via a translation dictionary. For Mabel, her liaison with the suave Vaquier may have been intended as nothing more than a passionate romantic interlude from the plodding pace of her life in a satellite town in Surrey, married to an alcoholic. Yet for Vaquier his love for Mabel became all-consuming.

The pair's fling was suddenly interrupted when Alfred sent a telegram saying that he was sick. Mabel began making her way home via Bordeaux and Paris. But Vaquier went with her. She arrived back in England on 8 February, and the next day her French lover followed, having told Mabel that he was planning to market his new sausage making machine in London.

At Mabel's suggestion, Vaquier stayed at the Hotel Russell in central London. Here, over the next few days, he would meet Mabel. It later emerged that a chambermaid had caught them together and told Vaquier: 'You have no business to have anyone here', to which Mabel replied: 'It is alright; I am his wife.'

On 13 February, Alfred left The Blue Anchor for a short break in Margate to recuperate from congestion of the lungs. Whether simply besotted or browbeaten into it, Mabel paid off Vaquier's bill at the Russell and invited him to stay at The Blue Anchor as her unpaying guest. He arrived on 14 February and would lodge there for the next six weeks. It's possible that by now the Joneses had some kind of arrangement when it came to their marriage, for when Mr Jones returned on 17 February he seems not to have minded Vaquier's presence. However, he was still sick and spent much of the following fortnight in bed, while Mabel and Vaquier dined together downstairs.

Yet the level of Mabel's commitment to Vaquier may also have been lost in translation. Over the course of his time as a resident, Vaquier repeatedly asked Mabel to leave her husband. She refused. Mabel even told her husband not to loan cash to the evidently hard-up Vaquier.

Then on the evening of 28 March there was a party at The Blue Anchor and, as usual, Alfred enjoyed one too many drinks and slept late on the 29th, a Saturday morning. It was 10.30 a.m. by the time he came down to open the bar and went to take his usual post-hangover pick-me-up – some bromo salt, which he kept in a blue glass bottle on a mantelpiece.

There, already sitting in the bar, was Vaquier, sipping his morning coffee and watching carefully.

Alfred measured out a teaspoonful of the salts and mixed it into a glass of water. But the moment he had taken a swig of the concoction, he cried out 'My God, that's bitter.' Mabel grabbed the bottle and, putting some of the salts to her lips, realised something was badly wrong, saying to Alfred, 'Daddy, they have been tampered with.' She gave him some warm salt water but by now Alfred was doubled up with pain. He was being sick and complaining of feeling numb and cold. Putting the bottle in a drawer in the kitchen for safety, Mabel then got some of the staff to help carry Alfred upstairs to bed before calling a doctor.

A Dr Carle arrived but Alfred's eyes were already bulging and he was racked with convulsions. There was little he could do. Half an hour after taking the mixture, Alfred was dead from asphyxiation, the usual result of strychnine poisoning. The doctor spotted the symptoms and asked to inspect the bottle containing the salts. But when he came to inspect it the bottle had evidently been washed out and dried by someone. However, Dr Carle was able to recover some of the salts that had fallen onto the bar room floor. He was later able to establish that these contained strychnine crystals. The bitter poison causes a quick, but horrible death.

Along with the rest of those at The Blue Anchor, Vaquier was questioned the same night and made several statements to the police. He was not immediately arrested, but a few days later, on the recommendation of the police, he moved to stay in The Railway Hotel in Woking. Mabel was now convinced that Vaquier was responsible for the killing and any sentimental feelings she'd held for him had disappeared. As he left, she accused him, saying: 'You have assassinated Mr Jones!' He, Mabel later claimed in court, replied: 'Yes Mabs, I did it for you!' to which she responded, 'I would have killed *you* if I knew you would have done a thing like that.' By now the case was national news and Vaquier's vanity got the better of him as he happily gave interviews to reporters and posed for pictures.

One of those who saw photograph in a newspaper was a chemist called Horace Bland. Bland remembered that a month before the murder, on 1 March, the same man had called at his shop in Southampton Row in central London to buy strychnine, purchasing enough to kill three or four people. He had signed the poison register under a false name – J Vanker. Yet he had given the correct address of the place he was staying – The Blue Anchor in Byfleet. Bland contacted the police and Vaquier was arrested on 19 April.

The Blue Anchor Hotel in Byfleet, Surrey, where Jean-Pierre Vaquier poisoned the landlord. (© *James Moore*)

Alfred Jones' body was subsequently exhumed and a post-mortem by the famous pathologist Sir Bernard Spilsbury confirmed that he had been killed by strychnine poisoning.

Vaquier's five-day trial opened on 2 July at the Guildford Assizes and he pleaded not guilty. He seems to have almost enjoyed being the centre of attention, perfuming his hair and beard every day of the proceedings and appearing immaculately dressed. Vaquier even entertained the court through an interpreter with a number of witticisms. When one witness was described as a builder and an undertaker, he said, 'Ah I see he houses them above and below ground.'

His defence, however, was less clever. Vaquier had originally told the pharmacist that he needed strychnine for his wireless experiments. But he then changed his story in court, saying that Mr Jones' solicitor had asked him to buy it so he could kill a dog.

After two hours of deliberation the jury returned. Vaquier was confidently smiling and clearly expected to be acquitted. When the guilty verdict was given he turned ashen. He pounded the dock with his fists and told the judge, Justice Avory, that he swore his innocence on his mother and father's grave.

While awaiting his death sentence Vaquier offered up new evidence, saying that he had discovered that there was a separate stash of strychnine kept behind a loose brick in a shed behind The Blue Anchor and that someone else might have used this to kill Jones. The Court of Criminal Appeal did not find this new evidence convincing, especially since Vaquier seems to have supressed it at his earlier trial. He went to the gallows at Wandsworth Prison on 12 August 1924. His last words are said to have been, 'Vive La France!'

LOCATIONS: *The Blue Anchor*, No. 155 High Road, Byfleet, Surrey, KT14 7RL, 01932 34630, www.the-blue-anchor.co.uk; *The Hotel Russell*, Nos 1–8 Russell Square, London, WC1B 5BE, www.hotelrusselllondon.co.uk

THE COBWEBS THAT CAUGHT A KILLER, 1927

The Lantern Pike, Little Hayfield, Derbyshire

Dubbed by newspapers at the time as the 'lonely inn murder', it was a crime that seemed as grisly and unpredictable as the weather that often gripped the isolated valley in which it took place. And the killing was all the more shocking because it occurred on Armistice Day, a time when the rest of the nation was marking the coming of peace at the end of the First World War, still fresh in the memory.

In 1927 The Lantern Pike, named after the glowering peak that towers over it, was known as the New Inn, though the eighteenth-century stone-built pub had been providing welcome sanctuary on a remote road through the fells of the Peak District for decades. It was a cosy, hospitable place serving a handful of locals from the tiny village of Little Hayfield and the odd soul passing through. The inn was run by a popular couple, Amy and Arthur Collinson, but much of the day-to-day running of the place was left to Amy, as Arthur also had another job sandpapering furniture which saw him set off on his motorbike early each morning for the nearby town of Glossop.

Returning at around 6 p.m. on 11 November, Arthur found a disappointed regular, Amos Dawson, on the doorstep, complaining that he had come in search of a pint on several occasions that day but found the place apparently shut up. Arthur let himself into the pub and made a horrific discovery: Amy was lying on the floor in the property's sitting room, surrounded by a pool of blood. Her throat had been cut from ear to ear. The scene was made even more gruesome by the fact that a white-handled carving knife was still sticking out of the wound. A cash box kept upstairs and containing change for the bar was light by around £40. This was apparently the only thing missing and the property had not been ransacked.

A policeman and a doctor were on the scene within twenty minutes, with Dr Lynch estimating the time of death as having occurred between 10 a.m. and noon. When senior officers arrived, they soon realised that they were dealing with a murder, which the perpetrator had clumsily endeavoured to disguise as a suicide. It was concluded that there was no way that Amy could have cut her own throat and left the knife in the wound. Plus marks on the head indicated that Amy had been bludgeoned with a blunt instrument, rendering her unconscious, before the knife had been used to finish her off.

Other clues gave rise to the belief that this was a murder. There was a second pool of blood near the fireplace – signalling that Amy's body had been moved so it could not be seen from the windows. Amy appeared to have been attacked whilst cleaning the fireplace, her attacker approaching from behind, giving her no time to defend herself. Yet there was no obvious clue to the killer. And though the knife was still present there was no sign of the weapon that had been used to hit Amy over the head.

Officers interviewed all the local drinkers and suspicion fell on one of them, George Frederick Walter Hayward, known as Jerry. Hayward was a desperate character. Aged 32, he had recently lost his job as a travelling soap salesman and was £70 in debt to his former employer. He owed money on the rent for his cottage, the White House, which he shared with his wife, Annie, located just half a mile from the New Inn. He was also in arrears on payments for furniture bought on hire purchase.

The lonely Lantern Pike Inn, Derbyshire, where the landlord discovered the bludgeoned body of his wife. (*Courtesy The Lantern Pike Inn*)

Described as a 'small wiry figure with keen piercing eyes', Hayward was friendly with the Collinsons. He knew that a float was kept at the inn and roughly where it was. But he was not alone in that. Any drinker sitting at the bar could easily surmise where it was from the telltale footsteps in the bedroom above every time one of the Collinsons went to get change.

Hayward clearly had a financial motive for stealing this money. But was he desperate enough to murder a friend for what was inevitably going to be a relatively small sum?

On the day of the murder he had told his wife he was going up to the nearby town of New Mills to collect his dole from the Labour Exchange. He had left at 10.05 a.m. and had been seen on the way by local Tommy Barr. By 10.45 a.m. Hayward had been seen at a nearby bus stop where witnesses confirmed he had caught the bus to New Mills Labour Exchange and duly collected his unemployment benefit. It was also known that he had gone on to Manchester where he paid off some of the money on his furniture and bought his wife a new pair of gloves.

This only gave him around fifteen minutes to have gone to the New Inn, kill Amy and make off with the cash. No one had seen him. Amy had been seen alive at 9.45 a.m. by a council road worker. Interviewed the same evening as the murder, Hayward admitted having gone to the New Inn on the morning of the 11th. He said he'd found the door ajar and stayed just ten minutes to buy some cigarettes but left Amy very much alive.

The police were unconvinced. The following day, they searched the pub looking for the weapon that had been used to hit Amy. For eight hours they found nothing. Then, at 1.15 p.m., one of the officers searching the outer kitchen found a disused toilet cistern that was covered in cobwebs. But what caught his eye was that in one place the webs had been broken. On further investigation a piece of bloodied lead piping was found at the bottom of the cistern.

Meanwhile a search was also made of Hayward's house. They noticed that a piece of lead waste pipe from the kitchen sink was missing. When the two ends of the pipe were compared they were found to match. They had found the weapon used to batter Amy to death. A bag of money, containing about £30, was also hidden up the chimney flue of the cottage. Hayward insisted he was innocent, telling detectives, 'I have not murdered the woman. You can examine my clothing if you like.'

The police duly took his clothes but already believed they had enough evidence to arrest him, which they did at 11.30 p.m. on the 12th. Blood was found on Hayward's tie and shirt. He claimed he had cut himself shaving, even producing an unwashed towel with his own blood on it. There was too little blood to match the samples to Amy's. But there were also bloodstains on Hayward's hat – blood was unlikely to fly upwards if it really had been caused by shaving. Then a 13-year-old witness, Maud Lilian McBain, came forward to say she had seen Hayward tinkering with a length of lead pipe outside his home on 5 November.

Five days after the murder, Amy's coffin was carried out of the pub as the local community gathered to pay their respects. The crowd simmered with anger. Most were already convinced that Jerry Hayward was responsible, but incredulous that one of their own could carry out such a pre-meditated and barbaric act virtually on his own doorstep.

Hayward was brought in front of Derby Assizes in February 1928 and pleaded not guilty.

On the first day of the trial there was more drama when one of the jurors collapsed as a Dr Lynch was describing Amy's injuries. A new juror had to be found and the whole trial had to be started again.

A fuller picture emerged of what had happened. Hayward had found Amy cleaning the living room floor and bashed her head in before moving the body behind a cupboard. He had then gone to the dresser in the kitchen to get a knife and make it look like suicide. Going upstairs to the trunk in the bedroom where the cash was kept, he had only taken £40 from the box, leaving £10 behind, possibly in the hope that police would think Amy had done away with herself because the books wouldn't balance.

And though the amount may not seem like much in today's terms, it was equivalent to a year's dole money back then. Hayward, who had been used to making £200 a year, clearly found being so hard up so impossible to bear that he had committed murder, not to get rich but simply in a bid to clear his debts.

The jury, who rejected the defence counsel's argument that he had not had time to kill Amy and find the money, took just half an hour to convict Hayward. The voice of Justice Hawke, conducting his first murder trial, was said to have wavered as he pronounced the death penalty. Hayward was hanged in March 1928 in Nottingham, by Albert Pierrepoint.

LOCATION: *The Lantern Pike Inn*, No. 45 Glossop Road, Little Hayfield, High Peak, Derbyshire, SK22 2NG, 01663 747590, www.lanternpikeinn.co.uk

Honeymoon Horror in the Lake District, 1928

Borrowdale Gates Hotel, Grange, near Keswick, Cumbria
Nestled in a beautiful Cumbrian valley, surrounded by majestic mountains, the comfortable Borrowdale Gates Hotel, built in 1860, is the perfect base for a romantic holiday. Yet in the 1920s it was at the centre of a murder investigation after a pretty, young Chinese woman was found strangled at a local beauty spot.

On Monday 18 June 1928 Chung Yi Miao, a handsome 28-year-old Chinese law student who had been living in America, arrived at the Borrowdale Gates with his new, wealthy wife, Wai Sheung Siu. She was a 28-year-old art dealer and hailed from a well-to-do family in China. The pair had met at a dragon dance in New York in October 1927 and married the following May. Afterwards, they had travelled across the Atlantic for a two-month honeymoon tour of Europe, intending then to go on to China to visit their families. Included on the couple's itinerary were stops in Glasgow and Edinburgh before a sojourn to the magnificent Lake District.

The day after the couple checked in, at around lunchtime, they left the hotel to go for a walk. A maid, Dorothy Holliday, saw them walking off into the countryside arm in arm. They seemed to be very much in love. Wai Sheung Siu was wearing a fur coat while Chung wore a blue overcoat and was carrying a camera. At approximately 4.30 p.m. Chung arrived back at the hotel alone. He seemed unruffled and told staff that, on a whim, his wife had decided to go on a shopping trip to the nearby town of Keswick to buy some warmer underwear.

At 7.30 p.m. that evening, a local farmer, Thomas Wilson, was walking through Cumma Catta woods not far from the hotel when he came across a woman wearing a fur coat lying by a rocky knoll above a popular bathing spot on the river. While he thought it strange, Wilson did not examine the woman closely as he thought she was sleeping. But when he got to the village of Grange-in-Borrowdale he happened to mention what he had seen to a local off duty policeman, William Pendlebury. By 8.45 p.m. Pendlebury and another local man had gone back down the footpath to investigate and discovered that the woman was, in fact, dead. She was lying on her back, partly under an open parasol. Her legs were apart with her knees drawn up. Pendlebury alerted senior detectives who raced to the scene.

They determined that the woman had been strangled. A chord had been wound four times around her neck and had cut 'deep into the flesh'. Next to the body lay a left-hand glove which was inside out. From marks on her hand, it was clear that a ring or rings had been wrenched from it, suggesting that she had been robbed. She was, however, still wearing an expensive watch. Her skirts were lifted above her waist and her underwear was awry.

The Borrowdale Gates Hotel, where the Chinese couple Chung Yi Miao and Wai Sheung Sui stayed. (*Courtesy of The Borrowdale Gates Hotel*)

Could she also have been the victim of a sexual assault? It was certainly clear she had been murdered. An examining doctor estimated the time of death as about mid-afternoon.

Meanwhile, at the hotel, Chung had taken tea alone in the hotel dining room. The maid reported that when she took some hot water to his room at 6 p.m. he observed, 'My wife has not returned. She said she would be back by six?' An hour later, Chung took dinner at the hotel on his own. A little later he spoke to the owner of the hotel, Mrs Crossley, saying he was worried about his wife and asked her to ring around shops in Keswick. Mrs Crossley told him that the shops were now closed but that she would go and meet the 9 p.m. bus to see if Wai Sheung was on it. Oddly, Chung suggested that she would probably come by private car. Mrs Crossley went to wait for the bus anyway – but Wai Sheung wasn't on it and she reported her guest as missing to the police.

Officers now had a probable identity for the woman they had found. They arrived at the hotel to find Chung comfortably tucked up in bed, which they thought suspicious given that his wife seemed to have gone missing. They told him that Wai Sheung was dead and took him to the police station for questioning. Meanwhile the couple's room was searched. Police found a locked jewel case – the key to it was discovered in Chung's bag, which police also found suspicious. Opening the box they found £3,500 of jewels belonging to his wife. Two of Wai Sheung's diamond rings – which she had been seen wearing earlier that day by a guest at the hotel – were found hidden, wrapped in two rolls of undeveloped camera film. Chung told police that his wife had placed them there for safety. The cord which had been found around Wai Sheung's neck was found to be similar to that used for the blinds in the hotel.

During questioning Chung behaved strangely. He seemed particularly keen to know from police officers whether his wife had knickers on when she was found. He also blurted out something like, 'It's terrible, my wife, assaulted, robbed, murdered.' Yet the police had yet to inform him of the exact circumstances in which they had found Wai Sheung's body or even the possibility that she had been robbed or assaulted.

Chung was charged with murder, appearing at Carlisle Assizes on 22 October for a three-day trial where he pleaded not guilty. The evidence was actually pretty circumstantial – there was no forensic evidence to link him to the body and no one had seen the crime take place. The defence claimed that Wai Sheung had, in fact, been attacked by a gang of Chinese jewel thieves. This was based on Chung's claim that the couple had been followed by two shady-looking characters during their honeymoon. The scenario seemed far-fetched, yet several witnesses did end up testifying to seeing two other Chinese men in the area (a somewhat rare sight in the 1920s) at the same time. One claimed to have seen them leaving by train the morning after the murder. Chung's defence counsel also said that the apparently incriminating phrases he had uttered to police had simply been misunderstood. Chung's command of English was not nearly as good as his wife's. None of this was believed by the jury. After ninety minutes they declared him guilty.

In November, Chung launched an appeal but it was promptly dismissed. The presiding judge said, 'It is impossible to say that there is not ample evidence to find that this appellant committed this crime.' Chung was dragged away still maintaining his innocence.

He was hanged by Thomas Pierrepoint at Strangeways prison in Manchester on 6 December 1928.

On the face of the matter it seems clear that Chung was the murderer. But what seems puzzling about the case is what motive he could have had for killing his wife. The prosecution case was that he had done it for money. There is evidence that he wasn't as well off as he immediately appeared but it seems unlikely that he should murder his own wife simply to get his hands on her £4,000. He could have easily lived off her savings.

Other theories were put forward. One suggested that he had done it because he had discovered that his wife couldn't have children and that if he didn't have an issue he would be cursed. Chung was supposed to have admitted as much in his cell before going to the gallows. Another possibility was that Chung had sexually assaulted his wife because she had refused him sex. Wai Sheung had recently undergone a gynaecological operation. Yet there was no actual evidence of rape. There was even talk that Chung had another wife back in China and that he killed Wai Sheung because his bigamy was about to be discovered. If Chung was guilty it was certainly a badly botched crime given his level of education. Perhaps he merely regretted marrying his wife after discovering that she couldn't gratify him sexually and was desperately trying to find a way out of the union.

In a sad postscript to the sorry affair, Chung's personal effects were auctioned in Keswick in February 1929. Madame Tussauds, the waxwork museum, was among the bidders. Today, at the Borrowdale Gates Hotel one of the bedrooms has been decorated with a Chinese theme in memory of the victim, Wai Sheung Siu.

LOCATION: **Borrowdale Gates Hotel**, Grange-in-Borrowdale, Keswick, Cumbria, CA12 5UQ, 0845 833 2524, www.borrowdale-gates.com

SHOT IN THE BACK BY A HOMEMADE BULLET, 1934

The Edisford Bridge Hotel & Red Pump Inn, near Clitheroe, Lancashire
Ordering a glass of gin, farmer Jim Dawson sat down to relax in the Edisford Bridge Hotel, near Clitheroe, a haven from the howling wind and rain which lashed down outside. It was 7.15 p.m. on Sunday, 18 March 1934 and Jim had left his home at Bashall Hall Farm around fifteen minutes earlier, taking a short cut across a field to get to his favourite pub. Inside it was business as usual. Jim, who was described as a 'quiet, inoffensive,

sober man', chatted to the pub's landlord, Jack Barnes, and struck up a friendly conversation about farming and football with an acquaintance called Matthew Hughes. He also bought another man in the pub, James Parkinson, a drink. Jim had a couple of pints of beer, and at 9 p.m., after a relaxed, cordial evening, he put on his bowler hat and overcoat. He bought a box of matches and left the Edisford Bridge to make his way home along the dark country roads. What happened next must be considered one of Britain's strangest crimes.

As Jim was walking along the road two cars passed him. In the headlights he saw the figure of a mysterious man silhouetted by a gateway but couldn't make out who it was. By the time he got to the gate the man had gone. Jim carried on and turned into the lonely lane that led to Bashall Hall farm. He walked along this for about 25yds when he heard a faint click. A moment later he felt a sharp pain in his back, which quickly went off, possibly thanks to the effects of the alcohol he had imbibed. Jim assumed that someone had thrown a stone at him as a joke. Shrugging off the incident he carried on home. Arriving at 9.20 p.m., he sat down to a hearty late supper of roast pork and apple sauce prepared by his sister Polly Pickles. Jim then took himself to bed.

The 46-year-old had a restless night but it was only the next morning that he realised something was badly wrong when he woke up in a pool of blood. There was a hole in his right shoulder blade. A veteran of the First World War, Jim was both tough and proud. He was reluctant to make a fuss and it was some time before he was persuaded that a doctor had to be called. The local GP sent Jim for an X-ray which revealed that there was an object buried deep in his body, just below the liver – about the shape of a small bird's egg. A surgeon extracted the object and it turned out to be a short piece of steel rod, around half an inch in diameter, which had been filed at each end. Jim, it was clear, had been shot, but with a homemade bullet which had been fired from no ordinary gun. Sadly, four days later, on Thursday 22 March, Jim died of blood poisoning in a Blackburn nursing home.

The police now had a murder enquiry on their hands. But in the days and months that followed Jim's death detectives were left baffled as they failed to identify any motive for the crime. Despite

The Edisford Bridge Hotel as it is today. Jim Dawson was shot on his way home from the pub. (*Courtesy of the Edisford Bridge Hotel*)

conducting scores of interviews locally, the police were hampered by a community apparently reluctant to always tell everything they knew. Superintendent Wilf Blacker, who was in charge of the investigation, complained, 'It was like talking to a brick wall.' Hedgerows, woods and fields were thoroughly searched and guns from across the district were called in, but no obvious murder weapon could be found. At the inquest into Jim's death it was suggested that the bullet could have been fired from a catapult, possibly by a youth as a misguided joke, but there was no suggestion as to who might have fired it or where it might now be. It seemed a woolly theory. However, as witnesses testified, no one appeared to have a particular grudge against Dawson and a policeman who had known him for three years testified that he hadn't a single enemy. An open verdict was recorded by the coroner.

Some say that Jim actually knew who had shot him and was keeping quiet, perhaps because it related to a relationship he may have been having with a woman in Clitheroe. The fact that he talked of someone having a 'joke' at his expense smacks of someone who knew that he had riled somebody local. Did Jim really not have any enemies? In such a close knit, but often tight-lipped community there may have been issues lurking in the background that the undemonstrative farmer kept to himself. Jim's reluctance to have medical help also seems strange – was he afraid that an embarrassing story would come out? Did he plan to take his own revenge on the person responsible? Did the person who fired the shot really intend to kill him, or was it just a warning? They must have been aware that, using such a crude weapon, Jim was actually quite likely to survive. And only one shot seems to have been fired.

Intriguingly, a neighbouring farmer, Tommy Simpson, killed himself ten days after Jim died. It's possible that, in the darkness, the bullet had not been meant for Jim at all and that one of his farmhands, Tommy Kenyon, was the intended target. He had been inside one of the cars that passed Jim on the night of the murder, heading into Clitheroe for a drink after supping at The Red Pump in Bashall Eaves, a pub that, intriguingly, Dawson avoided after an altercation three years previously. Simpson, it was said, suspected Kenyon of making his 17-year-old daughter Nancy pregnant. Others said that Simpson had committed suicide for more personal reasons and that, however coincidental, there was no link.

The death of Jim Dawson remains unsolved and a frustrating mystery to this day. No murder weapon was ever found. A recent book by Jim's great niece, Jennifer Lee Cobban, turned up a tale about an unusual gun found years later in a barn next to the Edisford Bridge Hotel. Some have suggested that Jim was shot with a type of airgun used by poachers or even an adapted walking stick. There also been talk of possible deathbed confessions among the local farming community. However, to this date, no definite culprit has been identified, leading to wild talk that supernatural forces may even have been at work.

LOCATION: *The Edisford Bridge Hotel*, Edisford Bridge, Clitheroe, Lancashire, BB7 3LJ, 01200 422 637; *The Red Pump Inn*, Clitheroe Road, Bashall Eaves, Clitheroe, Lancashire, BB7 3DA, 01254 826227, www.theredpumpinn.co.uk

A CHILD MURDERER, DUBBED THE 'MAD PARSON', 1937

The Lamb Inn, Burford, Oxfordshire

The beautiful town of Burford in Oxfordshire is built of mellow Cotswold stone, and The Lamb, tucked away on Sheep Street, is the quintessential English inn. It is a place where everything seems right with the world. Yet in the summer of 1937, the mind of John Edward Allen, an assistant chef at The Lamb, was seriously troubled. On Saturday 19 June, 25-year-old Allen had gone to the home of a fellow employee, waiter Frederick Woodward, with whom he was friendly. Allen had been to the house at Fulbrook, just to the north of the town, a number of times before. On this occasion he arrived at around 4.30 p.m., telling Mrs Kathleen Anne Woodward that her husband had asked him to take their 17-month-old baby out for 'an airing'. Taking the child in his arms, Allen rode off with her on his bicycle, promising to have her back for teatime. When they didn't return after two hours Mrs Woodward raised the alarm.

At around 10 p.m. that evening, the body of little Kathleen Diana Lucy Woodward was found by two boys lying in grass by the roadside about 50yds from her home. She had been strangled with a piece of clothes line taken from The Lamb which had been tied twice round her neck. Diana, as she was known, was still clutching the two pennies her mother had given her. There was no sign of any indecent assault. Allen had disappeared and a nationwide manhunt for him was launched. He was described as being 5ft 10in, of a fair complexion, with brown eyes and dark brown hair as well as 'noticeably white teeth'.

Two days after the crime, on 21 June, Allen turned up in London's Elephant and Castle. He calmly walked up to a traffic policeman, telling the surprised officer that he was the man who was wanted 'for the job in Oxford' and was soon charged with murder.

At his trial that October at the Oxford Assizes, Allen admitted that he had been in a mental institution twice in the past. But he maintained that it was Mrs Woodward, not he, who had killed the girl. Allen claimed that he and the mother were in

The Lamb Inn, Burford, where child murderer John Edward Allen worked. (*Courtesy of The Lamb Inn*)

love and that when he had arrived at the house the toddler was already dead, with a rope around its neck. He declared that Mrs Woodward had said to him, 'I did it for you' and that she wanted to run away with him. Allen then said he offered to take the blame for the killing, pointing out that since he had experienced mental problems he would probably get away with it. An outraged Mrs Woodward – her grief now compounded by allegations that she was both an adulterer and a murderess – strenuously denied the allegations.

Fortunately, the jury was not persuaded by Allen's story. And, on 21 October, they found him guilty. However, they recommended that enquiries be made into Allen's mental state. The judge, Mr Justice Finlay, pronounced the death sentence on Allen but said that he would write to the Home Secretary recommending that a psychiatric assessment be undertaken. That November, Allen was duly committed to Broadmoor, a high security criminal asylum in Berkshire.

Nothing more was heard of Allen publicly for another ten years and staff at Broadmoor found him a model prisoner. Then, on the night of Sunday, 20 July 1947, Allen sensationally escaped from Broadmoor by scaling a 16ft security wall. Police searching for him said that he was disguised as a clergyman and had taken with him a bible and money from the asylum canteen. It turned out that Allen had assembled his outfit by playing a vicar in a theatrical performance inside the asylum. In the following days, as he remained at large, newspapers soon dubbed Allen the 'mad parson'.

Few inmates ever escaped from Broadmoor and those who did were usually caught quickly. However, despite many sightings, Allen remained on the loose for the next two years, using a variety of aliases – including George Radcliffe and Michael James – a remarkable feat for a man who had been decreed mentally unstable. His staring eyes were said to be striking but Allen, originally from County Durham, repeatedly gave police searching for him the slip.

In August 1947 he was spotted working as a waiter at the Nansidwell Hotel near Falmouth in Cornwall, but when police arrived to arrest him he had disappeared. In early 1948 Scotland Yard received a letter from Allen saying, 'Ah, catch me if you can.' They didn't. Later that year he wrote another letter in which he claimed to have left notes in the waxwork model of serial killer Neville Heath at London's Madame Tussaud's. Police who searched all the models at the attraction failed to turn up anything.

It was only in May 1949 that police made a breakthrough when they found a man calling himself Kenneth Wallace living in London, just 200yds from a police station. He had been working at a bakery in the capital but his employer had become suspicious that he might be Allen. Using fingerprint records, detectives confirmed that Wallace was indeed Allen and he was taken back to Broadmoor. Yet Allen only remained there for another two years. He said that he had originally escaped and stayed on the run for so long in order to prove he was, in fact, sane. His skill at managing to outwit the police while holding down responsible jobs, not to mention securing ration books and other identity papers, could not be doubted.

In 1951 the authorities decided that the 39-year-old was indeed cured. He was released that September amid some controversy.

Allen went on to write a cogent book, *Inside Broadmoor*, about his time in the asylum, which was published in 1952. But was he really cured? In October 1953 police were again hunting Allen who had gone missing from his lodgings in Newcastle where he'd been working in a bakery. This time he was soon caught. In November that year he was tried at the Old Bailey and found guilty of obtaining money by forging Post Office saving books. Allen was sentenced to thirty months behind bars in an ordinary prison.

LOCATION: *The Lamb Inn*, Sheep Street, Burford, Oxon, OX18 4LR, 01993 823 155, www.cotswold-inns-hotels.co.uk

THE 'PERFECT CRIME' ON THE EVE OF WAR, 1939

White Hart, Flitton, Bedfordshire

In the spring of 1939, just as Britons were about to have their world turned upside down by the outbreak of the Second World War, the peace of a small village in Bedfordshire had already been shattered by the bloody murder of a much-loved farmworker. Flitton was, at the time, a sleepy village near Luton and home to just 500 people. The gabled White Hart was at its centre and the softly spoken George Stapleton had often enjoyed a quiet pint and a game of dominoes at the pub. It was at the White Hart that two Scotland Yard detectives set up their headquarters when Bedfordshire Police found themselves at a loss to explain why 66-year-old George had been viciously beaten around the head and left for dead whilst walking along a quiet country footpath.

At 12.30 p.m. on the afternoon of Saturday 22 April, grey-haired George, a man described as having no enemies, had left work at Ruxox Farm with his 34*s* in wages, taking the path across the fields back to Flitton and the cottage where he lived. It was a route he had trodden pretty much every day for two years. At about 12.55 p.m., walking close to the hedgerows, he got to a place called Cuckoo Corner when he was attacked from behind.

George was almost completely deaf and would not have heard his attacker coming.

The man George shared his cottage with, another bachelor called George Stanley, knew his namesake would be home soon and had a meal waiting for him. By 5 p.m. when his friend had failed to return, George raised the alarm at the White Hart, and the landlord, Harold Kingham, went with him to conduct a search.

They set off down the path via which they knew George would be making his way home. After crossing three fields they came across George's pipe. Then, a couple of yards away they found his brown cloth cap. In a ditch 6yds from the path they found George. He was lying in in a foot of water, groaning. Sadly, by the time a doctor made it to the scene, he was dead.

When police arrived they recovered a bloodied fence post from the scene as well as samples of wool from a cheap jacket that was found on barbed wire nearby. There was also a mysterious pile of old clothes. The ground was hard from a lack of rain and there were no footprints, though marks on the grass indicated George had been dragged to the ditch. While George's pay packet was gone, his watch chain was still about his person and 10s and 3d remained in his pockets. A post-mortem found that George had been hit over the back of the head six times and that one of these blows had fractured his skull.

County police quickly called in the experienced Scotland Yard to investigate the murder. Chief Inspector William Salisbury and Sergeant C. MacDougall began working on the basis that the culprit must have been local – and with good reason. George had been murdered on a quiet country path. His killer had surely lain in wait for him there in the bushes, knowing that he was likely to pass by at that time and that he wouldn't be seen. Salisbury also discovered that there was a rumour in the village that George didn't trust banks and was thought to carry a large amount of cash on his person. A local person would have known this and also that George was profoundly deaf and so wouldn't hear them coming if they attacked from behind at the secluded spot.

But there were some puzzling questions. If the motive was robbery, then why had the killer not taken everything? At one point the focus fell on local youths, with one quizzed for three hours by police. The idea was even put forward that George might have come across some boys bird-nesting who turned on him. This didn't really account for the frenzied nature of the attack, which police themselves described as 'maniacal'. With the focus still on a local killer, clergy in the district made appeals from the pulpit urging people to come forward if they knew anything. However, despite taking 250 statements, interviewing 600 people and dredging the local stream, police were left without a suspect. A man working on the other side of a hedge nearby at the time of the murder had heard nothing. Before long, the newspapers of the time were calling George's murder 'the perfect crime'.

On Wednesday 20 June 1939, with no further leads, an inquest at Ampthill recorded a verdict of murder by some person or persons unknown. In the ensuing months, the whirlwind of war seems to have seen George's case placed on the back-burner. It has never been solved. In the end it was assumed that the murder was the work of a tramp who had somehow come to know that poor George, a man who locals said wouldn't hurt a mouse, had money on him. However, it was also an intriguing fact that on the same day as he was killed there was a fair taking place at Greenfields, a neighbouring village, meaning that there may well have been strangers in the vicinity after all.

LOCATION: **The White Hart**, Brook Lane, Flitton, Beds, MK45 5EJ, 01525 862022, www.whitehartflitton.co.uk

A SUICIDE AT THE ADELPHI AND THE WHITE MISCHIEF MYSTERY, 1942

The Adelphi Hotel, Liverpool
There was a chill in the air as Sir 'Jock' Delves Broughton checked into the grand Adelphi Hotel in Liverpool on Wednesday 2 December 1942. He gave staff strict instructions that he was not to be disturbed and retired to his room. Some forty-eight hours later, the hotel's housekeeper found him in a coma, bleeding from the nose and ears. Delves Broughton had injected himself four-teen times with morphine and died in hospital shortly afterwards.

His suicide was a sorry chapter in an unsolved murder mystery which continues to be the subject of heated debate to this day. The case was the inspiration for a 1987 film, *White Mischief*, starring Greta Scacchi and Charles Dance.

The scene of the murder couldn't have been more different from the spot where Delves Broughton took his own life in a Blitz-ravaged city. It occurred in 1941, thousands of miles away in sun-drenched Kenya, and saw the philandering Josslyn Hay, the 22nd Earl of Erroll, shockingly shot to death.

Delves Broughton had married his second – and much younger – wife, Diana, in 1940. Then, at the height of the Second World War, the pair had moved to Kenya where they became part of the so-called Happy Valley colonial expatriate set, a hotbed of adultery and excess. Delves Broughton appeared not to mind greatly when the beautiful 26-year-old Diana openly began an affair with Erroll within months of arriving in Africa.

Then, at 3 a.m. on 24 January 1941, the 39-year-old earl was found dead in his Buick car at a deserted crossroads near Nairobi in the middle of the night. He had been shot at close range, the single bullet which killed him entering behind his left ear. Suicide was discounted as there was no gun at the scene. Erroll's body had been stuffed into the footwell of the car and there were some mysterious white marks on the back seat of the vehicle.

By that March, Delves Broughton had been arrested for the murder. Although he appeared to have every motive for wanting Erroll dead, Delves Broughton and Diana had actually dined with the earl on the evening of 23 January at the Muthaiga Country Club. When Erroll and Diana decided to go on to a nightclub, Broughton had apparently wished them 'every happiness' and simply told Erroll to have his wife back by 3 a.m. Erroll duly dropped Diana off at home at 2.30 a.m.

The ensuing trial, which began in May, became a sensation, temporarily elbowing aside war headlines in the papers back in Britain. But the evidence submitted against Delves Broughton at his trial was weak, despite the fact that he had no concrete alibi for where he had been at the time of the murder. Erroll had been shot with a .32 Colt revolver. Delves Broughton was known to have owned a similar gun but claimed that it had been stolen a few days before the murder. Police believed he had faked the theft in order to cover his tracks. But when it came to the forensic evidence, it transpired that Delves Broughton's pistol was apparently a six groove Colt while Erroll had been killed by a bullet with five grooves.

On 1 July, in the absence of the murder weapon itself, Delves Broughton was acquitted. Despite this he was shunned by the upper crust set that had once welcomed him with open arms, and a year later Delves Broughton snuck back into Britain a broken man. Diana, meanwhile, chose to stay in Kenya, having already taken up with another man.

By late 1942 Delves Broughton was suffering with depression. He was also being investigated by the police again, this time over insurance fraud. And when he took the decision to kill himself at the Adelphi – once described as Britain's most luxurious hotel outside London – he almost certainly took the secrets of what really happened in Kenya to the grave.

While the hotel has hosted figures such as Winston Churchill, Frank Sinatra and Judy Garland during its illustrious history, Delves Broughton was not a guest to boast about. Yet some said that the hapless aristocrat was indeed innocent. He was said to have been blind drunk on the night of the murder and had to be helped to bed. The prosecution's contention that the 57-year-old, who suffered from a bad leg and night blindness, had climbed down a drainpipe from his bedroom and walked 2 miles to the murder scene to kill Erroll was also branded implausible.

One theory had it that Diana herself had killed Erroll when he had actually tried to end their relationship. Another view was that he had been gunned down by a jealous former lover, of which there were many, the prime candidate being a woman called Alice de Janze who killed herself not long after the episode. A wilder theory posited that Erroll had been the victim of a secret service assassination because of his links with Oswald Moseley's fascists back in Britain.

Yet it seems most likely that Delves Broughton was indeed responsible for Erroll's murder. Juanita Carberry, a 15-year-old schoolgirl at the time, stated that he had even confessed to her a few days after the killing. She also claimed that she saw a pair of white plimsolls, like the ones linked to white scuff marks found in the back of Erroll's car, burning at Delves Broughton's home. In 2007 author Christine Nicholls even claimed to have discovered the identity of a driver who picked Delves Broughton up after the shooting. She put forward the idea that an incensed Delves Broughton, wearing a pair of white plimsolls, had sneaked into the back seat of Erroll's car while the earl was saying goodbye to Diana at his home on the fateful night. He had then shot him, before being picked up at a pre-arranged location by an unwitting friend.

LOCATION: *The Britannia Adelphi Hotel*, Ranelagh Street, Liverpool, Merseyside, L3 5UL, 0871 222 0029, www.britanniahotels.com

DARK DEEDS IN A HOTEL'S SUMMERHOUSE, 1943

Housel Bay Hotel, The Lizard, Cornwall

The site of the Housel Bay Hotel, which opened in 1894, was chosen because of its 'beauty of situation and salubrity of climate'. Its directors believed that the stunning location, above the cliffs on the rugged Lizard peninsula, could not be surpassed in all England. The site, at Britain's most southerly point, is certainly breathtaking. Yet even this remote eyrie could not avoid the shadow cast by a global conflict. During the Second World War it was taken over at first by the army and later the RAF.

The Housel Bay was surely one of the best places in the country to be billeted. In the summer of 1943 a new local air station commander, Flying Officer William James Croft, 32, from Bath, arrived. He, along with many of the men and women staying at the luxurious hotel, enjoyed the odd bathing party on one of the nearby beaches. It was at one of these that the married father of two met Corporal Joan Norah Lewis, 27, from Porthcawl, South Wales. She was a member of the Women's Auxiliary Air Force radar plotting team who were stationed nearby. Soon the pair fell madly in love, but their affair did not stay secret for long. Racked with guilt over the relationship, Croft revealed what had been going on to Freda Catlin, the officer in charge of the WAAFs. She told him that the liaison should end immediately. Reluctantly Croft agreed and arrangements were soon made for Joan to be posted to another station in Devon. Yet Croft, who had been married for thirteen years and had two daughters, was tormented by the idea of Joan's departure. In one of several letters to her he wrote, 'The thought of some other male sharing your company drives me to distraction.' She, too, was besotted, writing, 'I know it is really better I should go but the thought that I have to leave you is driving me crazy.' The couple went on seeing each other right until the date that Joan was destined to leave, Saturday 16 October.

At 11.30 p.m. on 15 October, Croft and Joan met for a final tryst at a romantic summerhouse in the hotel garden. The wooden building, which had a comfortable settee inside, looked out over the sea. It was the couple's favourite spot in which to spend time together and on this night they 'smoked, talked and dozed' until around 4.30 a.m. Suddenly, two shots rang out above the crying of seagulls and crashing of waves below. As the rain and wind lashed the Lizard, Croft ran back into the hotel where he informed the duty officer that he had killed Joan. Then he rang another officer saying, 'I have killed Joan Lewis!'

Dashing to the summerhouse, two RAF officers discovered Joan's body slumped on the floor in a pool of blood. She had been shot twice, one of the bullets passing through her chest, the other entering her head through the left temple. On a table was Croft's service revolver with two empty cartridges. The gun contained four other rounds that had not been fired. A post-mortem found that the shot to Joan's head had been the fatal one.

Following a police investigation Croft was charged with Joan's murder on 16 November. He was brought to trial on 14 December 1943 at Winchester Assizes. In his defence, Croft maintained that he and Lewis had made a suicide pact after becoming depressed about their impending separation. They had discussed the possibility of throwing themselves off the cliffs before settling on using Croft's gun. Croft said that the pair had sat on the settee together, clasping the gun, for some time that morning. The idea was that whoever had the courage to shoot first would fire and then the other would use the same gun to kill themselves. He swore that when the gun had eventually gone off it was Joan that had squeezed the trigger and that she had then said, 'Fetch some help quickly.' Croft testified that he had then rushed to get help, but that he had heard the gun fired again. Going back to the summerhouse he discovered that Joan had shot herself a second time. Seeing that she was dead he had then got down on the floor and put the gun to his own head. However, he had been unable to go through with the deed. Croft explained away the fact that he had afterwards admitted killing Joan to other officers, saying that he had simply meant that he felt responsible for the situation.

The prosecution insisted that medical evidence proved Joan could not have fired the shot that killed her. Dr Frederick Hocking, a pathologist who had examined the body, concluded that it would have been difficult for Joan to have fired the first shot as she would have had to hold the heavy gun 5in away from her body. It would have taken considerable strength – exerting 18lbs of pressure – to discharge it. To fire the second shot, he said, would have been impossible. Damage to her chest muscles from the first shot would have made her too weak to lift the gun. Joan would have needed to hold the gun 12–18in from her own head. This, he stated, was implausible.

It was also pointed out that if the jury believed that Croft had not killed Joan but had abetted her suicide, that also meant he was guilty of murder in the eyes of the law. After just twenty minutes of deliberation Croft was found guilty of murder and sentenced to death. He appealed and, in February 1944, received a reprieve from the Home Secretary. Instead of being hanged he was given a life sentence. We'll never know whether Croft really meant to kill Joan or whether the tragic event was indeed a suicide pact gone wrong. But some believe that Joan's spirit still lurks in the grounds of the Housel Bay. In the decades that have followed several visitors to the hotel have spotted the ghost of a young woman in a Second World War uniform sitting on a bench in the garden.

LOCATION: **Housel Bay Hotel**, The Lizard, Cornwall, TR12 7PG, 01326 290417, www.houselbay.com

WARTIME SHOOT-OUT AT A COUNTRY PUB, 1944

The Crown and The Swan, Kingsclere, Hampshire

By late 1944 the threat of invasion by Hitler's armies had waned and the Allies were well on their way to winning the Second World War. So the picturesque village of Kingsclere in rural Hampshire should have been one of the safest places to be. But that autumn the tranquillity of this rural idyll was shattered by a shocking shoot-out at the The Crown Inn. This largely forgotten chapter in the history of wartime Britain was more reminiscent of something from a gangster movie than the leafy Home Counties. Incredibly, the culprits were not enemy agents but a group of American soldiers who had gone on the rampage. One of those who survived would describe what happened as 'all hell let loose'.

It was just before 10 p.m. on 5 October when the dramatic episode unfolded. Time was about to be called at The Crown where a dozen or so locals and several military policemen were finishing their drinks. Some American soldiers inside were finishing a game of bar billiards. Meanwhile, ten GIs from 3247 Quartermaster Service Company were taking up their positions in the churchyard opposite the pretty Victorian pub. Suddenly, without warning, they opened fire on the pub, shooting indiscriminately with their semi-automatic rifles. By the time the guns fell silent, three people lay dead.

The soldiers of the all-black 3247 Company had only been in the area a few hours, having been moved earlier that day from their base in Devon to a new camp at Sydmonton Court, not far from Kingsclere. They had arrived at 4.30 p.m. and, having had some dinner, some of the men decided to go into the village.

There had already been some problems with discipline at Sydmonton Court and military policemen patrolled Kingsclere in case any of the men left camp without permission. So the renegade group, who were wearing their work clothes rather than their best uniforms, were heading for trouble. Arriving in Kingsclere in the early evening they called first at a pub called The Bolton Arms, which has since closed. There, just after 7 p.m., they were confronted by four MPs. The men were told to return to camp immediately as they were improperly dressed and had no passes allowing them out. One of the regimental policemen was said to have cocked his rifle to make his point.

The group headed back to the camp, hitching a lift in a lorry. Angered by how they had been treated, they now came up with a plan for revenge. The soldiers' rifles, which they had been carrying during their transition to Sydmonton Court, had not yet been collected for safe storage. All but one of them grabbed their weapons, along with 100 rounds of ammunition, and headed back to the village, intent on teaching the MPs a lesson.

It appears that, initially, they had only intended to give the MPs a beating. The situation soon got out of hand. At some point, some of the men boasted that they would kill the offending MPs. Wielding their guns, the GIs entered the Bolton Arms again looking for their targets. Not finding them there, they then headed to The Swan, another pub in the village. Finally discovering that the MPs were inside The Crown, just a few hundred yards away, the GIs took up their positions. Two of the military policemen who were having a drink at the pub, Privates Anderson and Brown, rushed out to see what was happening only to be met by a hail of bullets. Jacob Anderson, who was unarmed, was hit in the chest. He managed to run 150yds before collapsing, dead, in a nearby garden. Brown hurled himself back inside the door and survived.

At the sound of the firing, most people in The Crown had hit the floor while one dived through a window. But some could not escape injury as bullets ricocheted around the bar. One of the unlucky ones was private Joseph Coates, a black GI who was sitting with his back to the window. He was hit in the head and killed instantly. Another victim was the Crown's landlady, Rose Napper. She had been dragged to the floor by her husband, Frederick, but had nevertheless been hit in the jaw – the bullet passing out through her neck. A US colonel immediately drove Rose to hospital in Newbury but the 64-year-old died the next morning. Many others who had been drinking in The Crown were wounded.

At 10.17 p.m. the local police sergeant rang the larger station at Andover for help. Detectives who arrived found thirty-three

The Crown pub in Kingsclere, Hampshire, was the scene of a wartime shoot out.
(© *James Moore*)

empty bullet cases in and around The Crown. The walls of the gabled pub had been left pitted with bullet holes. Some of those responsible were rounded up that night and the rest weeded out over the next twelve days. On 9 November ten men were brought to a military court martial at Thatcham, Berkshire. They were Privates James L. Agnew, Ernest Burns, Willie J. Crawford, Hildreth H. Fleming, Herbert Lawton, John E. Lockett, Herbert Moultrie, Percy D. Oree, Willie Washington and Corporal John W. Lilly.

There is no doubt that in an era still tainted by casual racism, the treatment of black soldiers by MPs was not always respectful. Interestingly none of the accused had previous offences on their army records. Yet during their court martial some of the men seemed not to appreciate the gravity of what they had done – taking the lives of two of their fellow soldiers, who were, as it happened, also black, but the innocent Rose Napper too. By 7 p.m., on the first day of proceedings, two of the defendants displayed their contempt by sleeping in the dock. The men had pleaded not guilty but the evidence presented seemed damning and only one of those being prosecuted, Willie Crawford, took the stand to defend himself. He maintained that he had only joined the group later in the evening and had not actually taken part in the shooting. However, the next morning he and eight of his fellow defendants were found guilty of being absent without leave, riotous assembly and murder. Hearing the verdicts, the reality of the situation seemed to sink in for two of the men, Fleming and Lockett, who put their heads in their hands and began to sob. They were all given a dishonourable discharge from the army and ordered to serve life sentences with hard labour. One of the men, Lawton, was only found guilty of being absent without leave but later retried and given the same sentence as the others.

The GIs were quickly shipped off to serve time in American jails. Some reports written in the decades since the episode claim the affair was hushed up to preserve Anglo–American relations. In fact, what was remarkable is that the case was reported in some detail in several local and national newspapers. Indeed, General Dwight D. Eisenhower, who had just masterminded D-Day, was so appalled by what had happened that he sent a personal message of sorrow and regret to the people of Kingsclere.

LOCATIONS: **The Crown**, Newbury Road, Kingsclere, Newbury, Berkshire, RG20 5QU; **The Swan Hotel**, Swan Street, Kingsclere, Berkshire, RG20 5PP, 01635 298 314, www.swankingsclere.co.uk

THE DASHING PILOT TURNED PSYCHO KILLER, 1946

Strand Palace Hotel, London; The Norfolk Hotel, Bournemouth; Nag's Head, Belgravia, West London

As he went to the gallows, double murderer Neville Heath was offered a last tot of whisky by the governor of Pentonville Prison in London. He quipped back, 'Make that a double.' Heath downed the drink and was then hanged by the famous Albert Pierrepoint in just seven seconds. The manner of Heath's death at 9 a.m. on 16 October 1946 was typical of a man whose disarming charm

The Strand Palace Hotel where murderer Neville Heath assaulted a woman in February 1946. (© *James Moore*)

had beguiled women and lured two of them to their deaths. It was also resonant of the nonchalance he had displayed once finally caught for crimes that were startlingly cruel.

Heath, born in 1917, was a dashing former RAF pilot. But he was also the ultimate cad, with a failed marriage behind him and a less than illustrious military career in which he had been guilty of fraud, gone absent without leave and spent time in the South African Air Force before returning to England at the end of the Second World War. It was in early 1946 that he had embarked on a campaign of sexual assault and murder.

The story of Heath's descent into depravity begins at the Strand Palace Hotel located at the heart of London's 'Theatreland'. Built in 1907, the Strand Palace built a reputation for high jinks throughout the 1920s and soon exuded glamour with its stunning art deco decor and glittering entrance. During the Second World War the Strand Palace stayed open amid the air raids and was a famous haunt for wild socialising even as the bombs fell.

In the early morning of 23 February 1946, sounds of a struggle in room 506 of the Strand Palace were reported to the head

porter, who went to listen at the door. He heard a woman screaming for help. The room had been booked by a man calling himself
Captain James Robert Cadogan Armstrong. He returned with
the assistant manager and the pair opened the door. Inside they
saw a naked woman lying on the bed. Her hands were tied behind
her back and a naked man was standing over her. He demanded
to know what the staff meant by storming into his room, while
the woman, Pauline Brees, cried, 'Thank God you came in.' The
assistant manager asked the woman if he should call the police.
But, deciding that she didn't want any fuss, she got dressed and
left. Armstrong swiftly checked out of the hotel.

It would turn out that Pauline had a lucky escape that night.
She'd met Armstrong, who was really Neville Heath, a week
before, and on the night of the assault the pair had visited several
pubs in the capital before going to the Strand Palace for a night-
cap. The incident was quickly forgotten at the hotel. But had the
matter been brought to the attention of the police at the time,
Heath might not have been emboldened to carry out more
attacks on women.

In June of 1946, Heath moved into the Pembridge Court Hotel
off Notting Hill Gate in West London, this time under his real
name though posing as a Lieutenant Colonel. Heath was apparently never short of a date and had met an attractive 32-year-old
artist called Margery Gardner whilst drinking in the Nag's Head,
a pub in Kinnerton Street in upmarket Belgravia. Interestingly
the pub was also frequented by the serial killer John Christie.
Then on 20 June, Heath, now calling himself 'Jimmy', went for
dinner with Margery. The couple returned to his hotel together
at midnight.

The next morning Margery's body was discovered in Heath's
room. Her face had been savagely whipped and her nipples had
been violently bitten. Margery's wrists and ankles had been tied
and she had been suffocated. Neither Heath, nor the riding crop
which was judged by a pathologist to have inflicted many of
Margery's injuries, were anywhere to be seen.

Three days later Heath was in Bournemouth, Dorset, where
he had booked into the luxurious Tollard Royal Hotel, this time
calling himself Group Captain Rupert Robert Brook.

The Nag's Head, Belgravia, West London, was one of Heath's haunts. (© *James Moore*)

The police chose not to publish Heath's photograph and so he remained unrecognised on the south coast. And during his stay at the Tollard Heath he maintained his insouciant manner. He told one waiter, 'I haven't got a bean on me today … put it down, old chap, on my crime sheet.'

On 3 July Heath met Doreen Marshall, a 21-year-old former Wren from Pinner, on the promenade. She was staying at the Norfolk Hotel whilst she recovered from a bout of measles. They went for tea. Heath then invited Doreen to share dinner with him at the Tollard. That evening the couple feasted on duck and enjoyed a magnum of champagne. At around 11.30 p.m. Doreen said she would get a taxi back to her hotel. But Heath insisted he would walk her back to the Norfolk. Two days later, staff there reported her missing.

When police investigated they found witnesses who recalled her dining with Heath at the Tollard. Knowing he would be the prime suspect, Heath did not flee as might be expected but instead brazenly presented himself to police officers on 6 July. He admitted that he had walked Doreen half way back to the

Neville Heath, a debonair
former pilot who killed two
young women. (© *Getty
Images*)

Norfolk but that she had gone the rest of the distance herself.
He didn't get away with the argument. While his picture had not
been released publicly it had been made available to police sta-
tions, and one officer noticed the resemblance between Heath
and the man calling himself Brook. Heath had done little to cover
his tracks. Looking in his jacket, police found a ticket for a locker
at the local station. Inside they found a suitcase – and a leather
riding crop, stained with blood.

A few days later, Doreen's naked body was discovered in
Branksome Dene Chine, a wooded ravine near the beach. She was
naked and had been beaten over the head. Doreen also appeared
to have been tied up. Her throat had been cut, her nipples bitten
off and, as with Margery, her genitalia had been mutilated. Heath
had also stolen her watch and a ring to pawn.

The murderer seemed to care little what happened to him
after he was arrested and initially planned to plead guilty at his
trial. But in the end he told his barrister, 'All right, put me down
as "not guilty", old boy.' At his trial, held at the Old Bailey that
September, doctors testified that though Heath was a psychopath

he was not insane. He was found guilty in less than an hour and sentenced to death. In one of his final letters, Heath wrote, 'I don't know what time they open where I'm going, but I hope the beer is better than it is here.'

LOCATIONS: **The Strand Palace Hotel**, No. 372, Strand, London WC2R 0JJ, 020 7379 4737; **The Nag's Head**, No. 53 Kinnerton Street, Belgravia, Westminster, London, SW1X 8ED, 020 7235 1135; **The Norfolk Hotel**, Richmond Hill, Bournemouth, Dorset, BH2 6EN, 01202 551 521; The Pembridge Court Hotel is now a private residence; The Tollard Royal in Bournemouth has been converted into apartments.

IN THE FOOTSTEPS OF THE ACID BATH MURDERER, 1944–49

The Goat, Kensington, London; The Kensington Hotel, South Kensington, London; The George Hotel, Crawley, Sussex; The Metropole Hotel, Brighton

When he began his killing spree, the arrogant and cunning John George Haigh was already a convicted criminal. Haigh had been locked up for fraud, but while he was in prison he began to believe that he could get away with murder. After experimenting on mice in the prison workshop he had come to believe that he could destroy a body almost entirely with acid – and also that if he destroyed the evidence of murder in this way, he would avoid the noose.

Haigh was born in 1909 the son of an engineer and had a conservative Christian upbringing in Yorkshire. Rebelling against his strict moral upbringing he was soon up to no good, ending up in jail three times for dishonesty including setting himself up as a bogus solicitor. By 1943 he had been released, and in the summer of 1944 he turned to more serious crime, setting out to prove his murder hypothesis.

His opportunity came when he bumped into an old employer, William Donald McSwann, 34, who owned a string of amusement arcades. Haigh had once worked as McSwann's chauffer. The pair had renewed their acquaintance in The Goat pub in Kensington

High Street, a cosy hostelry with history dating back some 300 years. On 9 September the pair met up in The Goat again at about 6 p.m. They had a couple of glasses of wine together and a pub meal. Dapper Haigh no doubt used his considerable charm to lure McSwann back to No. 79 Gloucester Road nearby, where he had a workshop.

Haigh smashed in McSwann's skull with a pinball table leg, then drank his blood before putting his body in a 40gal barrel full of sulphuric acid. Within a few days most of McSwann's body had dissolved and Haigh poured the rest down a drain. Haigh told McSwann's parents, Donald and Amy, that their son had disappeared in order to avoid call-up for military service. They fell for this deception along with letters that Haigh faked in McSwann's handwriting asking them to forward cash through him. But Haigh was even more ambitious. On 2 July 1945 he invited the couple to his Gloucester Road workshop and killed them, disposing of them in the same way and drinking their blood too. Using forged documents, Haigh then managed to get his hands on the couple's property, amassing £8,000.

Callous Haigh's main motivation for the murders appears not to have been a vampiric desire to drink their blood but financial, and by 1948 he was in need of more cash to feed a gambling habit. By this time he was living at The Onslow Court Hotel, now renamed The Kensington Hotel, but he also kept a workshop in Crawley, Sussex.

He had got friendly with a couple called Archibald and Rosalie Henderson, and in February that year Haigh drove Henderson from the Metropole Hotel in Brighton, where they were staying, to the workshop where he then shot him in the head. The same day he returned to take Rosalie to the same workshop, saying that her husband had fallen ill. After shooting her too, he plunged their bodies into oil drums full of acid. Then he went back to the Metropole where he paid their bill and flogged their possessions. Haigh attempted to cover his tracks by writing letters to relatives claiming that the Hendersons had gone to South Africa.

By 1949 Haigh was on the lookout for another victim. But by now he was getting cocky. And the murder of his next target, a fellow guest at the Onslow Court Hotel, would prove his undoing. Claiming to be an inventor he befriended Olive

The Goat, Kensington,
West London, where
John George Haigh dined
with one of his victims.
(© *James Moore*)

Durand-Deacon, 69, and invited her to see his workshop so that
the pair could explore her idea of manufacturing artificial finger-
nails. On 18 February 1949 they travelled to Crawley where they
were spotted calling at The George Hotel – now the Ramada
Crawley Gatwick – before driving off. Once at his workshop,
Haigh shot Durand-Deacon and stripped her of valuables before
putting her body in another acid bath. At 9.30 p.m. he went back
to The George Hotel where he had dinner before driving back to
the Onslow Court. At his trial a witness also revealed that Haigh
had been spotted in The George earlier that day with a woman
matching Durand-Deacon's description.

Two days later a friend at the hotel insisted on going to the
police to report Durand-Deacon missing and Haigh went with
her. He told them how he had arranged to meet Olive to take her
to his workshop but that she hadn't turned up for the appointment.
Suspicious, officers looked into Haigh's criminal history. They went
to his workshop and found his gun as well as a dry cleaner's receipt
for Mrs Durand-Deacon's coat. It also emerged that he had tried to

pawn some of her jewellery locally. And it turned out that Haigh's acid baths had not entirely destroyed every scrap of evidence as efficiently as he would have wished. In the sludge at his workshop, a pathologist found human gallstones, Durand–Deacon's dentures, part of a foot and other bone fragments.

Quizzed by detectives, Haigh admitted to killing six people and boasted, probably falsely, that he had killed another three. But he taunted police, saying, 'How can you prove a murder if there is no body?' As it happened, he had not only misinterpreted the law but the evidence from his workshop was enough to convict him once their link to Olive had been proven.

Haigh was tried at Lewes Assizes on Monday 18 July 1949. His defence tried to claim he was insane, pointing to Haigh's desire to drink his victims' blood. However, it was revealed that during police interviews he had also asked, 'What are the chances of getting out of Broadmoor?' The very next day a jury swiftly found him guilty. He was hanged at Wandsworth prison by Albert Pierrepoint on 10 August 1949. When a waxwork of Haigh was put up at Madame Tussaud's, it turned out he had donated one of his own suits and a tie.

LOCATIONS: *The Goat*, 3A Kensington High Street, London, W8 5NP, 020 7937 1213, www.taylor-walker.co.uk; *The Kensington Hotel*, formerly the Onslow Court Hotel, Nos 109–113 Queen's Gate, South Kensington, London, United Kingdom, SW7 5LR; *The Ramada Crawley Gatwick*, formerly The George Hotel, High Street, Gatwick, RH10 1BS, 01293 524215; *The Hilton Metropole*, King's Road, Brighton, BN1 2FU, 01273 775432, www3.hilton.com

WHEN BLOOD MINGLED WITH BEER ON THE PAVEMENT, 1955

The Magdala, Hampstead, North London; The Crown, Penn, Buckinghamshire

On 13 July 1955 an attractive 28-year-old woman with bleached blonde hair and wearing a simple blouse, skirt and black court shoes went to the gallows at Holloway Prison in London. The hangman, Albert Pierrepoint, completed the execution of his slightly built 5ft 2in charge in just twelve seconds. Pierrepoint later said, 'She died as brave as any man.'

Ruth Ellis was to be the last woman hanged in Britain, convicted of shooting her philandering lover, 25-year-old racing driver David Blakely. There was no doubt about her guilt. She herself had admitted in court, 'It's obvious when I shot him I intended to kill him.' But in the years that have followed the case many have questioned whether the verdict was a just one, with many believing the background to her crime meant she should have been given a reprieve from the noose.

The dramatic killing, on Easter Sunday 1955, was played out at the entrance to the Magdala Tavern near London's leafy Hampstead Heath. At 9.20 p.m. Blakely, 5ft 9in with brown eyes and slicked back hair, emerged cheerfully from the pub with his friend Clive Gunnell. Blakely had only called in to the packed bar to buy some cigarettes for a friend and have a quick drink. The pair exited carrying three quarts of light ale and were aiming to head back to the party they had been attending.

Outside, Ellis, a nightclub hostess and part-time model, was waiting for Blakely, her back to the wall of the pub. Wearing a grey two-piece suit with a green sweater and horn-rimmed glasses she shouted, 'Hello, David' and then pulled a .38 calibre Smith and Wesson revolver from her handbag. When Blakely saw her with the gun he ran towards his car, parked just feet away. Ellis fired two shots. The first missed, but the second hit its mark. Blakely staggered round his car with Ellis following, firing another shot at point blank range. Her victim fell to the ground, trying to raise himself on an elbow before Ellis pumped another two shots into her on-off boyfriend.

The landlord of the Magdala, John Colson, remembered, 'We were very busy … and suddenly I heard this noise going on outside – shots. Nobody seemed to think it was shots, we all thought it was a car backfiring and nobody took a lot of notice of it.'

But an eye witness outside the pub recalled:

The man stumbled as he ran round the car and when he had completed a circuit of the car he fell face downwards on the pavement between the public house door and the car. All the time he was running the woman was pursuing at a distance of about 2yds and firing continuously. After the man had fallen on to his face the woman stood over him and I saw her fire the gun once; the gun was pointed at the man's body. After this she fired again, but this time all I heard was a click, as though the gun was empty. I heard a man who was standing beside the public house entrance shouting 'Look what you've done Ruth.'

As the blood pumped out of Blakely's lifeless body it mixed with the froth from the beer of the smashed bottles he'd been carrying. A last, sixth bullet, had injured bystander Gladys Yule in the thumb as she was walking with her husband to the pub. Gunnell burst back into the pub saying 'she's got him'. Colson phoned for a police and an ambulance. As chance would have it, an off-duty policeman, Alan Thompson, had been drinking in the saloon bar of the Magdala. When someone rushed in saying, 'A bloke's been shot outside,' he rushed outside and found Ellis still there. She was standing with her back to the wall of the pub, still holding the gun and trembling slightly. Thompson calmly relieved Ellis of the gun and arrested her.

Ruth Ellis, who shot her lover David Blakely outside the Magdala pub in 1955. (© *Getty Images*)

The Magdala pub in Hampstead, North London, as it is today. (© *James Moore*)

At her subsequent trial at the Old Bailey in June, Ellis was con-victed of murder in just twenty-three minutes. While her guilt was beyond question, the background to the case threw up questions about the verdict and the sentence. Just ten days before the shoot-ing Ellis, already a single mother of two, had lost Blakely's baby after he had punched her in the stomach. She'd already suffered sexual abuse at the hands of her father and physical abuse from her first husband. What is more, in between the trial and the hanging it had also emerged that another of Ellis' lovers, Desmond Cussen, jealous of Ellis' feelings for Blakely, had given Ellis the gun and even driven her to the pub on the day of the shooting.

Many felt that given her distressed mental state, Ellis should have been convicted not of murder but manslaughter. Or, at the very least, that she should have been allowed to end her days behind bars rather than at the hands of the hangman. Before she met her fate, Ellis wrote to Blakely's parents saying, 'I have always loved your son, and I shall die still loving him.'

There was fierce criticism of the decision by the Home Secretary at the time to deny Ellis a reprieve from the death sentence and her execution was widely derided. The American thriller writer Raymond Chandler branded it 'medieval savagery'. The furore surrounding Ellis' case helped lead to the permanent abolition of the death penalty in Britain in 1969.

If you look closely at the tiled wall of the Magdala today you can still see holes left by fragments of one the bullets fired by Ellis. In 2010 there were reports that Ellis' ghost had been spotted in a churchyard at Penn, Buckinghamshire, where Blakely is buried. It is across the road from The Crown pub in the village that the pair often frequented.

LOCATIONS: **The Magdala**, 2a South Hill Park, London, NW3 2SB, 020 7435 2503, www.themagdalanw3.com; **Crown Inn**, Church Road, Penn, Buckinghamshire, HP10 8NY, 01494 812640, www.chefandbrewer.com

WHERE RONNIE KRAY SHOT GEORGE CORNELL, 1966

The Blind Beggar, Whitechapel, East London; The Carpenter's Arms, Bethnal Green, East London

'Well look who's here,' said a sneering George Cornell as Ronnie Kray walked into the Blind Beggar pub in London's East End. They were the last words Cornell would ever say. Ronnie said nothing in reply. He simply took a 9mm Mauser pistol from his pocket, held it a few inches from Cornell and shot him in the head as he sat at the bar. The 6ft, heavyset Cornell spun sideways off his stool and fell fatally injured on to the floor. Still playing on the pub's jukebox was 'The Sun Ain't Gonna Shine Any More' by the Walker Brothers.

Cornell's killing on 9 March 1966 was not the first time that crime and the Blind Beggar on Whitechapel High Street had been bedfellows. The pub was rebuilt in 1894 on the site of an earlier inn and got its name from Henry de Montfort, who was wounded and lost his sight in the Battle of Evesham in 1265. It was outside the inn that William Booth, founder of the Salvation Army, had preached his first sermon. But by the turn of the century it had an association with a gang of thieves. And by the time George Cornell met his demise in the bar, there was already a legend about a former member of the gang called Bulldog Wallis. According to the story he had murdered a commercial traveller in a pub by thrusting an umbrella ferrule through his eye

Ronnie and Reggie Kray, London's most famous gangsters, photographed in 1964. (© *Getty Images*)

and into his brain. No witnesses were prepared to come forward and so he was acquitted, being carried triumphantly back to the East End from his trial at the Old Bailey. In fact this was a popular myth based on a real story from 1891 of a cabinet maker called Frederick Klein who had refused to fight with a 19-year-old gang member called James Ellis. Klein was fatally stabbed through the eye with an umbrella at Gower Street underground station. Ellis, whose real name was Paul Vaughan, did not get away with the killing. He was convicted of manslaughter and was sentenced to twelve months' hard labour.

While the Blind Beggar may have had local notoriety before the 1960s, it would become world famous after Ronnie gunned down 38-year-old Cornell. The pub was one of the many which were on the patch of the Kray twins Ronnie and Reggie. With their gang, nicknamed The Firm, they already had a reputation for armed robbery, running protection rackets and casual violence.

The Blind Beggar, Whitechapel, where Ronnie Kray shot George Cornell in 1966. (© *James Moore*)

The Carpenter's Arms in East London, a pub once owned by the Krays. (© *James Moore*)

But they were also mini celebrities in their own right, running their own nightclub in London's swanky West End and schmoozing with stars of the era including the actresses Barbara Windsor, Diana Dors and Frank Sinatra.

When the rival Richardson gang, based south of the Thames, began muscling in on the Krays' act, the mentally unstable Ronnie, in particular, was out for revenge. The killing of an associate called Richard Hart in Catford on 8 March was the final straw. On the evening of the 9th Ronnie had been in another pub, The Lion, on nearby Tapp Street when he got a tip-off that Cornell was having a drink at the Blind Beggar with a friend called Albie Woods. Cornell had been visiting a friend in a nearby hospital who had lost a leg in a shooting. But he must have known he was taking a risk by hanging around afterwards on the Krays' territory. He and Ronnie already had 'beef'. Cornell had once called Ronnie, who was gay, 'a big fat poof'.

At 8.30 p.m. Ronnie and another gang member, Ian Barrie, burst into the saloon bar, where only a few regulars were nursing drinks. Barrie was also armed and fired some shots into the ceiling of the pub. Along with the other drinkers, Cornell's friend, Woods, jumped to the floor for safety. Ronnie later recalled how he raised the gun towards Cornell: 'I shot him in the forehead. He fell forward … there was some blood on the counter.' He and Barrie then promptly made their exit, jumping into a getaway car which was waiting for them outside. They ended up at another pub called The Coach and Horses in Stoke Newington where Ronnie asked another member to dispose of his gun and told Reggie about the shooting.

Cornell died shortly after being shot but police were in doubt as to the culprits. They brought the Krays in for questioning and organised an identity parade. Sadly the barmaid of the Blind Beggar failed to identify Ronnie as the killer. She, and the other witnesses on the evening, had already been intimidated into silence by The Firm. For now at least the Krays were in the clear.

The year after Cornell's murder the Krays bought a pub for their mum, Violet, called The Carpenter's Arms on Cheshire Street. It was just round the corner from Vallance Road where they'd grown up. Keen amateur boxers in their younger days, the

Krays organised for boxing gloves to be hung behind the bar – which itself was said to be constructed out of coffin lids.

It was here that on 28 October the twins held a party for friends and family of The Firm. But Ronnie and Reggie were preoccupied with what to do about an associate called Jack 'The Hat' McVitie, a burly associate who had failed to fulfil a contract to murder a man despite being given down payment and a gun. They became determined that McVitie must get his comeuppance, and Ronnie was keen that Reggie should now notch up his own murder. McVitie was lured to a party on the promise of 'girls and booze' at a flat in Evering Road, Stoke Newington. Once he was inside, Reg pulled out his revolver, aimed it at McVitie and pulled the trigger. Nothing happened. McVitie tried to escape through a window but other members of the Firm wrestled him back. Reggie then grabbed a kitchen knife and stabbed McVitie to death while Ronnie held him down. The body was never found.

Meanwhile the police, under Inspector Leonard 'Nipper' Read, had been slowly building a case against The Krays. Finally, on 9 May 1968, the twins, along with their brother Charlie and fifteen other gang members, were arrested. As they had hoped, with the Krays now safely in custody, witnesses who had previously been too scared to testify now began to spill the beans.

Key to the case was the barmaid from the Blind Beggar who had originally maintained that she was in the pub cellar when Cornell had been shot. Only ever known as Mrs X, and something of an unsung heroine, she finally called time on the twins by identifying Ronnie and Ian Barrie as the men who had shot Cornell.

The Krays' trial at the Old Bailey began in January 1969 and lasted thirty-nine days. In the end both twins ended up convicted of murder. Each was given thirty years behind bars with no chance of parole. Their other brother, Charlie Kray, got ten years for helping to dispose of McVitie's body. Ronnie was subsequently certified insane and eventually died in 1995 from a heart attack. Reggie died in 2000 shortly after his release. On 11 October of that year his funeral cortège passed by the Carpenter's Arms, which is still serving. The Blind Beggar is also still open and is now thoroughly respectable, sporting a plaque recalling Cornell's shooting and welcoming in tourists who often drop in for a drink before embarking on Jack the Ripper tours. Another pub on Whitechapel High Street, where the Krays often drank, called the Grave Maurice, was recently closed and turned into a betting shop.

LOCATIONS: *The Blind Beggar*, No. 337 Whitechapel Road, London, E1 1BU, 020 7247 6195, www.theblindbeggar.com; *The Carpenter's Arms*, No. 73 Cheshire Street, London E2 6EG, 020 7739 6342, www. carpentersarmsfreehouse.com

HEAD TO TOE IN BLOOD – THE LUCAN MYSTERY, 1974

The Plumbers Arms, Belgravia, London

Thursday 7 November 1974 was a quiet night in the Plumbers Arms with just eight customers taking refuge from the rain outside and chatting at the bar. Suddenly, at 9.50 p.m., the door opened and a woman burst in wearing only her nightdress. As head barman Arthur Whitehouse would later testify, she was 'head to toe in blood' and in a state of shock. Rushing to her aid Arthur got the woman to lie down on a bench and as he did so she turned to him crying, 'Help me, help me, I've just escaped from being murdered.' She continued, 'My children, my children, he's murdered my nanny.'

The woman would turn out to be Lady Lucan, who lived at No. 46 Lower Belgrave Street, a six-storey townhouse located just a few doors away. She had run to the pub for help after being attacked by a man whom she later claimed was her husband, Richard John Bingham – 7th Earl of Lucan. He, so her account went, had already killed their children's 29-year-old nanny, Sandra Rivett, by bludgeoning her over the head in the basement moments earlier with a piece of lead piping. It seemed that Lucan had mistaken Sandra for his intended target – his estranged wife, Lady Lucan herself. She had been hit and half strangled by her husband before managing to free herself from his grasp by grabbing his testicles. Lady Lucan then pretended to want to help

Lucan. And, while her husband was getting towels to help clean her wounds, she slipped out of the house to raise the alarm.

That evening, once police had arrived at the Plumbers Arms, Lady Lucan was taken to hospital while officers followed a trail of blood from the pub to No. 46. There they found Sandra's body half stuffed into a mail sack and the murder weapon – a bloodied 9in section of piping – wrapped with tape. The Lucans' three children were still at the house but unhurt.

By this time Lord Lucan, known as 'Lucky' to friends in his high society gambling set, had fled the scene. The Eton-educated 39-year-old was a former banker who had quit his job to become a professional gambler, taking up with the well-heeled Clermont Club run by John Aspinall. In fact 'Lucky' was a failure at his chosen career and by 1974 had serious money troubles. Meanwhile his relationship with his wife Veronica, Lady Lucan, had deteriorated and he had moved out of the family home. A fierce custody battle for the Lucans' children had followed, with Lucan convinced that his wife was mentally unstable. In June 1973 a court ruled in favour of Lady Lucan.

On the night of the murder, Lucan had phoned his mother to report a 'catastrophe' at No. 46 and asked her to collect the children. Then he had driven a borrowed Ford Corsair to the home of some friends, the Maxwell-Scotts in Uckfield, Sussex, arriving at 11.30 p.m. There he told Susan Maxwell-Scott that he had been passing No. 46 earlier in the evening and had happened to see, through the basement window, a man attacking his wife. In a bid to come to her aid he had let himself in but slipped in a pool of blood while the attacker made his getaway. According to this version of events a hysterical Lady Lucan had then accused him of hiring a hitman to kill her. Lucan left the Maxwell-Scott house at 1.15 a.m. after writing some letters. In one, to his brother-in-law Bill Shand-Kydd, he wrote, 'The circumstantial evidence against me is strong in that Veronica will say it was all my doing.'

Three days later, police found the Corsair parked at the port of Newhaven on the south coast. Inside the bloodied boot was a piece of tapped lead pipe similar to the one found at the Belgravia house. Police issued a warrant for Lucan's arrest, but the trail went cold. Seven months later, in June 1975, an inquest into Sandra

The Plumbers Arms, Belgravia, London, where the Lucan murder was first brought to light. (© *James Moore*)

Rivett's murder found that after being hit over the head she had choked on her own blood. Forensic evidence revealed that the blood on the lead piping found at No. 46 came from both Sandra Rivett and Lady Lucan. Experts also revealed that the lead piping found in the boot of the Corsair was probably from the same section as that found in the house. Blood from both women was also found on the letters written by Lucan after the murder and one was found to have come from a notepad found in the car. The inquest jury concluded that the nanny had been murdered and that the person responsible for her death was likely to be Lord Lucan. This later led to a change in the law which meant that inquests could no longer name murder suspects.

Lucan had, however, disappeared without a trace, avoiding a trial. To this day, despite 'sightings' from as far afield as Australia and Mozambique his ultimate fate remains a mystery. In 1999 he was officially declared dead by the High Court. Many assumed that in the days following the murder he had committed suicide, probably by jumping from a cross-Channel ferry. Yet his body has never been found.

There are many theories about what happened to Lucan. One of the most popular is that he managed to escape to Africa. A personal assistant of John Aspinall recently claimed that she had helped arrange for his children to visit the peer there in the 1970s and 1980s. Another theory posits that he himself was killed by a hitman – hired by some of his rich friends to cover up their part in helping with the crime.

The person often forgotten in the debate about the whereabouts of the blue-blooded culprit is the victim, Sandra Rivett. She had been killed after offering to go and make tea for the family in the kitchen, located in the house basement. There, at around 9 p.m., with the lightbulb removed by her attacker, she was brutally murdered in the gloom. Twenty minutes later, when Lady Lucan went to see where Sandra was, she too was attacked. According to her account, when the attack was over, Lord Lucan admitted to her that he had killed the nanny. Sandra was supposed to have been on her night off, seeing her boyfriend, a 27-year-old Australian barman called John Hankins. But she had changed the night of her date to a Wednesday instead.

Ironically it was at the Plumbers Arms, in happier times, where she had met John. The couple had talked about starting a new life in Australia. Sadly for Sandra, she was to become the casualty of a domestic battle that had led the troubled and bungling Lucan to turn to violence, with disastrous consequences for all.

LOCATION: *The Plumbers Arms*, No. 14 Lower Belgrave Street, London, SW1W 0LN, 020 7730 4067, www.taylor-walker.co.uk

WHERE SERIAL KILLER DENNIS NILSEN LURED HIS VICTIMS, 1978–83

Golden Lion, Soho, London; The Salisbury, Covent Garden, London; The Black Cap, Camden, London; The Princess Louise, High Holborn, London

In the early 1980s The Golden Lion, in London's trendy Soho district, was a well-known venue for homosexual men to meet each other. Paul Nobbs, a 21-year-old student, headed to the pub in November 1981 and struck up a conversation with an apparently genial older man. The pair then went to a bookshop together before ending up back at Nilsen's flat. They went to bed together but were too drunk to have sex and fell asleep. The next morning Paul awoke with a terrible headache and bloodshot eyes. Paul left the flat, but felt so awful that he took himself to University College Hospital in Euston Road. When a doctor examined bruising around his neck, Paul was shocked to be told that he had been strangled. However, in an era when homophobia was still widespread, Paul decided against going to the police to report the crime.

It wasn't the first time that Dennis Nilsen had used London's bars and pubs to prey on and then attack young men. But many had not been as lucky as Paul Nobbs and escaped with their lives. Nilsen is now regarded as one of Britain's worst serial killers and is reckoned to have killed fifteen people in a five-year period. A former army cook, police officer and civil servant, the Scottish-born murderer unleashed his callous killing spree after moving to a flat in Cricklewood, North London, in the mid-1970s.

Already aged 30, his string of crimes appears to have begun in December 1978 after he met teenager Stephen Holmes in an Irish pub near his home called The Cricklewood Arms. Nilsen, who had been drinking heavily, invited Stephen, who was on his way home from a rock concert, to visit his home. The next morning he strangled the unfortunate youngster and drowned him in a bucket. Stephen's body was then stored under the floorboards of Nilsen's flat in Melrose Avenue for eight months before he burned the remains in his back garden.

Nilsen later said, 'I was desperate for company, even if it was only a body.' And he was soon seeking out more men to lure into his suburban web. In late 1979 he headed to The Salisbury, a smart pub with a long history in Covent Garden. It had been known as a place for homosexual men to meet since Oscar Wilde's time. There he met a student called Andrew Ho, from Hong Kong, and brought him back to Melrose Avenue. Nilsen attempted to put a tie around Andrew's neck but Ho escaped his clutches and fled from the property. He went straight to the police to report the attack. Although police did go on to interview Nilsen, the case went no further as 19-year-old Ho eventually decided not to press charges.

Despite this close call, Nilsen was undeterred. A couple of months later he met a 23-year-old Canadian tourist called Kenneth Ockendon in The Princess Louise, a pub in High Holborn. After offering to show Kenneth the sights of London, the pair left the pub and, after the tour, went back to Nilsen's flat to listen to music. Kenneth picked up a pair of headphones and was listening to a record when Nilsen put a flex round his neck and strangled him, then finished him off by drowning him in the bath.

Over the next two years there were many more victims – with The Golden Lion a favourite hunting ground. Nilsen's killing frenzy saw him murder homeless man Martyn Duffey, 16, Billy Sutherland, 26 and Malcolm Barlow, 24, as well as a string of other unidentified men. After their deaths Nilsen's victims were often bathed and dressed too, in a weird ritual which would later earn Nilsen the ironic nickname of the 'Kindly Killer'. Nilsen would keep the bodies, sometimes for months, storing them under the floorboards and having sex with the corpses before chopping them up.

In November 1980 there was another escapee, a barman called Douglas Stewart. But when he reported an attack by Nilsen to the police, officers appear to have accepted Nilsen's suggestion that it was a 'lover's tiff'.

By October 1981, Nilsen was running out of storage space for the bodies of his victims at his Melrose Avenue flat and neighbours were beginning to complain about a strange smell. He burned the remaining corpses he had kept in a garden bonfire and moved to another address, this time an attic flat in Cranley Gardens, Muswell Hill.

But his lust for more corpses showed no signs of waning. In March 1982, the year after his failed attempt to kill Paul Nobbs, he went to The Salisbury to seek out a new victim. He chose John Howlett, a man who claimed to be an ex Grenadier Guard. Finding the service in the pub slow, the pair left and went to an off-licence and then back to Cranley Gardens, where they watched television whilst drinking. When John nodded off he was strangled. Nilsen then made sure he was dead by holding

The Salisbury in St Martin's Lane, London – one of the pubs frequented by serial killer Dennis Nilsen. (© *James Moore*)

Howlett's head under the water for five minutes. He went on to dismember Howlett's body, hiding parts around the house and flushing others down the toilet.

In May of the same year, Nilsen met Carl Stottor who worked as a drag queen, Khara Le Fox, in a pub called The Black Cap in Camden. Carl was in a vulnerable state, having just come out of a turbulent relationship, and Nilsen comforted him as he poured his heart out over a lager and lime. In a taxi back to Nilsen's flat they held hands. That night Nilsen tried to strangle and drown Stottor but in the end, for some reason, let him go.

Two more men, Graham Allen, 27, and Stephen Sinclair, 20, would end up dead at Nilsen's hands before his crimes were finally uncovered. Nilsen's macabre method of disposal for his victims' bodies was to be his undoing. In February 1983, a plumber was called in by a neighbour to unblock a drain and found rotting human flesh. Police were called and when, on 9 February, they challenged Nilsen at his home, he finally admitted that there were human remains still in the flat. Detectives found them concealed in bin bags, including the partly-boiled head of Sinclair. Once arrested, Nilsen calmly told police that there he was responsible for a total of fifteen deaths. In November 1983, after a trial at the Old Bailey, Nilsen was convicted of six murders and two attempted murders and sentenced to life imprisonment. He is still in prison.

LOCATIONS: *The Golden Lion*, No. 51 Dean Street, London W1D 5BH, 020 7434 0661; *The Salisbury*, No. 90 St Martin's Lane, Covent Garden, 020 7836 5863, www.taylor-walker.co.uk; *The Princess Louise*, No. 208 High Holborn, London, WC1V 7EP, 020 7405 8816, princesslouisepub.co.uk; *The Black Cap*, No. 171 Camden High Street, London, NW1 7JY, 020 7485 0538, www.theblackcap.com

SELECT BIBLIOGRAPHY

Ashbridge, I., *Murder in Cumbria* (Carlisle, Bookcase, 2004)

Barber, J., *The Camden Town Murder* (Oxford, Mandrake, 2006)

Bardens, D., *Lord Justice Birkett* (Hale, 1962)

Begg, P., *Jack the Ripper: The Uncensored Facts – A documented history of the Whitechapel murders of 1888* (London, Robson, 1988)

Begg, P., Fido, M., Skinner, K., *The Jack the Ripper A–Z* (London, Headline, 1992)

Billingham, N., *Foul Deeds and Suspicious Deaths in Birmingham* (Barnsley, Wharncliffe, 2013)

Blundell, R.H., and Seaton, R.E., *Trial of Jean Pierre Vaquier* (London, William Hodge, 1929)

Boardman, C., *Foul Deeds and Suspicious Deaths Around Oxfordshire* (Barnsley, Wharncliffe, 2004)

Brandon, D., *Stand and Deliver!: A History of Highway Robbery* (Stroud, The History Press, 2011)

Brandwood, Davison and Slaughter, *Licensed to Sell: The History and Heritage of the Public House* (Swindon, English Heritage, 2011)

Bridges, Y., *How Charles Bravo Died* (London, Jarrold, 1956)

Briffett, D., *The Acid Bath Murders: A reconstruction of events that shook Britain in 1949* (David Brifett, 1997)

Bruning, T., *Historic Inns of England* (London, Prion, 2000)

Burke, J., *The English Inn* (London, Batsford, 1981)

Burney, I. A., *Bodies of Evidence: Medicine and the Politics of the English Inquest, 1830–1926* (London, Johns Hopkins University Press, 1999)

Butler, I., *Murderers' England* (London, Robert Hale, 1992)

Clark, P., *The English Alehouse: a Social History 1300–1830* (Harlow, Longman 1983)

Cobban, J.L., *Wall of Silence: The Peculiar Murder of Jim Dawson at Bashall Eaves* (Chatburn, Demdike Press, 2005)

Cole, B., *Crawley: History and Celebration* (Salisbury, The Francis Frith Collection, 2012)

Coysh, A.W., *Historic English Inns* (Newton Abbot, David and Charles, 1972)

Cullingford, C.N., *A History of Dorset* (London, Phillimore & Co Ltd, 1980)

Deghy, G., and Waterhouse, K., *Café Royal* (London, Hutchinson, 1956)

Douglas D'Enno, *Foul Deeds and Suspicious Deaths Around Brighton* (Barnsley, Wharncliffe, 2003)

Doogan, B., *The Guardian of Blackmount: a History of Kingshouse Inn, Glencoe* (Scotland, Highland Highway, 2004)

Donnelley, P., Essex Murders (Barnsley, Wharncliffe Books, 2007)

Downie, R.A., *Murder in London: Topographical Guide to Famous Crimes* (London, Littlehampton, 1973)

Earnshaw, S., *The Pub In Literature* (Manchester, Manchester University Press, 2000)

Easdown, M., *Foul Deeds and Suspicious Deaths Around Folkestone* (Barnsley, Wharncliffe, 2006)

Eddleston, J., *Foul Deeds and Suspicious Deaths in Reading* (Barnsley, Wharncliffe, 2009)

Fidler, K., *Stories of Old Inns* (London, Epworth, 1973)

Fido, M., A History of British Serial Killing (Mortimer, 2011)

Fido, M., *Murder Guide to London* (London, Academy Chicago Publishers, 1993)

Ford, K., *Keepers of the Monarch of Old Inns: The George of Stamford* (Bourne, Mad Publishing, 2006)

Fox, J., *White Mischief* (London, Vintage, 1998)

Fry, C., *The Krays: A Violent Business: The Definitive Inside Story of Britain's Most Notorious Brothers in Crime* (Edinburgh, Mainstream, 2011)

Fuller, P., and Knapp, B., *Welsh Murders: 1770–1918* (Llandybie, Christopher Davies Publishers, 1986)

Gibson, K., *Killer Doctors: The Ultimate Betrayal of Trust* (Glasgow, Neil Wilson, 2012)

Gordon, R.M., *The Infamous Burke and Hare: Serial Killers and Resurrectionists of Nineteenth Century Edinburgh* (Jefferson NC, McFarland & Co, 2009)

Haydon, P., *Beer and Britannia: an inebriated history of Britain* (Stroud, Sutton, 2001)

Haydon, P., *The English Pub* (London, Hale 1994)

Hayhurst, A., *Lancashire Murders* (Stroud, The History Press, 2004)

Hayhurst, A., *Staffordshire Murders* (Stroud, The History Press, 2008)

Helm, P.J., *Jeffreys* (London, Hale, 1966)

Heslop, P., *Cumbria Murders* (Stroud, The History Press, 2008)

Honeycombe, G., *Murders of the Black Museum* (Pub location?, John Blake, 2011)

Honeycombe, G., *More Murders of the Black Museum* (London, Arrow Books, 1994)

Hornsey, I.S., *A History of Beer and Brewing* (Cambridge, Royal Society of Chemistry, 2003)

Howse, G., *North London Murders* (Stroud, The History Press, 2005)

Howse, G., *Foul Deeds and Suspicious Deaths in South Yorkshire* (Barnsley, Wharncliffe, 2010)

Humphreys, C., *Seven Murderers* (London, Heinemann, 1931)

Jakubowski, M. and Braund, N., *The Mammoth Book of Jack the Ripper* (London, Robinson, 2008)

Jones, R., *Walking Dickensian London* (London, New Holland, 2004)

Jones, R.G., *The Mammoth Book of Women Who Kill* (London, Robinson, 2011)

Keverne, R., *Tales of Old Inns* (London, Collins, 1947)

Kray, R., *Our Story* (London, Sidgwick & Jackson, 1989)

La Bern, A., *Haigh: The Acid Bath Murderer* (Star, 1974)

Lane, B., *Murder Club Guides: Eastern and Home Counties* (London, Webster's New World, 1989)

Lane, B., *Murder Club Guides: Midlands* (London, Chambers, 1988)

Lane, B., *Murder Club Guides: North West England* (London, Harrap, 1988)

Lane, B., *The Murder Club: Guide to South-East England* (London, Harrap, 1988)

Lane, B., *The Murder Club Guides: South West England and Wales* (London Virgin Books, 1989)

Lee, C.A., *A Fine Day for a Hanging: The Real Ruth Ellis Story* (Edinburgh, Mainstream, 2012)

Long, R., *Historic Inns Along the River Thames* (Stroud, History Press, 2006)

Majoribanks, E., *Famous Trials of Marshall Hall* (London, Penguin, 1989)

Masters, B., *Killing for Company: The Case of Dennis Nilsen* (London, Random House, 1985)

McLaren, A., *A Prescription For Murder: The Victorian Serial Killings of Dr. Thomas Neill Cream* (Chicago, The University of Chicago Press, 1995)

Meeres, F., *Norwich Murder & Misdemeanours* (Stroud, Amberley, 2009)

Milne-Tyte, R., *Bloody Jeffreys the Hanging Judge* (London, Andre Deutsch, 1989)

Monckton, H.A., *A History of the English Public House* (London, Bodley Head, 1969)

Moore, P., *Damn His Blood* (London, Vintage, 2013)

Morson, M., *Norfolk Mayhem and Murder* (Barnsley, Wharncliffe, 2008)

Mower, M., *Suffolk Murders* (Stroud, The History Press, 2011)

Napley, Sir D., *Camden Town Murder* (London, Weidenfeld & Nicolson, 1987)

Nash, J.R., *Look for the Woman* (London, Harrap, 1984)

Oates, J., *Unsolved London Murders: The 1920s and 1930s* (Barnsley, Wharncliffe, 2009)

O'Connor, S., *Handsome Brute: The Story of a Ladykiller* (London, Simon and Schuster, 2013)

Philip, K., *Victorian Wantage* (Wantage, Kathleen Philip, 1968)

Ranson, R., *Looking for Lucan: The Final Verdict* (London, Smith Gryphon, 1994)

Root, N., *Frenzy!: How the tabloid press turned three evil serial killers into celebrities* (London, Arrow, 2012)

Rose, A., *Scandal at the Savoy: The Infamous 1920's Murder Case*, (London, Bloomsbury, 1991)

Roughead, W., *Trial of Mary Blandy* (Edinburgh, Hodge, 1914)

Ruddick, J., *Death at the Priory: Love, Sex and Murder in Victorian England* (Leicester, Atlantic, 2002)

Rumbelow, D., *Complete Jack The Ripper* (London, Virgin, 2013)

Sharpe, J., *Dick Turpin: The Myth of the English Highwayman* (London, Profile, 2005)

Shew, E.S., *A companion to murder: A dictionary of death by poison, death by shooting, death by suffocation and drowning, death by the strangler's hand, 1900–1950,* (London, Cassell, 1960)

Sly, N., *A Grim Almanac of Oxfordshire* (Stroud, The History Press, 2013)

Sly, N., *Hampshire Murders* (Stroud, The History Press, 2009)

Sly, N., and van der Kiste, J., *West Country Murders* (Stroud, The History Press, 2009)

Sly, N., *Wiltshire Murders* (Stroud, The History Press, 2009)

Smith, G., *When Jim Crow Met John Bull: Black American Soldiers in World War II Britain* (London, I.B. Tauris, 1987)

Spraggs, G., *Outlaws and Highwaymen* (London, Pimlico, 2001)

Stratmann, L., *Essex Murders* (Stroud, The History Press, 2004)

Stratmann, L., *Gloucestershire Murders*, (The History Press, 2005)

Stratmann, L., *Kent Murders* (Stroud, The History Press, 2009)

Storey, N., *Norfolk Murders* (Stroud, The History Press, 2012)

Stuart, D., *Old Sussex Inns* (Derby, Breedon Books, 2005)

Sugden, P., *Complete History of Jack the Ripper* (London, Robinson, 2012)

Torry, G., *Chelmsford Through The Ages* (Ipswich, East Anglian Magazine Ltd, 1977)

van der Kiste, J., *Surrey Murders* (Stroud, The History Press, 2009)

Wade, S., *Yorkshire Murders and Misdemeanours* (Stroud, Amberley, 2009)

Webb, S., *Execution: A History of Capital Punishment in Britain* (Stroud, The History Press, 2011)

Whittington-Egan, R., *Bedside Book of Murder* (Newton Abbot, David & Charles, 1988)

Wild, R., and Curtis–Bennett, D., *'Curtis' The Life Of Sir Henry Curtis-Bennett, K.C* (London, Cassell, 1937)

Wilson, D., *Mary Ann Cotton: Britain's First Female Serial Killer* (London, Waterside, 2013)

Worsley, L., *A Very British Murder* (Hants, BBC Books, 2014)

Wynn, D., *Lincolnshire Villains: Rogues, Rascals and Reprobates* (Stroud, The History Press, 2012)

INDEX

Note: italicised page numbers indicate illustrations.

Visit our website and discover thousands of other History Press books.

www.thehistorypress.co.uk